THE

GARDENER'S TEXT-BOOK:

CONTAINING

PRACTICAL DIRECTIONS

UPON THE

FORMATION AND MANAGEMENT

OF

THE KITCHEN GARDEN;

AND FOR

THE CULTURE AND DOMESTIC USE OF ITS VEGETABLES FRUITS, AND MEDICINAL HERBS.

BY

PETER ADAM SCHENCK,

FORMERLY GARDENER TO EDWARD C. WILLIAMS, ESQ.

"Hence Summer has her riches, Autumn hence,
And hence e'en Winter fills his withered hand
With blushing fruits, and plenty not his own."

NEW-YORK:

ORANGE JUDD & COMPANY.

41 PARK ROW.

CONTENTS.

ADVERTISEMENT.

The publishers introduce this little volume to the notice of the public, with confidence in its merits, and adaptation to the wants of that class for whom it is designed. The author has aimed to give thorough and practical directions upon the formation and management of the family kitchen garden, and upon the cultivation of our common vegetables, fruits and medicinal herbs, in a clear, simple manner, without any attempt at elegance of style. He here details what he has learned from personal experience, as compared with, and enlarged by, the published observations of others upon the same subject. For this reason, it is believed that the work will be found more generally useful, than though it were of a strictly local character. The numerous receipts scattered through the pages, will be appreciated by the housekeeper, and they add much to the value of the other matter. Many families do not derive half the satisfaction and profit from their gardens, which they might if acquainted with the best modes of preparing its vegetables and fruits for the table. The author and publishers have spared neither pains nor expense to render this treatise, although modest in price as well as in size, a complete and reliable Text-Book upon kitchen gardening; and they indulge the hope, that it will be received with that favor to which they think it entitled.

John P. Jewett & Co.

March 1st, 1851.

Henry S. Mahon
from his father
May 1872.

THE GARDENER'S TEXT-BOOK.

INTRODUCTION.

A Kitchen Garden is, properly, a piece of ground devoted to the culture of esculent vegetables alone; but, it has become customary also to include within its limits, several varieties of fruit, and such herbs as are considered most valuable for medicinal purposes. Large fruit trees belong of right to the orchard, because when placed in a garden, it will be found that their extended roots greatly impoverish the soil, while their overhanging branches are injurious to nearly every kind of vegetation which may be in their vicinity.

It is gratifying to notice among our population a growing taste for horticultural pursuits. Our wide-spread country embraces every variety of soil and climate, essential to the production of the choicest fruits and vegetables in their perfection. But, it would seem that, until within a few years, we have been strangely unmindful of these advantages with which we are favored by nature, and that in the management of the kitchen garden, we have been far behind the peasantry of some European states.

The common day laborer of England, a man of much less intelligence and shrewdness than the greater portion of our working classes, is distinguished by a remarkable degree of skill and taste in the cultivation and embellishment of the little spot of ground connected with his dwelling. Here it is that he spends the odd moments of time between his regular hours of labor; and while he bestows the greatest attention upon the vegetables which are afterwards to grace his humble board, he does not forget the excellent effect of a few flowers in the door-yard. The stranger who passes along the road cannot fail to infer that comfort and happiness preside in that cottage, however lowly may be its roof, and however rustic and unpolished may be its inmates.

The state of things in this country was formerly very different. Although gardens were common, yet from the little interest which they excited in their owners, there could not have been much pleasure or profit attending their cultivation. The farmer thought it necessary to devote himself exclusively to his farm, and the mechanic preferred buying from others, to the trouble of supplying his wants by the culture of his own ground.

This apathy with which we were once justly charged by intelligent travellers, is fast wearing away, and we are gradually becoming aware of the claims which the art of kitchen gardening has upon our attention. Much good has been accomplished through the agency of the horticultural societies that are now established in several sections. Intelligent and practical men have devoted their pens to the subject, and have already given us many treatises which are valuable alike for their originality, discrimination and good sense. Within a few years, several choice varieties of fruit have been propagated, and numerous additions made to our list of table esculents. Others with which we were little acquainted, have been brought into common use. The well-known tomato, which is now highly esteemed in all kitchens, was formerly raised in the flower garden under the name of love-apple, and was by some persons considered poisonous. We are thus awaking to the importance of the kitchen garden as an appendage to every country house; and we find that its cultivation is beneficial to health and morals, as well as productive of pleasure and profit.

To labor is our common lot—a universal duty prescribed by an all-wise Providence before the commission of sin. Adam, the father of us all, was placed in a garden "to dress it and to keep it." Man was never made to pass his life in idleness; the very organization of his mind and body proves conclusively that neither health nor happiness could be the portion of inactivity. The experience of physicians has demonstrated that the mind and the body should both be exercised, in a reasonable manner, and at suitable intervals; that the one ought not to be restricted to a single chain of thought, any more than that the other should be confined in one wearisome position. The author may kill himself by close application to his desk, giving his brain no rest, and yet keeping his limbs fixed in the chair. Where both are properly exercised, the muscular system is made strong, the blood courses through its accustomed channels with a healthful impulse, the appetite becomes regular, while the mind itself remains composed and tranquil. Thus the necessity for labor is of divine institution, and we find it not only the source of health and pleasure, but also the very basis of our worldly prosperity.

To be thus beneficial, our labor must have for its object some useful purpose, such an one as will be of advantage to ourselves, or to our fellow-men. The turning of a crank is of itself tedious, but so soon as the crank is connected with machinery, the task is rendered a source of gratification. What person with three ideas in his head, would be willing to sink a drill in the block of granite, unless it were for the reception of gunpowder by which the rock is to be shattered into fragments? What dairy maid would be willing to operate the churn without the expectation of making butter? Who would be content to trundle an empty wheelbarrow? Labor must be useful, in order to be thus blessed. In no other sense will the words of the poet be true:—

> "From labor, health; from health, contentment springs;
> Contentment opes the source of every joy."

And where, we may now with propriety inquire—where can be found any employment which is more worthy the attention of him who seeks after health and happiness, than the cultivation of the kitchen garden? The gardener has some useful object constantly in view. While turning over the stubborn soil—while cherishing the feeble plants in all stages of their growth; in the cold of winter, when he is making ready for the advent of spring—in the noon-day heat of summer; he is laboring in the hope of an abundant reward. He feeds himself, and he feeds others. That which his hard toil has brought to maturity, graces the table of the wealthy, as well as that of the humble day-laborer.

Gardening was man's first occupation, when in a state of innocence. He takes a harmless delight in the gradual progress of his crops. He acquires habits of industry, and learns to economize time, for his work is regulated by the succession of the seasons, that roll around in their wonted course. In adapting the soil to the wants of different vegetables, in arranging a rotation of crops, and in providing for future contingencies, he exercises forethought, and is taught to do nothing rashly, or without due reflection. When the insects have destroyed the plants of one sowing, he is led to persevere, and to sow again, in the hopes of better fortune. By the care of his beds and walks, he becomes orderly and neat in other things. Even his disposition will be improved. If an idle, worthless fellow can be coaxed into a garden, the work of his reformation is already commenced. The crabbed and stingy will in time become generous, for he soon learns the pleasure of giving of his abundance to those who are less favorably situated than himself.

We all like an occasional change, either in our mode of living, or in the objects by which we are surrounded. The same foot-path at length loses its interest for the pedestrian, and he wishes to turn his steps into an unexplored track. In the garden, there is a regular succession of new beauties and wonders to gratify the eye, or to elevate the mind. Not only has each season its particular characteristics, but on each day is there presented some unexpected novelty to attract the attention. The germination of the seed, the development of the stem and branches, the bursting forth of the flower, and the perfection of the fruit, are only a few of the many incidents of the horticultural year. The cultivator's interest is awakened at the outset of his labors, and it gradually strengthens with the progress of the months. As soon as the young plant rears its tiny head above ground, it is the object of his watchful care—to shield it from injury, and to hasten its growth. Every operation of culture, every natural phenomenon, is calculated to excite emotions of pleasure, and to direct the psalm of praise to the Giver of all good.

The mental and physical faculties are made strong, while the gentler feelings of the soul are quickened, and the strongest passions of our nature are subdued. For these reasons, a celebrated medical authority has said, "Horticulture and agriculture are better fitted for the promotion of health and sound morals, than any other occupation."

We cannot think less favorably of the products of a garden, in respect to their influence upon health. They furnish us with the substantials of life, and such of the delicacies as do not vitiate or corrupt. They have been considered by some anatomists as man's natural food, and that they should form the basis of every system of diet, is agreed by all. Nothing can be more nutritious, or more palatable—particularly in the summer months, when the free use of animal flesh is most hurtful to the system. He who has once been accustomed to good, fresh vegetables and fruits, knows how to estimate their value aright, and will admit how difficult it would be for him to get along without them. Their excellence is vastly increased, when they happen to be the products of one's own land, or have been watered by the sweat of his own brow, and nurtured by his care. No other person enjoys them so much as he. They seem to have an additional flavor, and it is reasonable to suppose that they are more grateful to the stomach. "Who so valueth," says an ancient worthy, "or eateth with so keen a relish, the fruit he buyeth of the stall-woman in a market, as that which his own hand hath gathered after great pains, and, it may be, peril, encountered in the search?"

Kitchen gardening is also a source of profit. To be sure, it is ordinarily looked upon as a very small and unimportant business. Men of large capital, who are engaged in gigantic speculations, may sneer at the idea of gardening being recommended on account of the profit which attends it. This is a mistaken notion, for it appears from statistics that no occupation is more certain of reward than the cultivation of the ground; while that Commerce is a great lottery, in which more than ninety-five out of a hundred adventurers draw blanks.

And, even the farmer looks down upon the kitchen garden as a small affair, almost beneath his notice. It is indeed of small size, when compared with the ample fields of a farm. But, this is not the proper way of estimating their relative importance. A farm is not valuable in proportion to the number of its acres, so much as in proportion to the quantity and quality of its productions. Hence a tract comprising a dozen acres, may be quite as valuable to the owner, as a tract of five hundred. In the same way, we should judge of the kitchen garden. If the annual income of a single acre, over and above the expense of cultivation, can be made greater than the net annual gain of five acres, which tract is most profitable?—which the most worthy of attention?

No land pays a higher rate of interest than the humble, despised garden. The quantity of vegetables which it can be made to produce, almost exceeds belief; and farmers may well open their eyes, when told that under good management two acres of a garden, will be more profitable than twenty acres of a farm, as it is usually conducted. In the vicinity of cities and large towns, the raising of vegetables for market is conducted on a large scale, and is said to be very lucrative.

Every person who is acquainted with the varied productions of the kitchen garden, the sustenance which they afford, and their cash value, will admit its importance to all living in the country, whether they be farmers or mechanics. For a family of moderate size, only a small space of ground is required for the supply of their table throughout the year. The labor and expense of cultivation may be rendered very light, so that while there is only a trifling outlay, the produce renders unnecessary the purchase of a substitute. This can, with propriety, be termed profit, because that consists of money *saved*, as well as of money *earned*. If the poor man, by his own labor at odd moments of time, can secure an abundance of nutritious food for his family, why it is plain that he thereby avoids the expenditure of just so much as other vegetables, or an extra quantity of meat, would have cost. The amount so saved is nothing else than clear profit. Should he raise more than he needs for his own household, he can generally dispose of it at good prices among the inhabitants of the next village; and in this way he will be remunerated for the necessary purchase of tools and seeds.

There are, however, other reasons why gardens should be common, of more weight than the mere commercial value of their productions. They contribute largely to the resources of good living. Their fruits and vegetables are considered necessaries on the tables of the rich. How insipid would soups be, if it were not for the vegetables of which they are composed. And, in the succeeding courses, there would be an insupportable monotony, if there were no potatoes, no peas, no beans, no cauliflower, no spinach, no celery; nor grapes, nor strawberries, nor gooseberries, nor raspberries. The poor can derive almost their whole living from the garden. Even the very food which is required to keep soul and body together, must unavoidably, when purchased, be of the cheapest description. If they have little money to spend in obtaining the substantials of life, they certainly cannot regale themselves with its delicacies, however agreeable they might be to the palate. By having gardens, they are enabled to feast upon nature's bounties with as much satisfaction as any nobleman can derive from his well-spread board.

But little need be said of the dignity of horticulture as an occupation. It has engaged the attention, and received the approval, of the most distinguished men in all ages of the world. The Creator assigned a garden, "planted" by Himself, as the abode of our first parents. The gardens of Gethsemane, and of Joseph of Arimathea, will never be forgotten as long as the history of the Divine Mediator continues to be read. The noblest families of Rome—the Cicerones, the Fabii, the Lentuli, and the Pisones—felt not ashamed to bear the names of the vetch, the bean, the tare, and the pea, common vegetables which had been introduced by their ancestors.

Socrates has called the cultivation of the earth, "an excellent employment, most worthy the application of man, the most ancient, and the most suitable to his nature; it is the common nurse of all persons, in every age and condition of life; it is the source of health, strength, plenty and riches, and of a thousand sober delights and honest pleasures. It is the mistress and school of sobriety, temperance, justice, religion, and, in short, of all the virtues, civil and military." Lord Bacon declared gardening to be "the purest of human pleasures;" another author called it, "the most rational of all recreations;" and Mr. Roscoe said, "If I was asked whom I consider to be the happiest of the human race, I should answer those who cultivate the land by their own hands."

Although it is easy to discover an increased attention to the kitchen garden, during the last dozen years, yet it must be acknowledged by every candid observer, that it does not at the present day excite that interest which it merits. We have shown that it not only is profitable in a pecuniary point of view, but is, moreover, conducive to health, happiness and good morals. Surely, no appendage to a country house can reflect greater credit upon the taste and judgment of the proprietor. We would have it more common—we wish its productions to be enjoyed as freely by the humble artisan, as by the man of wealth who employs others to cultivate it. We desire it to be connected with every farm house throughout the length and breadth of the land. It is better to have ground planted with useful vegetables, than to be overrun by pestiferous weeds. The occupation is a noble one, and we cannot think of any manual labor which is more worthy the notice of the gentleman and the student, or the farmer and the mechanic. It becomes us not to neglect those treasures of the vegetable kingdom, which a good Providence has appointed for our sustenance and enjoyment, and which He has been graciously pleased to place within our reach.

THE FORMATION OF A KITCHEN GARDEN.

THE SITUATION.

Not a little judgment should be exercised in the selection of the ground; for, as has been justly remarked, a poor situation cannot be improved, like a sterile soil, by skilful management. The choice, when once made, is generally final. It would be quite unprofitable, to say the least, for a person to depend upon actual experiment, and to keep shifting his frames and plants from one place to another, until he can find one perfectly satisfactory. A garden spot is intended for a life time, and it, therefore, behooves the owner not to make a selection of the site, until he shall have given due consideration to the respective advantages and disadvantages of such localities as present themselves to his notice. But we would, at the same time, remind him, that it is very seldom a situation can be found which is in every way desirable. He must select the best one that his premises offer, and then exercise his ingenuity in remedying the defects, as well as in improving the advantages of nature.

The first thought should always be regarding the aspect or exposure. Although authorities apparently differ much on this important point, yet, after all, it would seem that a preference is given to a gentle inclination towards the south-east. A northern aspect may then be considered as generally unfavorable; still, on some accounts, it is to be desired. Several kinds of vegetables,—such as spinach, cauliflower, and peas, yield more abundantly, especially in dry seasons, when not exposed to the full power of the sun. Vegetable growth is also in the same way retarded, and will thereby afford a long succession of crops, instead of running up to seed in the early part of summer. It might, therefore, be deemed advisable to select an exposure to two or three different points of the compass. Perhaps a small knoll in the centre of the grounds would be considered advantageous. The inclination should in all cases be slight. Where it is so great that there is danger of the soil being washed away by heavy rains, it would be well to throw up a series of terraces, faced with turf.

A moderate elevation should be secured, if possible. The garden ought to be neither on a hill, nor in a valley, as they are equally objectionable; the first being exposed to inclement winds, and the second to damp vapors, early frost, and that sourness of the soil which is so difficult to eradicate.

Convenience of access is by no means the most unimportant point to be borne in mind. The garden ought to be near the stable whence supplied with manure, and not far distant from the dwelling-house, "lest," as Dr. Deane quaintly observes, "being too much out of sight, it should be out of mind, and the necessary culture of it too much neglected."

THE SOIL.

The best soil for general purposes is a rich sandy loam, two or three feet deep, well drained, and sufficiently mellow to be easy of cultivation at any season of the year when not frozen. Some authors pretend to say, that in a good garden two varieties of soil are necessary. However desirable this may be on some accounts, we think that where a strict rotation is observed, a healthy loam of rather a sandy character will be sufficient.

Should circumstances render necessary the selection of a loose sand, a hard gravel, or a stiff, heavy clay—which may be considered the very worst kinds of soil for culture—their peculiar characteristics must first be corrected, before they can be cropped with success. The sand is so porous that it cannot retain manure and moisture for any length of time, while so permeable to heat that in hot weather its vegetation will be parched and almost burned up. The gravel is still worse, because when stirred by the spade, it becomes greedy, swallows every ounce of nutriment furnished, and then cries for more; so that it has acquired the name of a "hungry" soil. Indeed, the expense and difficulty of bringing it into good condition are such, that we can scarcely recommend the attempt. The heavy clay is bad for very different reasons. It is tenacious and retentive of water, a property which is injurious to almost every culinary vegetable; with the additional disadvantage that it cannot be worked when wet, thereby causing a great loss of time in spring.

As the sand is light and porous, and the clay stiff and heavy, by mixing them judiciously a very fine loam may be obtained. The first named is also improved by the addition of lime, plaster, ashes, and any kind of vegetable manure; and the second, by lime, litter, horsedung, or anything which tends to the separation of its particles. Lime and plaster operate favorably upon both, correcting the looseness of the one, and the tenacity of the other. Some persons even go to the expense of carting good soil from a distance; they should always select that which is rich and full of vegetable fibre, such as is found in a wood-lot, or a field which has long lain fallow. This practice is much followed in Great Britain, but labor is too dear for its general adoption in this country. We have read of the soil in the kitchen garden belonging to the Duke of Buccleugh, twelve acres in extent, having been filled in to the depth of three feet. It can easily be calculated by the reader, that for such an enormous labor, the revenues of none other than a duke would be sufficient. Nevertheless, it is a maxim quite applicable to this country, that a judicious expenditure at the outset, will do much for subsequent success and satisfaction.

If both situation and soil be good, then there will be little difficulty in obtaining a productive garden; if otherwise, their disadvantages must be overcome as far as possible by increased attention and perseverance.

SIZE AND SHAPE.

These particulars are to be determined wholly by circumstances,—the nature of the ground, as well as the wants and ability of the owner.

It may serve as some criterion for the reader, to state that a single acre will furnish steady employment for one man, who will probably need an assistant at the busy periods of the year. But the produce of that acre varies so much with locality, season and management, that it is impossible to make any estimate of the space required to supply the wants of a certain number of individuals. It must in every case be decided by the size of the family, their partiality for vegetables, and the fertility of the ground.

It is a primary principle in horticulture, to raise the greatest quantity from the smallest surface. Then, is it not better to start with a small garden, to till it well, and, if it be found insufficient, to add to its dimensions; rather than to attempt the culture of too much, so as to become discouraged at not receiving even interest upon the investment of capital and labor?

The amount which one rod of land can be made to produce, is truly astonishing. An old story tells the experience of a Roman vine-dresser, who had two daughters. When the eldest was married, he set aside for her portion one third of the vineyard; notwithstanding which, he still obtained the same quantity of fruit as before. And when the youngest was married, he gave her one half of the ground that remained, leaving to himself only a third part of the original tract; still the produce was undiminished. This illustrates the value of small holdings, and shows that a single rod may be made to yield as much as a lot several times larger, provided a reasonable degree of skill be exercised in its cultivation. We prefer seeing a small garden which is well managed, rather than a large one half overgrown with weeds.

As regards shape, that must be determined by individual taste, as well as by the position of the ground. However, it is well to state that the square and parallelogram are deservedly approved forms, because adapted to a cheap, easy and regular arrangement of the beds and walks. The parallelogram, if running east and west, has the further advantage of a long, warm border facing the south, with one of equal length facing the north; which borders, from the difference in their exposure to the sun, are excellent locations for early and late crops.

ENCLOSURE.

Shelter of some kind is needed upon the north and west sides. It is generally known, that on a north border protected by a high, close fence, small plants, like lettuce and radishes, may be brought forward from ten days to a fortnight earlier in spring, than when sown in an open compartment; and it is, moreover, an excellent situation for tender cauliflowers from the hot-bed, or for such hardy vegetables as are allowed to remain in the ground through the winter. Low buildings at the north-east corner, will do much in breaking the force of strong, piercing winds from that quarter. But the vicinity of large trees is to be avoided, because vegetation is injured by their shade, and the soil robbed of its most valuable properties by their spreading roots.

A high stone wall, laid in mortar, is considered the best protection; but the cost of its erection will influence most persons in favor of a wooden fence, made of either close boards, or open pickets. In many places, the entire enclosure of the garden is necessary, to guard against the encroachments of poultry or other two-legged animals. In this case, there will be a fine border, having a northern aspect, for currants, and such plants as lettuce and peas, which suffer when exposed to the full influence of a summer sun. The sides of the wall, or fence, may be covered with grape-vines, or trained fruit trees; thus, at the same time, being made to answer several important purposes.

INTERNAL ARRANGEMENTS.

"Strength may wield the ponderous spade,
May turn the clod, and wheel the compost home;
But ELEGANCE, chief grace the garden shows,
And most attractive, is the fair result
Of thought, the creature of a polished mind."

By the phrase "Internal Arrangements," we mean the division of the garden into quarters, borders, beds, walks, etc. This laying out the ground must be regulated wholly by the taste of the gardener, and we, therefore, venture to offer only a few hints in regard thereto, instead of giving precise directions. As far as our opinion may be worthy of notice, we should recommend regular divisions made by the square and line. Such are most easily laid out, and most conveniently kept in order. Serpentine walks, with crescent, star or bean-shaped beds, are all very appropriate for the flower garden, but they seem hardly suited for such humble tenants as cabbages, potatoes and onions. It is a rule to be constantly borne in mind by the proprietor of a kitchen garden, that his main object be utility, rather than ornament.

At least one path should be of sufficient width to admit the wagon or cart, which will be required at certain seasons to bring in dung, or to carry off produce. Foot-paths need not be over three feet wide, and the alleys between the beds not over twelve or eighteen inches. The border extends all around the garden, and is from six to ten feet wide, with a foot-path in front. The beds ought to be narrow—say four or five feet wide, such being the most easy to cultivate. The numerous alleys, of course, occupy a great deal of room, but they possess the advantages of convenience and neatness, in enabling the workmen to clean or gather the crops, without trampling upon the beds. The principal paths might be dug out to the depth of two feet or more, and then become places of deposit for the stones removed from the quarters. A thin layer of gravel, tan, or even common earth, would render the paths hard and dry to the feet at all seasons.

In connection with the above hints, a diagram or plan of our own garden may be deemed not out of place. It will be found on the following page. It is in the shape of a parallelogram, running east and west, with the entrance on the south side. The border inside the fence is about eight feet wide; that part facing the west, south and east, is adapted for such plants as require a warm exposure, and the other for such as need shelter from the mid-day sun. In front of the border is a foot-path three feet wide. Directly in the centre of the garden is the tool-house, beneath which is a good location for a cistern. Here meet the four principal paths, which divide the large plat into four equal parts, or "quarters" as they are generally called by English gardeners. These paths are of sufficient width to admit the wagon, which can turn around the tool-house, and return through the same path, so as to avoid the necessity of having more than one entrance. The quarters are of equal size, so that a four-year rotation of crops may readily be observed. The tool-house and cistern being in the centre, are convenient of access from every part of the grounds. Currants, gooseberries, raspberries and quinces are set out on the edges of the principal paths running north and south, and the grape vines are trained upon the fence. Dwarf fruit trees might be placed in the border, where neither their roots nor their tops would be likely to occasion much injury. This

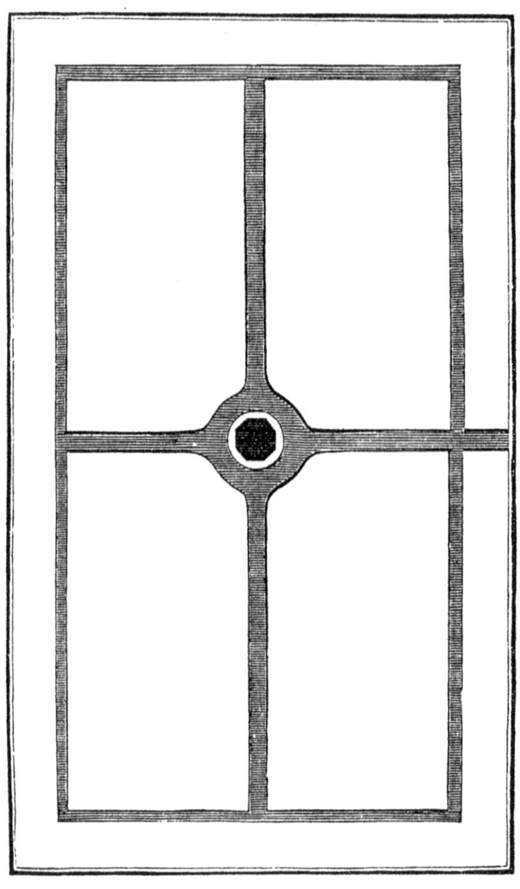

short description will enable any intelligent reader, who approves of the plan, to adopt it, with such modifications as his own taste may suggest.

Although in this business of laying out a garden, ornament is a mere secondary consideration, yet perfect regularity and neatness are attained with little extra labor, and they will certainly add much to the gardener's interest in the spot. The eccentric William Cobbett said, that it is quite as reasonable for a man to take pleasure in a garden which is tastefully arranged, and tidily kept, as it is for a woman to delight in a fine dress; and he will be as anxious to preserve the neat appearance of the beds and walks, as she to protect her gown from dust or grease, from being faded by the sun, or eaten by moths. We all take best care of that which is most pleasant to the eye.

THE CISTERN.

An abundant supply of water is of great advantage. Vegetables recently transplanted often droop, and, if they do not die, are much retarded in their growth for the want of moisture. And in the middle of summer, the heat is sometimes so excessive that the most promising plants "wilt down," as it is termed, and nothing but prompt attention will save them. In our own grounds, we have often experienced the advantage of applying water in such cases, even after the heads had fallen over, and the stems had turned yellow for several inches above the roots.

Loudon remarks, that "many kitchen crops are lost, or produced of very inferior quality, for want of watering. Lettuces and cabbages are often hard and stringy; turnips and radishes do not swell; onions decay; cauliflowers die off; and, in general, in dry seasons, all the *cruciferæ* become stinted or covered with insects, even in rich, deep soils. Copious waterings in the evenings, during the dry seasons, would produce that fulness and succulency which we find in the vegetables produced in the

Low Countries, and in the Marsh Gardens at Paris, and in England at the beginning and latter end of the season."

The Marsh Gardens here spoken of, are so called from being in a low district which was formerly a swamp. The soil is naturally a poor sand, but it has become by careful cultivation a very rich mould. From its porous nature, and the frequent recurrence of dry summers, it would produce little without constant and abundant watering. The raising of water from numerous wells dispersed through the grounds, and conveying it to the growing plants, is the most laborious part of the whole process of cultivation. By such means, the growth of vegetation is accelerated, and crop succeeds crop with astonishing rapidity. We notice these Gardens thus particularly, to show how a poor situation may be made productive by the regular supply of moisture. We are not disposed to recommend any reader to the adoption of such a task upon his own premises; for, aside from the actual labor required, the vegetables thus obtained have not the agreeable flavor of those raised by a more natural process.

And we think, further, that the wholesale mode of applying water practiced by some gardeners, is positively detri mental to the objects of their care. Our own experience has satisfied us, that it is only when given moderately and with discretion, that water becomes a useful assistant. We are not prepared to recommend its regular application through the growing season, as, of however much benefit it may be, it is scarcely practicable by the majority of our readers. But we have no hesitation in suggesting, that it be applied at certain periods in the growth of particular plants, which can not be brought to perfection without an abundant supply of moisture, applied either naturally or artificially, viz. when in the seed-bed, when removed to the open compartment, in time of drought, and when perfecting their seed-vessels. There can be no doubt of the real advantage to be derived from such a mo derate course.

When the garden is small, it can be supplied, by two or three hours' labor in the evening, with water brought from the kitchen cistern—especially if it be not far distant. This can be done in the watering pot, or in the large garden engine, or in a common barrel. (See article on "THE TOOL HOUSE AND ITS CONTENTS.") But where the grounds are extensive, the gardener will look for a supply within the limits. "They are happy," says Dr. Deane, who can resort to a pond or rivulet. When these are wanting, recourse must be had to a cistern receiving the rain water which falls upon the dwelling-house and outbuildings. Indeed, rain water is preferable, because containing those gases which are of most benefit to the plants; the application of pond or spring water, on the contrary, is sometimes attended with injury.

If the buildings be upon elevated ground, the cistern may be located there, from which the water will descend by its own weight, through a pipe, to the garden below. In this case, hose can be attached to the hydrant, and the grounds sprinkled without the labor of raising the water by a pump, and then carrying it to the spot where it is required. Or, if this be not practicable, the cistern must be located in the garden itself, as near the centre as possible, and the water conducted thereto by a pipe, and raised by means of a pump or windlass. Any such work as this will, of course, be intrusted to a skilful mason. In the description of our own garden, we remarked that a cistern might be put under the tool house, as that is a central position, and convenient of access from every part of the grounds. The reader, before he makes any such arrangements for a supply of water, will ask himself whether the extra labor of bringing it for a short distance, in the engine or barrel, will justify the cost of a second cistern with its necessary appendages. Economy should in every case be regarded, for "a penny saved is a penny earned."

THE FORCING-PIT.

Fig. 1.

This is used in bringing vegetables forward at unnatural seasons of the year, and is by most persons considered an essential part of every good-sized garden. We, however, do not think so highly of its merits. About all of its advantages are common to the hot-bed, which is vastly more convenient, and less expensive. But, that all classes of readers may be satisfied, we here append a short description of its appearance.

It is a rectangular frame or bin, partly sunk in the ground, and covered with sash-lights. It may be built of heavy plank, brick or stone; the first named is objectionable, because it will have to be renewed every few years. The rear, or north wall, is about four feet high, and the front one is some ten or twelve inches lower. The width is six or eight feet, according to the size of the sashes used, while the length will be regulated by the wants of the owner. Light rafters to support the sashes, are thrown across at proper distances. It has been suggested by Mr. Buist, that these rafters be movable, so that the glass can be raised as soon as it shall be touched by the plants within. This is effected by taking out the rafters and placing them in a wooden framework—say twelve inches high—which is then set upon the pit walls. The pit, when covered with mats, forms an excellent winter apartment for house plants.

We quite agree with Dr. Lindley, the celebrated horticulturist, in thinking that however desirable it may be to have fresh vegetables throughout the year, those which are forced will be found less palatable and less nutritious than those grown in the natural way. Their excellence is sacrificed to the merits of rarity and extraordinary size. It is with them as with flowers, which always lose their beauty and fragrance when subjected to great artificial heat.

THE TOOL HOUSE AND ITS CONTENTS.

A gardener ought no more to be without the proper implements of his art, than a tailor should be without his press-board, a mason without his trowel, or a professional man without his library. There are a few tools which are indispensable; these are the spade, the hoe, and the rake. The others mentioned in the following list, though they may not be considered absolutely necessary, will be found valuable assistants. Money spent in the purchase of those which will economize time, or will render labor less severe and irksome, is by no means thrown away. He who has charge of a large garden, will require many which another person can very well get along without. In making the selection of the most useful, much discrimination must be exercised; as many articles are yearly brought forward, and highly praised by persons interested in their manufacture, which have little to recommend them besides novelty of construction.

In buying tools, the gardener should bear in mind, that the lowest-priced is not always the most desirable. It may be of very inferior character,—the materials being of poor quality, or put together upon wrong principles. In either of these cases, it will be found less serviceable than another which would have cost perhaps only a trifle more. The woodwork should be straight-grained, and well seasoned: the metal properly tempered, and free from flaws. Neither ought to be heavier than is essential to durability. The extra weight of an ounce in a hoe or a spade, causes the laborer to exert many pounds of strength unnecessarily during an hour's work.

Good care should always be taken of tools, because they then last longer than they would if exposed to the weather, besides standing in less danger of being lost or stolen. When not in use, they ought to be stored in a shed, or some old building, where they will be guarded from the influences of sun and storm. And then too, it will be known where they can always be found. It is a bad plan to spend an hour in hunting after a spade every time it is wanted. The decay of the wood will be prevented by an occasional coat of paint.

In a garden of moderate size, the tools may be kept in any convenient place about the premises, where they will be secure. But in a large piece of ground, it is desirable to have everything near at hand. Any old shed will answer, but a very tasteful building can be specially erected for the purpose, at a small expense.

In the diagram of our own grounds, it will be seen that the tool house is located in the centre, where it is convenient to the persons employed in either quarter. To the eye it is nothing more than a rustic summer-house, overgrown with vines; but we have little hooks and shelves beneath the seats, on which the smaller tools are placed when not in actual use. The large articles, such as the wheel-barrow, engine, sash-lights, hot-bed frames, &c., which occupy considerable space, are put in another building.

A set of rules for the guidance of the workmen, is hung in a conspicuous position. The first one is that old standard maxim—"*Have a place for everything, and everything in its place.*" The second is scarcely less important—"*No tool shall be put away when dirty, or out of repair.*"

Fig. 2

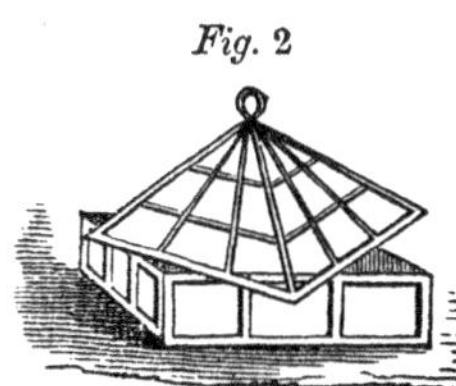

The HAND-GLASS is made either of hard wood, or cast iron. It is a glass case, with a pyramidal-shaped cover; and is used for forwarding early plants, or sheltering such as are taken from the hot-bed and set out in an open compartment. When air is to be given to the plants, the cover is placed in the manner represented in Fig. 2.

The HOT-BED FRAME should always be of good sound plank, with close joints to prevent the admission of air and water. It may be made of any required length, but in width should conform to the length of the sash lights. The front side is usually nine or twelve inches high, and the back side from six to ten inches higher, so that the glass may be inclined towards the south, as well for the benefit of the sun, as for allowing the water to run off. Cross-pieces will be required at suitable distances for the support of the sashes; they may be about one inch thick and three inches wide, and dove-tailed into the planks. Where the hot-bed is made with an inclined surface, (see the article on "FORCING VEGETATION,") the sides of the frame should be of equal height. It is a very good plan to have the planks fastened together by hooks and staples, so that when not in use, they can be taken apart and piled up for protection from the weather.

Fig. 3.

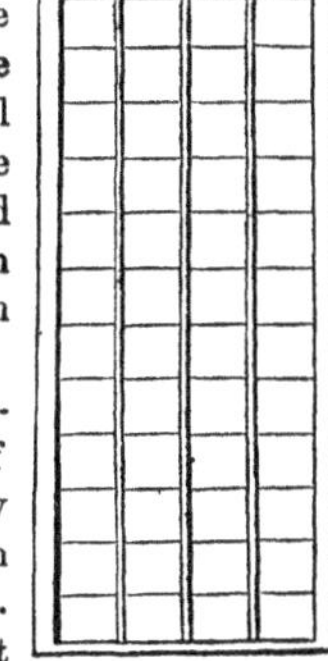

SASH-LIGHTS should be made of well-seasoned wood, about one and a half inches thick, and small, cheap glass. They may be of any length desired, but a width of three feet and a half is most convenient. The wood must have two coats of oil paint before glazing, and one afterwards. This care will preserve it many years. This precaution is very important.

Fig. 4.

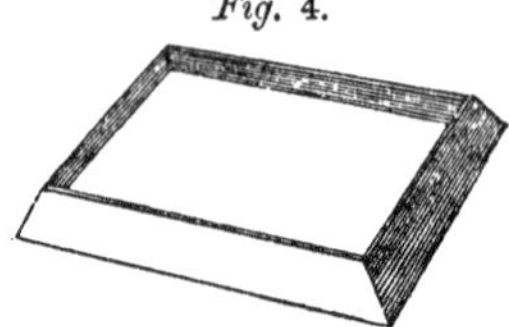

The Vine-Shield (Fig. 4) we have found of great use in protecting young plants from the cold, and the attacks of vermin. It costs little, and will last many seasons. It is merely a small frame, made of thin boards, with a pane of glass in the top. The sides should be bevelled so that one screen can be set inside another without touching the glass, and by this means they will occupy less room when stored away. The size we find most convenient, is four inches high, and large enough on the top to accommodate eight by ten inch glass.

Fig. 5.

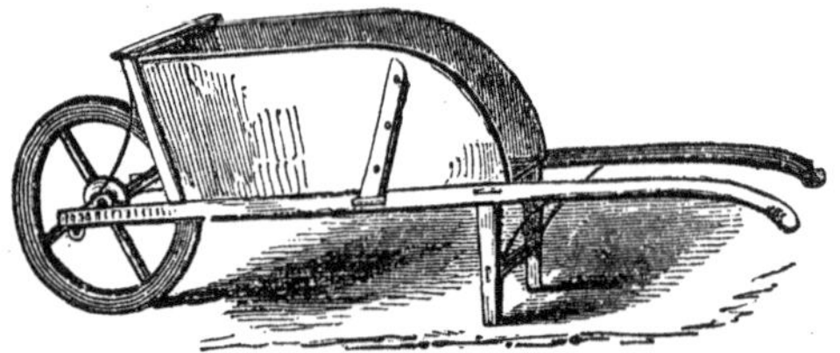

The Wheelbarrow may be considered as very essential. In fact, no piece of ground, meriting the name of garden, can be cultivated without its assistance. It should be made of the best materials, and then it may be light and easily moved from place to place. Nor should an occasional coat of paint be neglected, if its preservation be deemed important.

Fig. 6.

Fig 7.

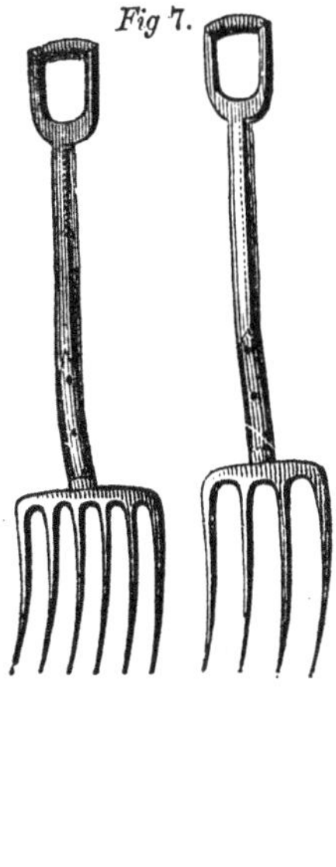

SHOVELS AND SPADES are too well known to require description. We can only advise the gardener to purchase the best articles, although costing more than those of an inferior quality.

FORKS are by many persons preferred to the spade, because in digging with them, the labor is diminished, and the pulverization of the soil better effected. They are also necessary for the manure heap, as well as for breaking up the surface of beds in spring.

HOES are of various shapes and sizes. Fig. 8 includes several different kinds. The two marked *d* and *f* are the *Dutch*, *Thrust* or

Scuffle hoes, useful for cleaning walks, cutting weeds, and stirring the soil. That marked *c* is called the *Forked-back*, which is a very efficient implement for loosening the soil without danger of injuring the plants. The hoe has been termed the gardener's best friend. It is often unnecessarily heavy, and the purchaser should be careful to pick out one which is both light and strong.

Fig. 8.

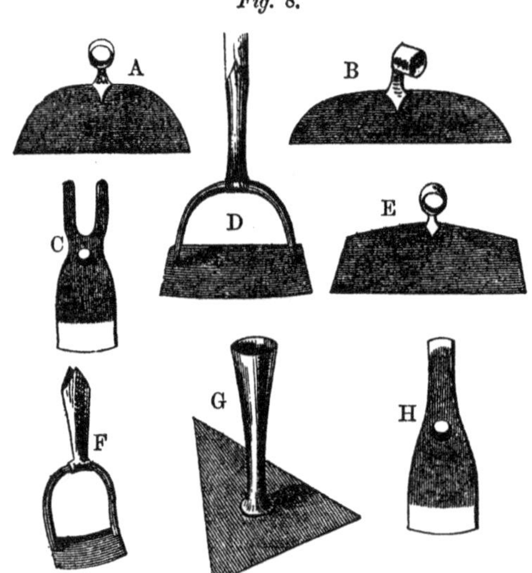

The Hand-Cultivator (Fig. 9) is made of iron, and expands from ten to eighteen inches. By being drawn between the rows of vegetables it performs the work of several men with hoes, in stirring the soil, and cutting up weeds. It will be found of great advantage in a large garden.

Fig. 9.

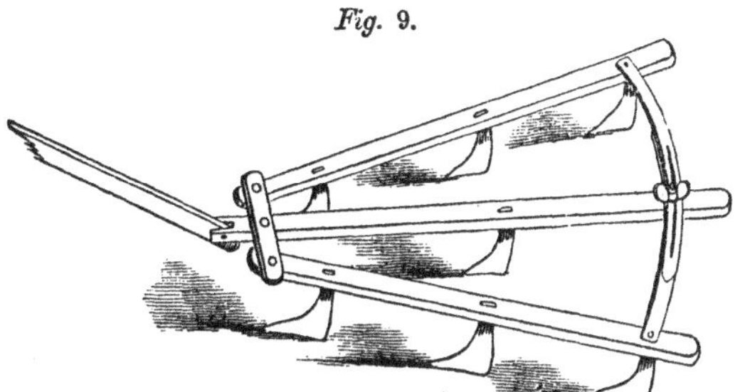

Fig. 10.

The RAKE ought to be of the best wrought iron. There are many different kinds, varying in the length and number of their teeth. For general use, perhaps one having teeth about two and a half inches ong and one and a half inches apart will be most suitable. The handle should be as light as consistent with strength, and made of sound, straight-grained wood.

Fig. 11.

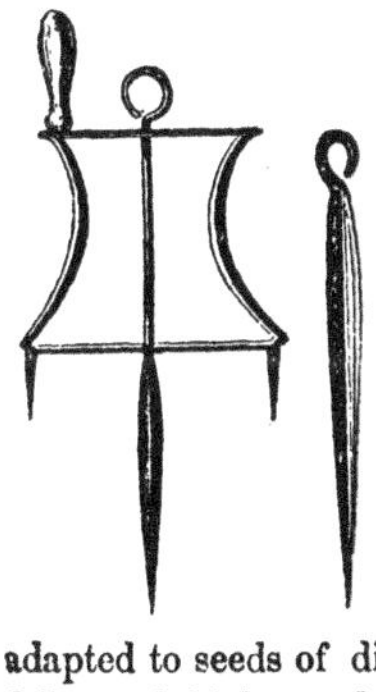

The REEL AND LINE are used for laying out beds and walks. The reel ought to be made of iron or strong wood, and the line should be of medium size. When not in use, they are to be kept under cover, as exposure to the weather would soon rot the line.

The SEED SOWER, is very serviceable in a large garden. It is quite light, durable, and not likely to get out of order. As it is pushed forward by the operator, the ground is opened, while the seed is dropped, covered and rolled all at the same time. It is easily adapted to seeds of different sizes, and drops them in hills or drills, and thinly or plentifully, just as may be desired.

Fig. 12.

Fig. 13.

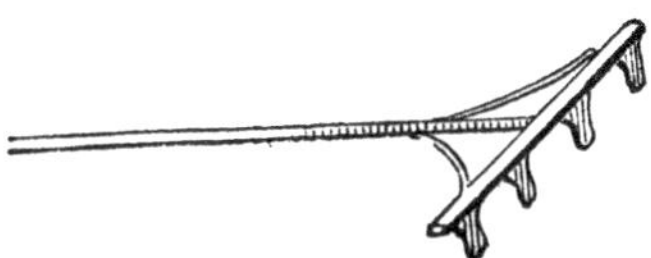

Drill-Rakes are for marking drills in seed beds. The gardener may have several sizes, with the teeth set at various distances apart, as six, eight, ten, twelve, and fourteen inches. The whole may be made of wood, or with a wooden head and steel teeth. By this effective implement four or five drills can be drawn at the same time, thus greatly facilitating labor at the most important season of the year, and securing the neat appearance of the bed.

Fig. 14.

The Dibble is used for making holes in which to set out roots or plants. It is generally made of an old spade handle, having the lower part sharpened, and sometimes shod with iron. The depth of its insertion in the ground may be regulated by a small peg, which can be placed at various heights.

Pruning-Shears are of several patterns. They are found useful in trimming currant bushes, raspberries, gooseberries, and especially grape vines.

Fig. 15.

Garden-Shears are convenient for trimming box and hedges, and grass borders. They are found of various sizes. Each one may consult his own taste for that; but it is important that they should be of the best metal, as they are liable to lose their edge from cutting hard substances. They should be kept dry to prevent rust.

Fig. 16.

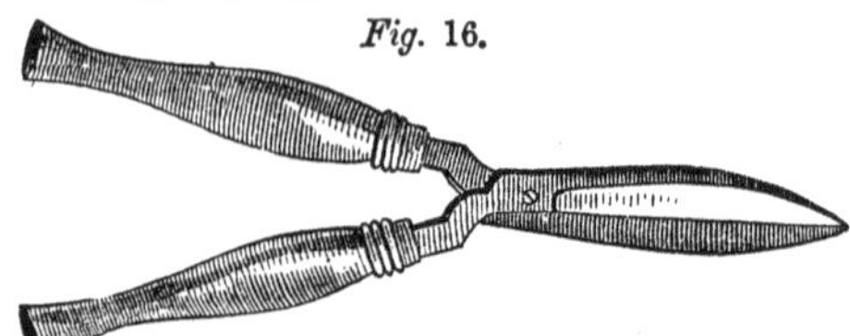

THE TROWEL is a very valuable tool for transplanting cabbages, &c.; as the plants can be taken up with balls of earth attached, and set out in another part of the garden with but little danger of injuring the roots.

Fig. 17.

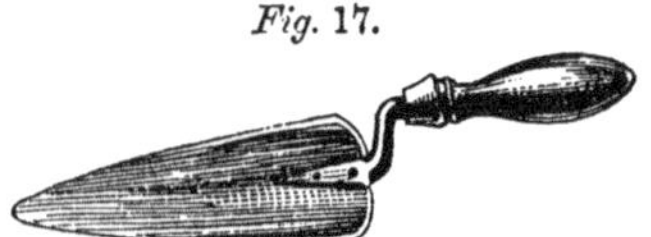

The WATERING POT will be found necessary, where watering the plants is practiced. It is made of different sizes When not in use, hang it so that the water can run out of the rose. If well taken care of, and occasionally painted, it will last a long time.

Fig. 18.

The WATER-CARRIER is a tight barrel or cask, attached to a pair of old wheels, and used for carrying water about the grounds. When large quantities of water are wanted, this is far less tiresome work than to carry it in buckets. Besides it makes a great saving of time. No one who has ever made use of one would willingly be deprived of it. The cost of it would be saved in one season.

Fig. 19.

The GARDEN-ENGINE is adapted to the wants of a very large garden. The one represented in Fig. 21, will hold about forty gallons, and can be easily wheeled around and worked by one person. It will throw water to the height of forty feet, and to the distance of seventy feet horizontally. It may, therefore, be found of use in extinguishing fire in buildings.

Fig. 20.

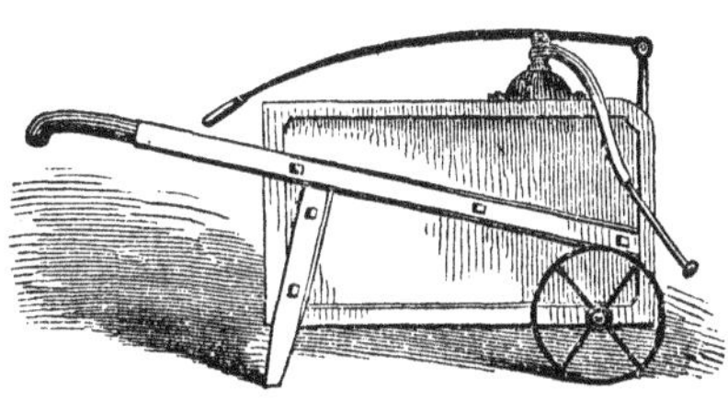

GENERAL MANAGEMENT.

THE EMPLOYMENT OF TIME.

The object of the gardener is to bring his vegetables forward to perfection, in the shortest period of time, and at the smallest expense. His success depends mainly upon the observance of certain principles, which are few in number, and easy of comprehension, viz.: depth and fertility of soil; a proper rotation of crops; selecting the best varieties of seeds; sowing at the most suitable seasons; a strict attention to the wants of the growing plant; the destruction of weeds and insects; keeping the soil open to the beneficial influences of the atmosphere; the application of water in time of drought; and care in raising seeds for future use. Under such management, unless there be some unusual natural occurrences to prevent, he may be sure of an ample return for his industry. In this chapter we propose to illustrate these principles more in detail; but, by way of preface, shall offer a few practical suggestions upon the employment of time, which, perhaps, may not be unworthy of the reader's attention.

An old proverb declares that "time is money." And, indeed, he who makes an improper use of it, is as little deserving of pity as the prodigal who wastes all his substance in riotous living. Of all men who earn a subsistence by the sweat of the brow, the gardener can least afford to be idle. The seasons of the year roll round in their course, and make no pause for the footsteps of the sluggard. In the garden there is always something to be done; each month has its appropriate duties; and the workman must not suffer himself to fall behind hand, with the idea that he can at any hour catch up with his work. Not so; for of all things lost, time is about the most difficult to regain, if what Poor Richard says be true,—"Lost time is never found again. He that riseth late must trot all day, and shall scarce overtake his business at night."

Procrastination may cause serious injury;—the proper season for committing the seed to the ground may pass by; or the labors of months may be destroyed in a single day. The gardener should not suffer his work to get in arrear. If he be so unfortunate, his troubles increase at every turn; he finds himself unprepared for the duties of the present moment, because lost time must first be redeemed. And, ten chances to one, after striving hard to regain his former position, and after battling manfully against the encroachments of weeds and insects, he becomes discouraged, throws aside the hoe, and permits the crops to come to maturity as they will.

But, good reader, our advice is not only "to keep up with your work," as it is familiarly termed, but also to keep in advance of it, whenever that be practicable. "Defer not until evening what the morning may accomplish." The numerous advantages of such a course are so evident, that they here need no exposition. In the winter, you should prepare yourself for the approach of spring, so that you may welcome it with a cheerful spirit. There are numerous things which may be done at that season of the year, when the earth is locked up in the chill embraces of frost, that will facilitate labor at other times; such as bringing manure from the stable, and piling it up in a convenient place, getting the different implements in order, hunting up bean poles and pea brush, &c., &c. As soon as the ground opens, and the weather becomes sufficiently mild, you will be in readiness to make the first sowing. There will be no hurry and confusion. If you be in advance of the regular time, you will gain much if the season prove auspicious; but, if obliged, by unfavorable circumstances, to repeat the labor, you can still secure a crop. Thus, an eminent author has said, "The management of a garden consists in attention and application; the first should be of that wary and provident kind, as not only to do well in the present, but for the future; and the application should be of so diligent a nature, as 'never to defer that till to-morrow which may be done to-day.'"

What is the proper time for work? The most important duties of the year are crowded into a few weeks of spring, yet there is much to be done at every other season. Industry at that particular period is generally considered most unnecessary, because if the ground be once planted and afterwards neglected, there is always a possibility of the vegetables being able to live through the various attacks of their enemies. But, should the owner of the garden be then idle, he has afterwards no chance to retrieve his error. "The sluggard will not plough by reason of the cold; therefore, shall he beg in harvest and have nothing."

From these remarks, however, we must not be considered as discouraging labor at other seasons, or recommending the mere preparation of the ground, and then leaving the result to nature. Not by any means. The person who thus wastes time and money, deserves not the honorable title of a gardener. During the summer and autumn, and even during a part of winter, there is always something to be done. The truly industrious man will not find himself at a loss for work. The ground is to be stirred, weeds to be cut down, vermin to be destroyed, walks to be cleaned, manure to be prepared,—and so on from one year's end to another. If the duties of each season and each month be not punctually met in their turn there can be little ground of hope for a generous reward. The gardener must not suffer himself to be idle, so long as a single green thing is to be seen upon his premises. Many an estimate of his character will be drawn from nothing else than the neat, or slovenly appearance of his beds. Self-respect, even if there be no other consideration, should prompt him to the formation of industrious habits, and to the exercise of perseverance under every discouragement.

He should also learn to economize time. The farmer, or a person who is engaged in other business, has only a few spare minutes each day to devote to the culture of his garden. Even this short allowance may be made productive of the best results. We know several merchants, who, by rising early and devoting an hour or two to their vegetables before breakfast, not only preserve their bodily health, but have the satisfaction of supplying their own tables with the most nutritious food throughout the year. One hour in the cool of the morning, is worth three or four in the heat and dust of mid-day. Beware of the "yet a little sleep, a little slumber, a little folding of the hands to sleep," when your plants are making loud calls upon your attention.

It is only by such judicious management, that one having the care of a garden, can hope to derive profit or pleasure from its cultivation. He who makes no effort at success, surely deserves not the reward. He little merits the prize, who is willing to see it snatched from his hand without a struggle to detain it. Nature is lavish of her bounties, but she gives them to none but those who base their claims upon untiring industry and perseverance.

A PROGRAMME OF LABOR.

Before he ventures to leave port, the mariner decides upon the course he is to pursue across the trackless ocean; not waiting for circumstances to determine whither he shall direct his vessel. The architect, who is engaged in building a house, before he suffers the first stone to be laid, draws up his plans, and makes an estimate of its cost. The several advantages of doing this are sufficiently obvious. Now, it seems to us, that it is scarcely less important for the farmer and gardener to lay down plans of their work, than for the sailor to mark out his voyage upon the chart, or for the builder to design the elevation of his house. It is with each an object to economize time and prevent disappointment. He is always a shiftless fellow, who works without any settled plan, and shapes his course by contingencies as they arise. We never like to see a farmer delayed in the spring, merely because he don't know where first to insert the ploughshare; it is perfectly clear that he has no system nor method, and that he is liable to many defeats in consequence. The success of the gardener who is thus situated, is even yet more precarious.

What we would earnestly recommend, is for the reader, at the commencement of each year, to draw up a programme of its operations. By this means, he need never be at a loss what to do next; when the season of spring fairly opens, he is not obliged to waste time, so precious at this juncture, in deciding how the ground shall be laid out, or where particular plants are to be cultivated. This programme should be a neat diagram of the garden, with its borders and principal compartments apportioned out among the different vegetables. Of course, many alterations will be made in this plan, from time to time, as unforeseen circumstances may render advisable; and to avoid defacing the paper, it might be best to use a lead pencil for inserting the names, so that they can easily be rubbed out by india-rubber. When no further corrections are to be made, the names can be written in ink. This is a very pretty employment for long winter evenings, when the gardener has plenty of time at command. The trouble and expense are nothing, compared with the actual benefit to be derived from the use of such a programme. It lightens and expedites labor, besides saving much trouble and perplexity, at the busy seasons.

DEPTH AND MELLOWNESS OF THE SOIL.

Depth and mellowness of soil may be considered the principal characteristics of successful gardening. In our school-boy days, we have all read of the dying husbandman, who told his son never to part with the vineyard, as there was a valuable treasure lying within a few inches of the surface. The young man, in the expectation of finding a bag of money, carefully turned over the soil, but found nothing. In the subsequent harvest, however, he was astonished at the extraordinary luxuriance of his crops, and then understood for the first time the enigmatical meaning of his father's words.

The most obvious advantage of having a deep, mellow soil, is that the roots of plants are thereby enabled to extend themselves further, and with greater facility, in search of nutriment. The delicate fibrils of the onion have been traced to the depth of two feet, and those of the Swedish turnip to the depth of five feet, below the surface. And long after they become invisible to the naked eye, they may be detected, by the aid of a microscope, pushing down deeper and deeper their thread-like extremities. Downing remarks, "I have seen the roots of strawberries extend five feet down in a rich, deep soil; and those plants bore a crop of fruit five times as large, and twice as handsome and good, as the common product of a soil only one foot deep." Every one who knows for what purposes roots are designed, viz.: to gather food from the soil, as well as to support the stem in an upright position, will perceive that as their foraging ground may be extended, so the health and vigor of the plants to which they belong will be increased.

A deep loam derives much benefit from the atmosphere, in the development of its natural powers of productiveness. It has also been ascertained, that the air we breathe is charged with a large per centage of the elements of vegetable growth, which it readily yields to a light, porous soil. Such a soil permits the immediate escape of water after heavy rains, and yet, by its capillary attraction furnishes a supply of moisture during a protracted drought. By its friability, it is more capable of absorbing heat during sunshine, and, therefore, more sensible of the early approaches of spring; and yet, it radiates heat so rapidly, that the deposit of dew in the summer nights is greatly facilitated. These latter two properties are very important, because the warmth of the sun is necessary for the roots, and because the free deposit of dew protects them from the fatal consequences of continued dry weather.

In fact, the only soil suitable for gardening purposes, is one which is both deep and mellow—one which allows the roots to penetrate far below the surface, and is at the same time open to the meliorating influences of the atmosphere. A rich loam of but a few inches in depth, resting upon a cold, compact substratum, is hardly worth the trouble of cultivation. When the substratum is broken up, and made fertile by a regular process of tillage, then—and not until then—will its full powers be developed. Hence it appears, that the gardener's first care, after he has got his ground properly laid out, is to pulverize it thoroughly for the reception of the seed.

If you have not much experience in these matters, you will inquire, good reader, how this is to be accomplished? In the outset, it may be as well to call in the assistance of a subsoil plough, which pulverizes the substratum without bringing it to the surface. This will answer a very good purpose, especially if you be in a hurry to get the ground in readiness for planting; but, at all times afterward, avoid the use of a plough. The paths will be broken up, the small shrubs injured, and early plants destroyed, by the awkward movements of the team; and, in addition to all that, the work will be done neither neatly nor thoroughly. You must, therefore, resort to the spade, which is the honorable badge of your profession. Some persons prefer the fork, because in consequence of its being much lighter, it diminishes the labor, while it effects a more thorough pulverization of the soil. In this book, we shall always use the word spade, and let the reader take either implement, according to his own fancy.

Many works on this subject recommend "trenching," as it is called, by which the surface soil changes places with the barren subsoil. It is truly said, that in course of time, the whole will become of equal depth and fertility. But a very important fact is overlooked, viz.: that until this be accomplished, the labor and expense of cultivation are much increased, and that the plants obtain only a scanty subsistence in their early stages, before the roots have penetrated to the rich soil.

We consider the following a much better plan. It is sometimes termed the "bastard system" of trenching, and is thus performed:—you commence at one corner of the bed, and open by the side of the path a trench two feet wide, and one spade deep, throwing the dirt into the path. Dig the bottom of the trench as thoroughly as possible, and mix with it the dung which is to be applied at this time. Run the spade down deep, and pulverize all the large clods. Then open a second trench of the same width and depth, throwing the dirt into the first one. Dig over the bottom in the manner above directed, and cover it with the top spit of the third trench; and so proceed until you reach the other side of the bed, where you find yourself with an open trench, which must be filled by the earth lying in the path.

By this method, the whole piece of ground is spaded about two feet deep, and manure is intimately mixed with the lower spit. The good surface soil is retained in its old position, while the improvement of the substratum is left to the gradual mixture of the two, as well as to the influence of manures and the atmosphere. This thorough digging should be repeated every four or five years. To avoid the inconvenience of being obliged to do the whole at one time, it will be well to take one quarter every year, by which means the whole garden will be gone over in the required period. After this course has been pursued several times, and the whole soil has become moderately fertile, it may be well to try the trenching system; but, never at the formation of a garden. In trenching, you dig the first trench two spades deep, and fill in from the adjoining one—the top spit being placed at the bottom, and thus completely reversing the position of the surface and sub-soils.

In addition to this quadrennial overturning, every bed will require an annual spading previous to the reception of the seed. It is performed somewhat in the way above described. Open a trench of the depth and width of the spade, and fill it by opening a second one, and so on to the other edge of the bed. Endeavor to raise about the same quantity of earth at each insertion of the spade, and deposite it in the trench with the bottom side uppermost. As you proceed, break up all the lumps, and keep the surface level, by a peculiar stroke which is soon acquired by practice. The work will be much facilitated by digging in a perfectly straight line, and to a uniform depth. If manure is to be applied, when old and well rotted, it may be spread upon the bed, and spaded under; but if long and troublesome, it should be placed in the bottom of the trench.

The two kinds of trenching may be performed late in autumn, or in winter before severe cold weather sets in. At that time, the gardener will not be hurried, and there will also be the advantage of exposing grubs and larvæ to the frost. The annual spading, or pulverization of the surface soil, had best be done in spring; or it can be done roughly in autumn, and dressed over with the rake just previous to sowing. Dry weather should always be selected for this work, when the earth crumbles easily; because, if wet or heavy, on being stirred thus by the spade, it becomes a kind of mortar, and the operation, instead of being advantageous, is in reality productive of much injury.

MANURES.

Giving manure to the soil, so as to furnish it with the constituents of vegetable growth, is quite as important as its thorough pulverization. Jethro Tull, the celebrated English agriculturist, more than a century ago maintained that the latter only is necessary to ensure abundant crops. This doctrine, however, has long since been proved fallacious. The application of manure is essential to fertility, and unless the soil be fertile, the gardener cannot derive much profit from its cultivation. Where the raising of vegetables is conducted upon a large scale, as in market gardens, the land is not allowed to remain idle, but there is a regular succession of crops, one taking the place of another as soon as removed; and yet, by the process of manuring, the land is all the time becoming better. Manure is all important;—with it, the gardener can do everything; without it, nothing. By its power, the most sterile spot can be made fertile, and the wilderness made to blossom as the rose. But, the idea of producing vegetables without manure, is about equal to that of the farmer who expects an ill-fed cow to give milk. Both the animal and the soil must be liberally supplied with food of good quality, before they can be expected to yield a return.

A garden of common size can, by proper management, be kept in good tilth at a small annual expense. Where connected with a farm, the principal supply of manure will be drawn from the barn-yard, or the stable. Everything which will act as a fertilizer should be carefully husbanded; as cents will by accumulation become dollars. The refuse matter of the grounds, such as decayed stalks, leaves, weeds, &c., should be turned to good account. About the best purpose to which a weed can be put, is to place it in the compost heap or pig pen. Forest leaves, after being thoroughly worked over by swine, are excellent food for vegetables. Let nothing be wasted upon your premises; for your manure heap may be likened to a cash capital, which, when invested, returns to you with interest.

If you have a large supply of manure, it will be best to mix it with the soil whenever it may be spaded or trenched. A portion should be incorporated with the substratum, every time it is dug over, so as to hasten its gradual improvement. Another portion, however, should be kept near the surface, that the young roots may not have far to travel in search of nutriment. Should your supply be small, or not large enough to admit of this broadcast application, you must put it in the hills, or drills, for the larger vegetables. But, in every case, it ought to be *thoroughly incorporated with the soil.* The autumn, or winter, is the best time for doing this, as there will be less danger of the plants being injured by its heat, than if it were applied late in the spring. We fear that the parched appearance of the ground in some gardens, at midsummer, is from ignorance of this fact. In the remaining part of this article, we shall enumerate the several kinds of manure most valuable for horticultural purposes.

Horse-dung is placed at the head of the list, because most generally used. There can be no doubt of its superior fertilizing effects. In an experiment with beans, in which six acres were manured with horse-dung, and nine with cow-dung, the six acres yielded more abundantly than the nine. Its value is dependent upon the food given to the animals, and the proportion of dung to straw, which absorbs the fluids, but reduces the value of any given weight of the manure. It ferments quickly, and to prevent the loss of the volatile matters, should be composted soon after being taken from the stalls.

Cow-dung is chiefly dependent for its value upon the condition of the animals, as well as the care which may be taken in its preservation. That from half-starved beasts, and which is suffered to remain for months exposed to sun and rain, is by no means the best for the gardener's use. It is colder than the dung of the horse, and, fermenting more slowly, retains its virtue longer. Its effects are, therefore, of greater duration.

Pig-dung is very good when used alone, although its strong odor sometimes imparts a rank taste to the vegetables. It also forms an excellent compost with the excrements of horses and horned cattle. They should be thrown into a heap, in alternate layers, and receive the urine and slops from the house. A hog kept on the premises can be made to earn his living, by converting grass-sods, leaves and refuse vegetables into manure.

POUDRETTE is very exciting, and is peculiarly adapted for the advancement of early crops. Much of that purchased by farmers and gardeners is of an inferior quality. Care should always be exercised in securing the best, as it costs no more than the other.

BIRDS'-DUNG has long been known as an active and powerful fertilizer. It is excellent for melons and plants of the same family. That produced by the poultry on the premises can be gathered with very little trouble. The real guano is exceedingly powerful, and must be applied with caution. We strongly suspect a great part of that in market to be nothing more than common dirt, perfumed with brine or something of the sort;—at least, its effects upon vegetation are about the same.

GREEN VEGETABLE MATTER may be considered of great value. Much that is carelessly wasted on farms, or even in gardens, would be beneficial to the succeeding crop. Every large weed, useless vegetable, and decayed stalk, should be carried to the compost heap, or pig pen, or else dug immediately into the ground. In the latter case, it ought not to be buried so deep as to prevent fermentation by the want of air.

CHARCOAL. It is within a few years, that a knowledge of the value of charcoal for manure has become general. And it seems to be specially adapted to garden use. Being porous, it has the power of absorbing various gases from the atmosphere, and, when subsequently placed in the soil, it readily yields them to the plants. It is excellent for mixing with night soil, as it retains the offensive—but valuable—ammonia, which would otherwise escape in the air. Besides this absorbent action, charcoal will loosen tough soils, and by its black color increase their warmth. It is applied in the shape of small lumps, or dust, and at the rate of one bushel to four square rods.

Ashes are among the most economical manures. Containing every element of vegetable growth, their return to the soil is very advantageous. They attract moisture from the atmosphere, and are somewhat useful as a protection against the ravages of insects. From the free use of wood as fuel, every gardener will probably have a supply of ashes in his own dwelling; if not, he can purchase them at a moderate price from his neighbors.

Salt, applied in small quantities, is strongly recommended by modern writers,—especially for such plants as sea-kale and asparagus. In addition to its influence as a manure, it is also useful in destroying slugs, worms and larvæ, which are hidden in the ground. Its effects are so powerful, that it must be applied with caution;—perhaps, for general purposes, at the rate of half a pound to the square yard; it is, however, frequently used in much larger proportions. When the weather is dry, the salt should be forked into the soil immediately after being spread.

Sea-weed can be easily obtained by gardeners who live in the vicinity of the sea coast. It is found very suitable for marine plants such as the artichoke, asparagus and sea-kale. Its effects are transient. It is applied either fresh as a top-dressing, or after being composted with dung and earth.

ROTATION OF CROPS.

Although instances are frequently cited, of certain plants being raised on particular spots of ground for year after year, without any apparent diminution in the produce; yet, it is generally allowed, that a rotation of crops is always of advantage, and often of the greatest importance. We consider it as necessary as depth and mellowness of soil, and the regular application of manures. Gardeners are sometimes heard to complain of vegetables becoming "tired" of the ground where they have been long cultivated. They are attacked by numerous diseases and insects, while a deficiency is to be discovered in the amount of the produce. As soon as this is known, some wiseacres will send many miles, in order to procure new varieties of seed, because the old ones have "degenerated."

A more certain method of relief, would be to adopt a good rotation of crops, which is based on the well known fact, that the several families of plants not only strike their roots to different depths and in different directions, but draw different kinds of nourishment from the soil. When one particular element of a vegetable is removed from the soil, the vegetable cannot be again raised there, until that element be restored. It is, therefore, advisable to alternate the crops, by which means the land will have opportunity to regain its original strength and fertility. This is illustrated by Dame Nature herself. If old pastures were to be attentively observed, it would be found that the grasses gradually change from season to season; and in wood-land, it would be discovered, that an entirely different kind of tree takes the place of such as have decayed, or have been cut down. Thus the pine and others of the coniferæ will succeed the oak, the chestnut, and other deciduous trees.

A rotation is designed to prevent a too frequent recurrence of the same species upon a particular spot. Some authors lay down regular plans for the guidance of their readers; but as the space annually appropriated to different plants depends upon circumstances, it will be readily seen that all such courses or plans are difficult of application. Instead, therefore, of following this practice, we shall content ourselves with some general rules, which possess the merits of simplicity and briefness, so that the reader can adapt them to his own wants.

In the first place, vegetables of the same species shall not follow each other, but return at as distant intervals as the case will allow. Tuberous or tap roots should be succeeded by those of a fibrous character; perennials by annuals; and plants of a dry, solid texture, or those left for seed, by such as are succulent and juicy. Ground which has necessarily been devoted for a number of years to the artichoke, asparagus, rhubarb, strawberry, and the like, should, as soon as they are removed to other parts of the enclosure, be subjected to a strict rotation, and allowed to recover those elements of fertility of which it has been exhausted. Where the garden is divided into quarters, the vegetables can easily be made to take a circuit in every four or eight years.

A little reflection will satisfy the intelligent reader, that by observing an alternation of crops, digging his soil to a proper depth, and manuring it abundantly, he need have no fear of its losing its fertility, or of his choice vegetables degenerating.

INDICATIONS OF RAIN.

Changes in the weather affect the gardener much more than the farmer. As will be seen from the following pages, the operations of sowing small seeds and transplanting, are most successful if performed just before gentle showers. Persons who are exposed to these natural phenomena, such as agriculturists and sailors, in time acquire much practical knowledge of the subject. Many rules have been published by which one can discern an approaching change in the weather that we would like to insert in this place, did our limits admit of it. For the sake of awakening the reader's attention, we append the following "Signs of Rain," said to have been sent by Dr. Jenner to a friend, with whom he had planned an excursion:

"The hollow winds begin to blow,
The clouds look black, the glass is low;
The soot falls down, the spaniels sleep,
And spiders from their cobwebs peep.

Last night the sun went pale to bed,
The moon in halos hid her head;
The boding shepherd heaves a sigh,
For, see, a rainbow spans the sky;
The walls are damp, the ditches smell,
Closed is the pink-eyed pimpernel.
Hark! how the chairs and tables crack,
Old Betty's joints are on the rack;
Loud quack the ducks, the peacocks cry;
The distant hills are looking nigh.
How restless are the snorting swine,
The busy flies disturb the kine;
Low o'er the grass the swallow wings;
The cricket, too, how sharp he sings;
Puss, on the hearth, with velvet paws,
Sits, wiping o'er her whisker'd jaws.
Through the clear stream the fishes rise,
And nimbly catch th' incautious flies;
The glow-worms, numerous and bright,
Illum'd the dewy dell last night.
At dusk the squalid toad was seen,
Hopping and crawling o'er the green;
The whirling wind the dust obeys,
And in the rapid eddy plays;
The frog has chang'd his yellow vest,
And in a russet coat is drest.
Though June, the air is cold and still;
The black-bird's mellow voice is shrill.
My dog, so alter'd is his taste,
Quits mutton bones, on grass to feast;
And see, yon rooks, how odd their flight,
They imitate the gliding kite,
And seem precipitate to fall—
As if they felt the piercing ball.
'Twill surely rain, I see with sorrow,
Our jaunt must be put off to-morrow."

SELECTION OF SEEDS.

Every one ought to know that there is a great difference in the productiveness and flavor of our common garden products. In fact, some of the varieties are scarcely worthy of notice. Therefore, when you go to the expense of laying out a garden, you should endeavor to procure none other than the choicest kinds of vegetables, and such as will afford a succession of crops. It is a great object with market men to raise the earliest and latest varieties, which always command the best prices. And it is no less important for families, who can, by proper management, derive the greater part of their living from the garden. The labor and cost of cultivation are no greater, while the profit and satisfaction are much increased.

In the beginning of your labors, you must of necessity procure the seeds from some enterprising neighbor, or a regular seedsman. In the latter case, go to a well known and responsible person,—if possible, one of your acquaintances. It is generally understood, that of the seeds annually exposed for sale, a very large part are worthless, having lost their vitality, or being of inferior varieties. The vexation of preparing land and realizing nothing, is equalled by waiting patiently for several months to obtain nothing but a small, tough, stringy product. It is not a fine sounding name which makes a valuable variety.

But, with all your care, you may get deceived. Perhaps the seed will not vegetate, or it proves different from what it was represented. Even then you must not hastily impute blame to the seedsman. It cannot be expected that he should raise all that he sells, and he may have been deceived as well as yourself. In the absence of proof, or very strong grounds of suspicion, it would certainly be wrong to believe him guilty of fraud. You must not jump at a conclusion. Because the seed *did* not vegetate, is no evidence that it *would* not have done so if placed in favorable circumstances. That plants do not appear above ground, may have been caused by your own ignorance; perhaps the seed was buried so low that its tender stem could not reach the surface, or else covered so slightly that the germ, as soon as it manifested itself, was killed by the heat. Defect of germination may have been the result of natural causes, such as excessive heat or cold, or the extreme dryness or dampness of the ground. For these reasons, you should be positively certain, before you dare level a blow at a man's reputation.

To discover whether seeds possess the power of vegetation, is quite as important for your own benefit, as to test the seedsman's honesty. Sowing dead seed will occasion the loss of much time and patience. You should, therefore, take a little of that which you consider doubtful, and steep it in warm water for several hours, when, if it show unmistakable signs of sprouting, you may sow as soon as you please. The only way to discover whether you have been cheated in the quality of the plant, is to wait patiently until the crop comes to maturity.

SOWING.

> "Then plant the germinating seed,
> And reap an honest, grateful meed."

This is, undoubtedly, the most important operation of the whole year. In the want of personal experience, the young beginner is obliged to rely upon the instructions of others.

The first inquiry will naturally be as to the most suitable time for sowing. By an examination of the DICTIONARY in the succeeding part of the volume, it will appear that there are varieties ripening at different seasons, and which require to be sown at different periods. Those intended for autumn and winter use are, as a general thing, to be sown two or three months later than those which are wanted during the summer.

Some cultivators prefer sowing in autumn, and protecting the plants through the winter, by which course the crop may be expected many days earlier, than where the opening of spring is waited for. Whether this gain will counterbalance the extra trouble and risk, the student must determine for himself. Others recommend sowing in a hot-bed about the latter part of winter, and transplanting to the open ground as soon as the weather becomes mild. The earliest sowing in the open air should be in a warm border, to be protected during cold nights by means of mats or straw. Should the plants be cut off by frost, there will still be plenty of time to secure a crop. There is an old English saying, that "the early sower never borrows of the late."

Sowing should always be performed in dry weather, particularly when the soil is of a tenacious character. In working ground just after a heavy fall of rain, it adheres to the spade, or other implement, and becomes a kind of mortar, which is baked by the sun into a hard crust with difficulty penetrated by the tender stem. We, therefore, prefer to sow when the earth is light and free, and when there is a prospect of a shower or gentle rain. This wakens the germ into life, and brings it up to the surface a vigorous plant. The soil should be finely pulverized, so as to come in contact with the very smallest seed. And it should, moreover, be freshly stirred, because it will then be full of atmospheric air, moist and permeable to heat, which are the three essential requisites for germination.

In gardens, it is customary to form beds of convenient width for subsequent cultivation. We think that an average width of four feet is suitable. Although, by this arrangement, there will be a great deal of ground in the shape of alleys and paths lying idle, the ease of taking care of the plants will thereby be much increased. It is well to have the beds as nearly as possible of a uniform size, because regularity of lines adds to the general appearance of the whole. The tops of the beds should be levelled smoothly, and the sides made sloping, so that they will not crumble down at the first rain. The rake is a very effective implement for such work; it brings all the small stones into the alleys, and breaks up the lumps of earth which the spade has left. Let all this be done neatly, because the owner will then take greater satisfaction in the after-culture.

Broadcast sowing is deservedly falling into disrepute, for with a gardener its only recommendation is that of expedition at the most hurried season. In reality, however, it causes an actual loss of time. The plants must be thinned out and transplanted at a period when every moment should be spent in resisting the encroachments of weeds and insects. There is considerable risk in this removal from the seed bed;—the fibrous roots are broken and injured, so that unusual care is necessary in their protection, until they become fairly established. The drill system is certainly much more tidy and convenient. The hoe can be used freely, while the beneficial influences of light and air are effectually admitted to the leaves and soil. The good effects will be discovered, not only in the increased product and its improved quality, but also in the better preparation of the land for the succeeding crop.

A seed requires heat, air and moisture to ensure germination. In the absence of either of these three conditions, it may remain dormant for centuries. When wakening into life, moisture is absorbed, the seed swells, the starch is converted into sugar, the germ bursts its integuments, and the stem pushes its way towards the surface, while the root buries itself downward in search of nutriment. Now, it is surely an object to hasten this process, for thereby the crop will be accelerated, and the young plant sooner placed beyond all danger from the attacks of its enemies. The mere putting the seed into the ground is not always sufficient. With certain kinds, it is well known that days, or even weeks, will elapse before the plant is developed; by which time the weeds may have taken undisturbed possession of the bed.

A great deal has been said lately about steeping the seeds before planting, so as to hasten vegetation. Various steeps have been proposed, among which are solutions of saltpetre, nitrate of soda, muriate of ammonia, sulphate of ammonia, guano, and chloride of lime. Warm water answers a very good purpose. The length of time for each kind of seed to remain in the steep varies, and must be determined, together with many other things of equal importance, by experiment. If suffered to remain too long, putrefaction will commence, which either weakens or destroys the vitality of the germ. We do not think it prudent, as a general thing, to delay sowing after the seed swells and gives unmistakable signs of sprouting. Should the ground be very dry, and continue so, the moisture in the seed will probably be abstracted, and the germ will perish; in such case, it is advisable to apply water every day until all danger is over. Perhaps the ground may be wet and cold, and then the gardener need not be surprised if, after waiting patiently a week for the plants to discover themselves, he should find that the seeds have rotted. Therefore, this plan of steeping seeds must be used with caution; or delay and vexation may result instead of benefit.

The manner of sowing next demands attention. If broadcast, the seed may be covered by a rake, or a branch of a tree, or a roller—which, indeed, is preferable in dry weather, as it makes the surface compact, without leaving any hiding places for insects. If in drills, the drill-rakes should be used for marking out the ground. For example, say the seed is to be sown in drills eight inches apart;—take the rake, having its teeth set at that distance, and draw it across one end of the bed, by which means several drills (according to the number of teeth) will be made at the same time. Then place one tooth in the last drill, and again draw the rake over the bed; and so on, until the whole be marked out. The depth of the drills will be regulated by the force with which you bear upon the rake. Then sow the seed, either thinly or thickly, as directed for the different vegetables in the DICTIONARY. Let the work be done well, as "Seeds are great tell-tales; for when they come up, we discover all the carelessness that may have prevailed at the sowing of them."

The surface of the bed should be pressed into close contact with the seed; it can be done by beating it gently with the back of the spade, by the use of the roller, by treading down the drills, or by walking upon a board. In using the board, place it lengthwise of the bed, and walk on it from end to end; then move it, and so proceed until the whole surface be made smooth and compact.

If the weather continue dry, the ground may be gently watered soon after sowing, and regularly afterwards until the young plants become established. This has been proved of decided benefit. But, when this artificial watering has induced the germ to start prematurely, and is then withheld, the consequences are fatal; the plant dies for want of moisture in the surrounding soil. In this, as in several other matters, we cannot too often repeat, that the reader must depend more upon his own judgment, than upon any written directions.

CULTIVATION WITH THE HOE.

As soon as the young plants appear above ground, they require attention. They will probably come up very thick in the drills, and need being thinned out whenever the seed-leaves are well developed. This should by no means be neglected. With a narrow hoe, loosen the soil to a moderate depth, cut down all weeds, however small, and thin the plants so that they will stand about an inch distant from each other in the drills. It is not advisable, in this early stage of their growth, to pull up more; as you may lose many by the depredations of vermin. It is even better to go over the ground half a dozen times, than to make a second sowing to fill up vacant spaces. In a few days' time, the stems will acquire considerable size, so that you must give them another—and, if much hurried, the final—thinning. As to the distances to be observed for the different vegetables, we refer you to the DICTIONARY.

The hoe has frequently been called the gardener's best friend. We do not know that it can be too often used. An old distich runs,—

> "The more we hoe,
> The more we grow."

Hoeing is of benefit even when there are no weeds to destroy; and in fact it should be the object to *keep*, rather than to *get*, them out of the beds. Hoeing makes the ground sweet, and open to the atmosphere; whereby the crops are much sooner brought to maturity, and in greater perfection. Strange as it may seem, keeping the surface light and porous, will prevent the parching effects of drought. Thus, in a dry season, a well-tilled garden suffers less than a field of grain on the opposite side of the fence.

During the day time, the loose soil imbibes heat freely, and transmits it to the most distant rootlets, securing to them that warmth which is so essential to a vigorous growth; but, at the approach of evening, when the temperature of the air falls, a reversed action takes place, and the heat is radiated or thrown off quite as rapidly as it was received. If, on a hot day, you fill a pitcher with cold water, in a few moments you will find the outside covered with drops of moisture, and it is a common expression that "the pitcher sweats." Instead, however, of the drops having been drawn through the pores of the vessel like perspiration through the skin, they are drops of vapor condensed from the surrounding air upon the cold pitcher. So with the soil at evening; as soon as by the radiation of heat it becomes colder than the atmosphere, that moisture which we call dew is condensed, and transmitted to the roots. The extent of this beautiful operation is just in proportion to the looseness of the surface. Thus Cobbett says, "A man will raise more moisture, with a hoe or spade, in a day, than he can pour on the earth out of a watering pot in a month."

We shall say nothing upon the chemical action of the air upon an open soil, which might involve us in some tedious disquisition, but, instead thereof, relate an experiment made by Curwen, an eminent agriculturist. He planted cabbages upon a piece of ground so stiff and forbidding, that the neighbors considered his labor lost. Not discouraged by their sneers, he took a horse and cultivator, and subjected the land to almost constant stirring throughout the season. The end of the matter was, that he gathered an immense crop,—some of the heads weighing over fifty pounds each. The beneficial results of such treatment are so well attested, that one of the most noted horticulturists in our country, writes in the following strain:—"If I had 'a call' to preach a sermon on gardening I should take this for my text, '*Stir the soil.*'"

The reader needs not to be informed of the worthlessness of weeds. Every one takes up as much room and robs the soil of as much nutriment, as a useful plant. It should be the intention to keep them out of the garden limits. But, this is scarcely possible. With all your care, they will obtain an entrance, and you then have no other course to pursue, than to commence the work of extirpation. The moment a head peeps above the surface, cut it off with the hoe, or, where found in a drill, do not hesitate to use the thumb and forefinger.

Do not neglect so important a duty; for, as "ill weeds grow apace," a few hours' labor at this period will effect more than whole days of hard drudgery, after they have acquired a mastery. You cannot commence too soon; and it is even better to give up sowing late varieties, than to neglect those which are already suffering from the want of your care. Keep

6

your hoe polished brightly, and your vegetables free from such unworthy associates. But, by no means allow one of the foul intruders to go to seed upon your premises. Tear it up, root and branch, and carry it to the compost heap, as that is about the only beneficial purpose to which it may be applied. If the seed vessels have already perfected themselves, do not put it on the heap, nor throw it in the pig pen; but burn it up, or dispose of it in such other way, as will prevent the seeds being returned to the land. Recollect that "One year's seeding makes seven years' weeding."

> "All hate the rank society of weeds,
> Noisome, and ever greedy to exhaust
> Th' impoverished earth ; an overbearing race,
> That, like the multitude made faction-mad,
> Disturb good order, and degrade true worth."

Thus keep your ground in a good state of tilth, and you may be assured of ample returns for your industry. Do not grumble if you, or your laborers, wear out half a dozen hoes in each season, if you can be satisfied that it was caused by good honest labor. The cost of a hoe is but little compared with the increased produce of a dozen bushels of vegetables.

DESTRUCTION OF VERMIN.

> "A feeble race ! yet oft
> The sacred sons of vengeance ; on whose course
> Corrosive Famine waits, and kills the year."

Nothing is more vexatious and discouraging for the gardener, than to see the objects of his care actually swept away by vermin of all kinds and sizes, of whose habits he is wholly ignorant,—unless their partiality for tender vegetables be excepted. He may have labored diligently for weeks, perhaps months; yet in a single night, his choicest plants will be destroyed. Of the whole vegetable kingdom, there is scarce a useful member which is not liable to these attacks at different stages of its growth. Some vermin prey upon the root, others choose the stem and branches, a third class prefer the leaves, a fourth select the flowers, while a fifth reject everything but the fruit or seed. For example; if the seed of the common turnip is so fortunate as to escape a minute weevil, another enemy awaits the unfolding of the first leaves; another buries itself in the bulb and rootlets, so that they become diseased, and covered with unseemly excrescences; and the mature foliage falls the prey of caterpillars. It is, therefore, the duty of the gardener to study the character and habits of these depredators, so as to guard against their attacks. The reader who may desire a thorough acquaintance with the subject, must refer to works of greater pretensions than this volume. We have room for only a few practical hints.

An ounce of prevention is said to be worth a pound of cure and the student will naturally first inquire for the best modes, of protecting his plants. This will in a measure be secured by high culture,—having the ground rich, sowing healthy seed, and hastening the maturity of the crop. As the young stems and leaves are sweetest, so are they most liable to injury; and everything that accelerates their growth, adds to their security. It is the policy of some cultivators to turn over the soil late in autumn, in order that the grubs and insects which have taken up their winter quarters may be exposed to the action of frost. We are acquainted with many gardens which have thus been almost entirely rid of these pests. The application of salt at the rate of two or three bushels per acre, in spring, or the occasional use of strong brine, is highly recommended; but, salt is a very powerful agent, and in every form must be applied with caution, lest vegetation should also be injured. Rolling or pressing the surface of the ground compactly, after sowing, is an excellent plan, as the flies are thereby deprived ' hiding places around the little lumps of dirt.

Reproduction should be prevented as much as possible. When ushing a grub under foot, or stifling a beetle, the gardener lessens the number of his enemies by millions *in embryo.* The aphides, or plant lice, multiply with astonishing rapidity, and a single butterfly has been estimated to produce thirty millions of descendants at the third generation! The butterfly, which is the parent of destructive caterpillars, will deposite its eggs upon pieces of woolen cloth laid upon currant bushes or around cabbage plants. It is even good policy to employ little boys and girls in this work, giving them a bounty on every worm, chrysalis, moth or nest of eggs, which they may discover. Children have very sharp eyes when their industry is stimulated by hopes of a pecuniary reward. Large gardens have thus been kept free from vermin at the annual cost of a few shillings. Bonfires of shavings or brush, just after twilight in the evening, will attract and destroy immense numbers of flying beetles.

The next inquiry will be, what is to be done after the vermin, in spite of all the above precautions, have actually made their appearance. The war against them must be vigorously prosecuted. The most certain, and therefore the best, mode of attack, is by hand-picking; but, the difficulty of capturing the minute and most agile insects by the fingers, will prevent its general adoption. However repulsive may be its personal appearance, the common toad is a very valuable assistant in this work. The writer who termed it "the most deformed and hideous of all animals," could scarcely have known its use in the vegetable garden. Its eye is active, and its long, viscid tongue moves so rapidly, that it will destroy twenty or more wood-lice in two or three minutes. It lives almost entirely upon small worms and insects, and in a very unostentatious and quiet manner relieves the cultivator of many of his most troublesome enemies.

But, still other plans are required. These are numerous;—such as dusting the plants, when covered with moisture, with soot, ashes, snuff, charcoal, sulphur, road-dust, powdered hen-dung, air slacked lime, etc.; or watering them and the ground with soap-suds, solutions of saltpetre, guano, hen-dung and whale oil soap,* decoctions of tobacco and elder, etc ; or fumigating them with sulphur and tobacco. Soap-suds from the wash-room is excellent for this purpose, and it likewise proves an excellent fertilizer. Whale oil soap is very cheap and efficient; care must be taken, however, not to make the solution too strong, lest it injure the plants. Of soap of an average quality, one pound may be put to seven gallons of water; but, as its strength varies much, the gardener should determine the proportions by experiment.

We have long used a solution of hen-dung with success, and we recommend it because it is always easily obtained. We have a tub standing in a convenient part of the garden, and, at the time when the insects are expected, put in the bottom about one bushel of hen-dung, upon which we pour several pailfuls of boiling water. When the mixture has become semi-fluid, by frequent stirring, we fill the tub up with water. After remaining twelve hours longer, the liquid should be of a dark green color, and somewhat offensive to the nostrils, as upon that particular depends its efficacy. It may then be cautiously applied upon melon and cabbage hills, and, in fact, every place liable to the attacks of insects.

We also make use of the vine-shield, (Fig. 4,) which not only protects the plant, but greatly accelerates its growth. Could the scratching propensities of poultry be restrained, their assistance would be of no little value. Broods of young chickens will do much good,—the hens being confined, and the chicks suffered to roam over the beds; as soon, however, as their claws become troublesome, a new brood should take their place. Whatever mode may be adopted, much depends

* *To make Whale Oil Soap.*—Take eighteen pounds of potash and thirty pounds of foot oil, and mix them together in a barrel. Every other day add twelve quarts of boiling water, and stir the whole for a few minutes every day, until the barrel be full, when the mixture will be fit for use.

upon the time when operations are commenced. The moment the enemy appears, the signal for a general onslaught should be given. By such prompt action only, may the cultivator have cause to expect a crop.

After these general directions, we think it well to give short notices of the most important vermin :—

CATERPILLARS are the young, or larvæ, of butterflies. Their appearance and habits vary so much, that it is impossible to give any particular description. They are very destructive, and should be diligently looked after. The various remedies proposed—such as lime-water, tobacco-water, brine, ashes, &c., are partial and uncertain; nothing is so effectual as hand-picking.

CUT-WORM, or BLACK GRUB. This is about the size of a goose-quill, and ash-colored with a dark stripe upon the back. During the day time, it lies snugly buried in the ground, about an inch below the surface; but emerges at night to eat off the stems of young plants. Common remedies are of no avail; lime and salt have no perceptible effect upon it. The only efficient plan is to examine the beds every morning, and by digging around those plants which have been destroyed, the worm may most generally be found. As a preventive, it is advised to wrap a burdock or walnut-tree leaf, or a small piece of writing paper, around each stem when transplanted. The vine-shield is also a good protection.

The ANT is very mischievous, and sometimes occasions considerable damage. It would be scarcely worth while to destroy a single one wherever found. In the evening, the nest may be discovered by observing the course of those returning from their day's labor. When the whole family are collected, hot water may be poured upon them, and few will escape. When the nests are numerous and this mode is thought too troublesome, they can be dug up by a spade, at any time in winter when a hard frost is anticipated, so that the inhabitants shall be exposed to the severity of the weather.

Turnip Fly.—This appears to be a general name for several kinds of agile and destructive insects which attack the turnip, the cabbage, &c., when in the seed leaf, and either totally devour them, or kill the centre buds. Their devastations are kept up with so much spirit, that the sowing of seed must in some years be repeated four or five times. Burning brush upon the ground before sowing, is an excellent preventive. Some gardeners steep the seed in sulphur-water; others put lime, slacked by urine and mixed with a treble quantity of soot, in the drill; others dust the plants with air-slacked lime, gypsum, soot, ashes, &c.; while many are satisfied with frequent sprinklings of soap suds, or even pure water. A brood of chickens is very useful.

Aphides, or Plant Lice. Almost every kind of vegetable seems to have a species of the louse peculiar to itself. They multiply with astonishing rapidity, and are of various colors—as green, brown, black, blue, red and purple. They fasten upon the tender buds, and render them incapable of development. Sometimes the entire bean crop will be thus destroyed. Sprinkle the parts affected with tobacco-water, a solution of whale oil soap, and soap suds; or dust with lime and snuff. As the ends of the branches are generally first attacked, they may be bent over into one of the above solutions; and bean or pea vines will be benefited by nipping off those parts, as the crop is thereby much increased.

The Cucumber Bug is yellow, striped with black. It eats the tender foliage and flowers of the cucumber family.

The Squash Bug has an orange-colored belly, with a turtle-shaped back. It collects under the leaves and upon the fruit of vines. In a morning when a heavy dew has fallen, the cucumber and squash bugs have not the free use of their wings, and may easily be caught by hand. We often take the trouble of knocking them, by a sly stroke, into a little dish of suds carried in the left hand.

Rose Bugs are beetles about half an inch long, with slender bodies tapering to each end. They come from the ground in June, when the rose is in blossom. Coming like a cloud of locusts, they destroy foliage and fruit of almost every description; but are remarkably fond of young grapes. We have tried several plans for their destruction, such as sprinkling them with a very strong solution of whale oil soap, and fumigating the leaves with turpentine or sulphur. About the only result of our experiments, was the loss of a fine cherry tree for which we would not have taken a ten dollar bill. The most effectual remedy is to go the rounds of the garden several times a day, and knock every trespasser into a cup of water or turpentine. When the cup is filled, it may be emptied on the ground, care being taken that none escape with a mere bath. By pursuing this course regularly and faithfully, day after day, the gardener will stand some chance of a crop; and by following it up yearly, the bugs will at length be almost exterminated.

MICE are sometimes troublesome. They may be caught in traps, or killed by arsenic—which is a certain, but not always a safe, way of getting rid of them.

SLUGS are very annoying and destructive. Thorough handpicking should be daily practiced. They are frequently caught upon cabbage leaves, or slices of turnip, laid in their way, and then committed to the fire.

The MOLE, and his burrowing habits, are too well known to need description. He is in reality an innocent trespasser; for, when undermining the gardener's smooth beds, he is in search of insects, without the least intention of injuring the seeds and plants. But as this is often a consequence of his extensive galleries, when they become numerous, some method must be contrived to get rid of his friendly visits. Traps may be purchased at the stores, but a very simple and cheap plan is to put tarred sticks in the burrows, which drive him away in disgust.

TRANSPLANTING.

Transplanting is the process of removing a plant from one situation to another. Thus, cabbage seed is generally sown broadcast, and the plants, when three or four inches high, are set out in the compartment where they are to come to maturity. As with the process of sowing, upon the time when, and the manner in which this labor may be performed, depend a successful result. The intention is, that the roots shall suffer from their change of locality as little inconvenience as possible. They ought not to be exposed to the air for any length of time, particularly in hot weather, and the ground should, therefore, be properly prepared—by being spaded deep, and manured,—before the plants are taken from the seed bed And, moreover, this preparation should be very recent, because the delicate fibres most readily attach themselves to a freshly dug loam.

Select for the operation, an evening, or a damp, cloudy day, or when a shower is expected; but not soon after a heavy rain, because the soil, if stirred when wet, is apt to become stiff like mortar, and to be baked into a hard crust by the next rays of the sun. The most successful transplanting is performed with a trowel. Push it down so as to reach below the root, and, by a dexterous movement of the hand, draw up the plant firmly set in a little ball of earth, which can be put wherever desired, and the plant will scarcely experience any check in its growth.

In transplanting with the dibble, you must go over the ground, and insert it at the proper distances, in such a manner as to leave deep, smooth holes. Draw up a sufficient number of stout, healthy plants, and carry with you, in a small vessel, a semi-fluid mass of cow-dung and water. Dip each root into the mixture, so that the dirt will adhere to the small fibrous extremities; and place it in the hole so that it will run down perfectly straight, without being turned up at the bottom

This latter caution is particularly necessary in the case of the beet, carrot, and other tap-rooted vegetables. When the plant is at the right depth, insert the dibble, or a pointed shingle, at a short distance from the stem, and push the earth up close to the root. Many people imagine that if the crown or the body be firmly set, it is quite sufficient; they surely cannot have reflected, that it is only the spongioles at the ends of the fibres which are capable of collecting nourishment from the soil, and that the body is nothing more than the channel for conveying it to the branches.

Should the weather become warm, the leaves and stem will suffer greatly from the sun's rays, unless some kind of shelter be given. A celery trench can be covered with boards during the day time. The vine-shield, with a piece of cloth, or paper, lying upon the glass, forms a good protection for cabbages which stand some distance apart. Indeed, we have often used pieces of old newspaper, laid over the plant, with a heavy stone at each corner to prevent their being blown away by the wind; this is troublesome, and not practicable in large plantations, but is well adapted for a few choice varieties, when no other means for protection are at hand. Or, a little brushwood may be thrown upon the ground, and overlaid with thin mats or straw. Whatever plan may be adopted, do not omit taking off the covering at the approach of evening, that the leaves may be favored with the usual deposite of dew. With many kinds of plants, it is advisable to apply tepid water, soon after being set out in a new bed, and every subsequent evening until the roots become firmly established. Keep the soil well stirred by the hoe, carefully eradicate every weed which springs up, and guard against the ravages of vermin. Nothing but a little attention at the proper time is necessary to ensure success.

APPLICATION OF WATER.

"The thirsty earth soaks up the rain,
And drinks, and gapes for drink again.
The plants suck in the earth, and are
With constant drinking fresh and fair."

In the article called "THE CISTERN," as well as in several distinct paragraphs, we have set forth the most important advantages of applying water to garden crops. We, of course, do not approve of its indiscriminate or excessive use; but have no hesitation in saying that, when properly given, it hastens the growth of the plant, and secures it from injury at the most trying periods of its existence, besides improving the size and flavor of the product.

With strawberries and the like, the practice of mulching or of covering the ground with hay, straw or litter, so as to check evaporation, as well as prevent the parching effects of the sun's rays, is vastly more convenient.

The following judicious remarks are from the pen of J. J. Thomas, the well known correspondent of the "Albany Cultivator," and who is one of the most eminent horticulturists in the country. "From repeated experiments, we are induced to draw the conclusion, that next to manure, the great prime mover in successful culture, there is nothing more important to vegetable growth, in many cases, than irrigation. Practical gardeners, in countries far more moist than our own, regard it as indispensable, and a large share of their success depends on copious waterings.

"Some interesting instances, which have recently occurred, may be worth stating. Two rows of raspberries stand on ground in every respect alike, except that one receives the drippings from a wood-house, and the other does not. The watered row is fully four times as large in growth as the other. Again: the berries on the bushes of the Fastolf and Franconia raspberries were at least twice as large when the soil was kept well moistened, as afterwards, when allowed to become dry; a repetition of the watering again doubled their size. Again: a near neighbor, who cultivates strawberries for market, and who uses a water cart for irrigating the rows, raised at the rate of one hundred and twenty bushels to the acre on common good soil by this means; and he noticed that where the cart was left standing over night, so that the water gradually dripped from it for some hours upon a portion of the plants, the fruit had grown to double the size of the rest, in twenty-four hours."

Cold water ought never to be given, as it chills both the ground and the vegetables. It should have been exposed to the atmosphere for several hours, and may in the morning be put in a tub or trough, so that it can be sufficiently warmed by the sun to apply at evening. As to the most suitable time for its application, authorities are divided between morning and evening, and we dare not recapitulate the arguments on either side, but advise the reader to settle the question by his own experiments. For our own part, we can truly say, that we have as yet seen nothing to change our preference for the evening. A garden engine, or a watering pot, may be employed, according to the dimensions of the garden and the fancy of the owner.

Frequent sprinklings are of more benefit, than an occasional saturation of the ground. Excessive watering is positively injurious, because it puddles the soil and chills the roots. The quantity given must be regulated by the nature of the plant and the character of the season. And, when the practice of watering is once begun, it should not be discontinued so long as the necessity for it remains. The seed is sometimes induced to germinate, and in consequence of the artificial watering being suddenly suspended, the young stem is killed by the drought. The benefit is temporary, and has the effect of exciting the plant so that it is afterwards more liable to injury, in case the regular supply of moisture should be withheld. Whenever the soil shows a disposition to bake, the hoe must be promptly used, so as to keep the surface always open and light. In adapting these rules to his own grounds, the gardener should recollect, that written instructions cannot suit all localities, or all seasons of the year. He must depend mainly upon his own good sense.

SAVING SEED.

We have in another place shown the importance of sowing sound, healthy seed, and that, moreover, of the choicest varieties. In the beginning of the gardener's labors, he must apply to some neighbor or to a well known seedsman; but, subsequently, he should endeavor to supply himself, with some few exceptions, from his own premises.

It is a well attested fact, that if two different varieties of a vegetable are permitted to blossom, at the same time, within a short distance of each other, they intermix, and produce a hybrid partaking of the character of both parents. The fertilizing dust of the stamens in the flowers of one plant is conveyed by the wind or insects, to the pistils in the flowers of the other. The distinctive features of each are thereby lost while the new variety may possess not a single point to make it worthy of cultivation. It is seldom that such a chance hybrid proves of much real value. The origination in this way of any choice esculent, is almost ever the result of study and long experiment.

A knowledge of this fact is of peculiar importance to the gardener, whose object is to raise several different varieties of the same vegetable upon a small piece of ground. It is by this only, that he can satisfactorily account for the rapid deterioration of the choicest sorts. Where, for example, he cultivates the melon, the cucumber and the pumpkin in close companionship, but a few seasons will elapse before he finds the juiciness, perfume and delicate flavor of the first named, exchanged for the coarse flesh of the last. And the celebrated

Brassica tribe, among which are our cabbage, cauliflower, &c., are supposed to number several hundreds, produced by intentional or chance intermixture. We, therefore, consider it as dangerous to allow plants of a particular family to run to seed in the vicinity of each other, as to turn a rough, scrubby, "Native" bull among a herd of thorough-bred Durhams.

You will now very naturally inquire, good reader, how you are to raise seed, and yet preserve the several varieties distinct. We first answer, that you ought to reduce the number of varieties to the very choicest—such as are desirable for being early or late, or of unusual size, or having a fine flavor, or distinguished for great productiveness,—instead of keeping a selection large enough for a seedsman. They are in reality very few, for the majority of the fine-sounding names in catalogues are given to plants of an inferior character.

Such as you select for seeding, should be located as far apart as the extent of your territory will admit, so as to lessen the chances of intermixture. And where the vitality of the seed will remain unimpaired for two or three years, you may allow only a part of the varieties to blossom in each year. Thus, by reference to the table at the end of this article, it will appear that cabbage seed preserves its germinating power for four years, and by permitting only one kind to perfect itself in a season, you may have four distinct kinds in perfect purity. This rule is good as far as it goes, but you will perceive that it is not of general application. Where you are obliged to have two or more kinds in flower at the same time, as with members of the cucumber family, place them as far asunder as possible. We think it better to raise only one valuable sort of seed, and depend upon a responsible seeds man for the balance, than to run the risk of getting mongrels.

Of such varieties as you select for seeding, choose the best plants only,—those which are healthy, and have their peculiar characteristics most perfectly developed. To insure earliness, only the most forward plants should be taken. Let the soil be rich and well cultivated; allowing plenty of room to the roots. Attend carefully to the subsequent growth, for the leaves and shoots are very apt to be injured by insects, and are often choked by rank weeds. It will be the best policy to look at the plants at least once a week, and, when the weather gets very dry, it becomes advisable to apply water in moderate quantities. The seed stalks will be thrown up in the early part of summer; being high and having many branches, they are liable to be broken down by heavy rains or strong winds. The labor of tying them up to stakes is trifling, and ought on no account to be neglected.

When the seeds are ripe, gather them without unnecessary delay; otherwise, the pods will split open, and their contents be scattered upon the ground. Do not gather indiscriminately, but take only the finest looking heads. By this selection of the best plants and the best seed, good varieties may be even improved, and they certainly will not deteriorate. In this way many of our choice vegetables have been obtained. The practical stock-breeder's motto is, that "Like produces like," and he breeds from those animals only which possess the points he wishes perpetuated. Thus, if you select the earliest peas from the earliest vines, for a number of seasons, you can obtain a variety ripening several days earlier than that with which you commenced. It has been done once, and may be done again.

Place the seed vessels, as soon as gathered, upon a cloth in the shade, so that they may become perfectly dry, at which time thresh out the seed, by means of a small stick. Winnow out the chaff and small or defective seed, and put the remainder in drawers or small paper bags. Every kind should be labelled with its name and the year when raised,—in this manner, "*Early Salmon Radish:* 1850." This will prevent all possibility of the inexperienced cultivator mistaking beet for cabbage seed, or sowing that which by the lapse of time has lost its power of germination. Keep these drawers or bags in a cool, dry apartment, where no injury may be apprehended from moisture or the attacks of mice. With care, seeds may be preserved for several years, according to the annexed table.

THE VITALITY OF SEEDS, under favorable circumstances, can be depended upon for the following periods:—

Parsnip,—Rhubarb,—and other thin scaly seeds,—for *one year.*

Balm,—Basil,—Beans,—Cardoon,—Carrot,—Cress,—Indian Cress,—Lavender,—Leek,—Okra,—Onion,—Peas,—Pepper,—Rampion,—Sage,—Salsify,—Savory,—Scorzonera,—Thyme,—Tomato,—Wormwood,—and small herbs generally,—for *two years.*

Artichoke,—Asparagus,—Corn Salad,—Egg-Plant,—Endive,—Indian Corn,—Lettuce,—Marigold,—Marjoram,—Mustard,—Parsley,—Rosemary,—Rue,—Skirret,—Spinach,—and Tansy,—for *three years.*

Borage,—Borecole,—Broccoli,—Brussels Sprouts,—Cabbage,—Cauliflower,—Radish,—Sea-Kale,—Tarragon,—and Turnip,—for *four years.*

Beet,—Burnet,—Celery,—Chervil,—Cucumber,—Dill,—Fennel,—Hyssop,—Melon,—Pumpkin,—Sorrel,—and Squash,—from *five to eight or ten years.*

EARLY PLANTS FOR SPRING USE.

Every reader can understand the value of early crops. They are less liable to injury from weeds and insects, and cause the "season" of each vegetable to be much extended. On his own table they are esteemed luxuries, while in the market they command extraordinary prices. They thus increase the profit, as well as the satisfaction, of gardening. For these reasons, it has become a matter of interest, and sometimes a matter of laudable rivalry, to procure early plants in the spring, instead of then sowing the seed, whereby the maturity of the crop is hastened several days.

These early plants are obtained in various ways. To save expense, a few seeds may be sown at mid-winter, in a box to be set in a warm kitchen window; this method, however, is troublesome to the occupants of the room, and cannot be practised to any considerable extent. It is most common to make a hot-bed, as described in the succeeding article, towards the latter part of winter, and to sow the seeds either upon inverted pieces of turf, or in small pots.

A third plan is to raise the plants in the previous autumn, and protect them through the winter. This bids fair to supersede the old fashioned mode of obtaining them from a hot-bed, because they are quite as early, and are certainly much more hardy. The seed is sown during September or October, in a shaded border, where it will not suffer from drought or excessive heat. Before cold weather sets in, the stems will have acquired sufficient size and strength to bear removal to a cold frame, which is nothing more than a hot-bed frame placed on the ground. The earth should be banked up around the outside of the box, so as to prevent the entrance of water, and sudden alterations of temperature. The plants may be set out by a small dibble, at such distances apart as will be indicated in the DICTIONARY. When frost is expected, the frame is to be covered with shutters or boards, so placed that the rain will run off. Every pleasant day, the covering must be wholly or partially removed, for the free admission of air, which is positively essential to the health and vigor of the plants.

To avoid the trouble of transplanting, the frame might be set upon the seed bed, and protected in the manner above described; or the bed could be enclosed by a rough box of boards, supported by stakes, and banked with earth on the outside. The north side of this frame or box should be several inches higher than the south side. The covering may be of boards or shutters. Some gardeners adopt a still more simple cold frame, viz: heavy mats laid upon bent hoop poles, somewhat like the covered top of a Pennsylvania wagon. In either plan, however, great care is necessary to give light and air, whenever the weather will permit; or else the plants will acquire a weak, spindling growth, which ill fits them for removal to the open ground.

When spring has fairly opened, a part of these early plants in the hot-bed or cold frame, may be set out in a warm, sheltered border. They will, at first, require the shelter of hand-glasses or vine-screens at night, as well as during cold days; this protection should be gradually withdrawn, when the weather becomes so mild that no danger of late frost is to be apprehended. In the course of a week or fortnight, another parcel may be set out and treated in the same manner, so as to insure a succession of crops. Should there be more plants than the gardener will want for his own use, he may readily dispose of them for cash, or give them away to his less fortunate neighbors.

FORCING VEGETATION.

Forcing is the art of accelerating the growth of plants, by the warmth afforded by certain fermenting substances, so as to obtain vegetables at unusual seasons of the year. The practice appears to be as old as the time of the Romans. We consider its chief value to be in raising young plants for removal to the open ground in spring. It is, undoubtedly, very curious, and speaks well for a person's horticultural skill, to have an abundance of fresh vegetables when the earth is locked in the chill embrace of winter; but, after all, it is attained only after long practice, and is attended with considerable risk—to say nothing of the trouble and expense. In this book, we have aimed to lay aside our individual opinion in regard to this matter, and to give the reader full information of the process. The

Fig. 21.

following remarks are general;—particular directions will be found under the appropriate heads in the DICTIONARY.

In American gardens, forcing under glass is generally conducted in frames and pits. There are several substances employed in obtaining this artificial heat, such as tanner's bark, leaves and grass, but the fresh dung of well-fed animals is generally preferred.

The first object is to get rid of the violent heat and rank vapor produced when fermentation is most powerful. For this purpose, a certain degree of moisture and air is necessary; and, therefore, it will be the gardener's business to place the dung in a conical-shaped heap near the place where wanted for use; to turn it over about once a week, shaking it well together, so that all parts may be equally exposed to the atmosphere; and to apply water when the materials appear at all dry. In cold, wet, or boisterous weather, the heap ought to be covered to a moderate depth, with coarse stable litter.

There is considerable difference of opinion, with regard to the time that stable dung shall be permitted to lie thus in the heap. Care must be taken that the process is not carried too far, as in that case there will not be sufficient heat left for the bed, and the plants will be rendered small and sickly. Perhaps it is a good rule, to wait until the greater part of the straw assumes a dark brown color.

The hot-bed should be in a place free from the shade of trees or buildings, and having an aspect rather a point eastward of the south. Shelter on the north-west is particularly necessary. The next labor will be to mark out the dimensions of the bed, which, on all sides, ought to be at least ten inches larger than the frame, and a stake should be driven down at each corner as a guide for keeping the edges perfectly straight. It is sometimes recommended to dig a trench from six to eighteen inches deep for the recep ion of the manure, as the dampness of the ground will prevent the too rapid escape of heat; but, as excessive moisture chills the bed, and as by this mode it is difficult to apply linings when they become necessary, we think the foundation had best be on the surface. Generally, the foundation is level, but Mr. Knight, the distinguished horticulturist, recommends a gentle inclined plane towards the south, as in the accompanying Figure.

Fig. 22.

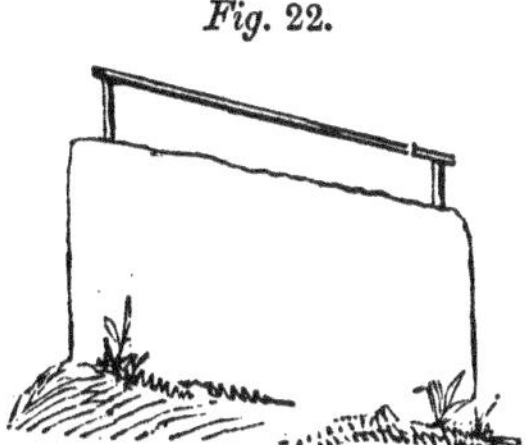

Some persons will require a board set up edgewise, as a guide in keeping the sides of the bed perpendicular, but the professed gardener trusts to the accuracy of his eye. The dung must be well shaken by the fork before being used, and a layer of the longest, or littery part, should be laid at the bottom of the bed. Every layer, as it is put on, should be beaten down by the fork, and the outer part especially, because that will have to sustain the weight of the frame. If the dung be not moderately moist, it ought to receive a gentle sprinkling of water. Ashes, tan and leaves, are often mixed with the dung of hot-beds, and are supposed to promote the steadiness and duration of the heat; indeed, it is generally found that if one-third part be of tan, the heat will be less violent and last longer. The sides ought to be carried up regularly, and combed with the fork, to prevent any unsightly appearance.

When the heap is built up to a proper height, which varies with the season of the year, and the kind of vegetable to be forced—but ranging between two and four feet, the edges ought to be several inches higher than the centre, because they will sink in a short time under the weight of the frame. If the foundation be inclined, as in Fig. 22, the top of the bed should be equally inclined. The frame and sashes can then be placed, and remain closed for three or four days; at the end of which time, they should be opened for the escape of steam and vapor. After these seem to have fairly passed off, the mould can be applied in such manner, and to such depth, as will be indicated in the DICTIONARY. Any good, rich soil, will answer; but that taken from an old wood lot, or well-rotted grass sods, which were piled up for the purpose a year previous, are considered best adapted to the wants of the plants. The sashes must then be closed, and kept tight for two or three days, until the mould shall have acquired a suitable degree of warmth for the reception of the seed. Should the heat be so violent as to bake the earth, a portion ought to be removed, and its place supplied by fresh mould. But even this precaution occasionally proves unavailing, and the tender germ is either injured or killed outright. To prevent which, the seed may be sown in pots plunged in the mould, and if the heat then prove too violent, each pot may be raised up by putting a stone at the bottom of the hole. The outside of the bed may be protected by a bank of earth, or coarse litter, during cold winds and storms, to prevent sudden changes of temperature within the frame.

The general rules of management are:—to keep the sashes covered with boards, mats or straw, during cold nights and severe storms; to admit air freely in pleasant weather, by sliding down the sashes for an inch or two, or by raising them up with wedges at the back part of the frame; and occasionally to apply water in moderate quantities, after it has been kept in the frame for at least twelve hours. When the bed is first made, great care is necessary to prevent the plants being injured by extreme heat, and at that time the protection of mats, &c., should be much lighter than afterwards, when the danger is passed. To ascertain this, the temperature of the bed ought every day to be examined. The most correct instrument for the purpose is a thermometer, but, in the want of that, a trying-stick will answer very well. It is a smooth lath of wood, about two feet long, which is to be thrust into different parts of the manure, and then drawn out and grasped quickly by the hand. Sometimes the heat is found so violent that, in addition to raising the sashes, several holes must be opened in the pile of dung, by means of a large stake or crow-bar, in such a manner that they can be filled up with hay or dung, when they are no longer necessary.

The air within the frame should be frequently renewed, or the plants will become spindling, with a sickly, yellowish color. They cannot be expected to grow hardy, unless the steam from the dung is permitted to escape, and fresh air to take its place. A hot-bed needs ventilation quite as much as a crowded church. The sashes ought to be opened in all pleasant weather, by the insertion of wedge-shaped props, so that the glass can be raised to any height desired, according to the heat of the bed or the temperature of the atmosphere. When there is a sharp, cutting wind, it will be advisable to hang a mat over the opening, in such a way that, while the plants will not suffer from the blast, there may be ample opportunity for the admission of fresh air. No effort must be spared to keep the plants stout and healthy, the stems strong, and the leaves of a fine green color.

As soon as the heat is found to decline, " linings," as they are called, should be applied. The litter having been first removed, the edges of the bed are to be cut down by a spade close to the frame. It may, perhaps, be best to take only one side at a time, by which means the heat will be rendered more regular and permanent. Several holes are to be opened in the manure by the crowbar or a large stake, and a bank, or "lining," of fresh dung, is to take the place of that which has just been removed. The width of this "lining " will vary from ten to twenty inches, according to the coldness of the season; and it should not be carried up much higher than the bed, lest the violent heat escape directly into the mould, and thereby injure the roots of the plants. To prevent the heat being wasted in the air, it will be necessary to cover the lining with a few inches of earth. This process may be repeated once or twice, until the maturity of the crop, or the increasing warmth of spring, shall render it useless.

A DICTIONARY

OF

THE VEGETABLES, FRUITS, AND MEDICINAL HERBS USUALLY CULTIVATED IN A KITCHEN GARDEN.

ARTICHOKE.—*Cynara.*

The artichoke is a perennial from the south of Europe, which was cultivated in England as early as the year 1580. It is naturally a marine plant, and has been greatly improved by domestication. The botanical name, according to Columella, is derived from the Latin word *cinere,* because the ancients were accustomed to apply ashes to the land in which the plant was grown. It resembles a gigantic thistle, and its flower-heads, before blooming, have somewhat the appearance of a small pine-apple, at which time they are highly prized on European tables, particularly by the French. There are two varieties, viz :—the *Oval green* or *French* (*C. scolymus*),—and the *Red* or *Globe* (*C. hortensis*). The latter has a purple head, and is generally most esteemed; but the first has the advantages of greater hardihood and productiveness.

Culture.—The artichoke is propagated by seeds, or by suckers from old roots. It flourishes best in a soil which is deep, light and rich; dry in winter, but somewhat moist in the summer season. The situation should be open, and free from the influence of trees.

When you wish to raise seedlings, you may sow as soon as the frost leaves the ground in spring. One ounce of seed will produce about six hundred plants. Sow in drills one foot apart, and two inches deep. When the stems are an inch high, they may be thinned out to distances of ten inches in the drill. Keep the ground light, and free of weeds, by the occasional use of the hoe. At the approach of cold weather, protect the bed by a covering of litter, and in the following spring, remove the plants to their permanent location, in the manner directed for suckers.

The suckers are afforded by the old roots, early in spring. They are fit for transplanting when eight or ten inches in height. After the ground for a bed has been selected, it should be spaded deeply, and manured with good rotten dung, sea-weed, salt, or anything of a saline character. Slip the young shoots from the parent root, and reject all that are tough and woody. Those only should be selected for a plantation, which are tender, with a general appearance of health, and having many fibrous roots attached. The loose outside leaves ought to be pulled off, so that the heart can be seen. If the shoots have been for some time exposed to the air, they are much benefited by being placed in water for three or four hours before planting. They may then be set out by the dibble, in rows three by four feet apart, with about half their length below the surface. They ought to be watered every evening until they become firmly established, and subsequently during times of drought; by which means, the size and succulency of the edible parts will be much increased.

The only cultivation needed during the spring and summer, is to keep the soil clean and mellow, as well as to apply water in dry weather. Under such treatment, a few heads for use may be expected between August and November, although in subsequent years the maturity of the crop will commence much earlier in the season. In addition to the principal head, there will be several smaller ones on the lower part of each stem; but, if the quality of the produce be more regarded than its quantity, these lower buds should be removed when quite young. The head is permitted to grow until the scales spread, and the flower seems about to open. The stem must then be cut off close to the ground, so as to encourage a new growth of suckers before winter.

Although apparently possessing a hardy constitution, this vegetable is very sensitive to the frost, requiring winter protection in the northern states. In order that the roots may strengthen themselves as much as possible, this protection may with propriety be delayed until there is a prospect of hard frost—say in November or December, according to the season. Cut away all the decayed leaves, with care not to injure the young growth. Then dig over the surface soil, and draw it up into a kind of ridge along each row of plants, in such a manner that their hearts will be clear. An application of dung before this process of earthing up, sometimes causes the shoots to decay. In all severe weather, the plants ought to be sheltered by a layer of leaves, branches or coarse litter.

When spring opens, all danger of hard frost being passed, and the young buds having fairly started, the litter or other protection is to be removed, and the ridges levelled. Make a selection of the suckers for new plantations, and, as they will not be wanted until they are eight or ten inches in height, they may be suffered to remain on the roots, together with two or three of the strongest shoots, which are to be left for heading. All other shoots, and every bud, must be removed by a knife, or by the simple pressure of the thumb and finger. Dig the ground thoroughly, and mix with it a quantity of good rotten manure, fresh sea-weed or salt. As soon as the suckers intended for transplanting acquire sufficient size, they may be taken up and treated in the manner before described.

An artichoke bed seldom continues in perfection for a longer time than six years; after that period the flower heads become gradually smaller and less succulent. For which reason, and because it so happens that the first cutting season of young plants commences about the time when the old stocks cease bearing, many gardeners make a new plantation every spring, whereby fine heads for the table may be obtained from June to November.

For seed,—select some of the best heads, and permit them to flower. To prevent water settling in the expanded calyx, the stalk must be somewhat bent over, by being tied to a small stake. The seed will be ripe in the fall. Gather it when dry; rub it out of the husk; and store it in a cool, dry apartment. Its vegetative power may be depended upon for at least three years.

USE.—As a vegetable, the artichoke is wholesome, but, probably, not very nourishing. It is used in various ways. In Italy, the young tender heads are eaten as a salad, with oil, salt and pepper. The edible parts are the receptacle of the flower, called the "bottom," and the fleshy substance on the bottom of the calyx scales. In England, the whole head is usually boiled plain, and the scales are pulled off at the table, one or two at a time, dipped in butter and pepper, and stripped of their fleshy part by the teeth. The stalks are eaten in France and Germany, after having been boiled and pickled. The flowers have the property of rennet in curdling milk, and the juice of the leaves and stalks, when prepared with bismuth, imparts a permanent gold color to wool; and, when mixed with an equal quantity of white wine, is said to have been successful in the cure of the dropsy.

To boil.—Scrape the artichokes, and put them into boiling water, with an allowance of a tablespoonful of salt to every two dozen heads. In about two hours' time they will become quite tender, when they may be taken from the fire, and seasoned with butter and salt.

To pickle.—Soak the artichokes in salt and water for several days. Drain them, and afterwards rub off all the outside skin. To one gallon of vinegar, add one tablespoonful oi alum, and a teacupful of salt; and turn it over the artichokes when it is scalding hot. After remaining a week, it should be drawn off, scalded, and then returned: the process being repeated, at intervals of six or seven days, until the heads appear to be thoroughly pickled.

ARTICHOKE (JERUSALEM).—*See* JERUSALEM ARTICHOKE.

ASPARAGUS.—*Asparagus officinalis.*

A well known perennial, the young shoots of which are highly esteemed as a culinary vegetable. It grows wild in great luxuriance on sandy plains near the sea; and is found indigenous in Great Britain, as well as on the saline steppes of Russia and Poland. In this natural state, however, the stem is usually not thicker than a goose quill, and only a few inches in height, whilst the roots penetrate to but little depth. One of the most interesting paragraphs in its history, is the account of the gradual enlargement in its size and the improvement in its quality, which have been effected wholly by the process of cultivation. The original plant could not now be recognized by any other person than the botanist. It was raised by the ancient Romans with such success, that we are told three of the shoots sometimes weighed as much as a pound. At the present day, it is considered one of our greatest delicacies, and is particularly valuable on account of the early season in which it comes forward for the table. Of the many varieties to be obtained from nurserymen, those best adapted to general culture are—the *Purple-top*, and the *Green-top*, so named from the color of the shoots. Much has been said in favor of several new kinds, but it is believed that they are indebted for their extraordinary size chiefly to skilful management,—deprived of which, they would soon resume their original character. A good soil, plenty of manure, and careful culture, are the only requisites to success.

Culture.—The seed—one ounce being sufficient for nine or ten hundred plants,—is to be thinly sown, in drills sixteen inches apart, early in the spring—say from about the middle of March to the beginning of April, due regard being had to the forwardness of the season. If you have no drill-rake with the teeth set at that distance apart, you can mark out the bed with the rake intended for eight inch drills, and in sowing pass over every other one. Cover the seed about an inch and a half deep. If the weather continue dry, the ground ought to be covered with straw or brush during the middle of the day, until germination takes place. Or, water may be frequently applied in small quantities, until the same end is accomplished. When the young plants are a few inches high, they must be thinned out to distances of six or eight inches in the drill. The surface should be kept open and free from weeds. By the middle or latter part of November, remove the withered stalks, by cutting them down close to the ground, and then cover the bed with two inches of rotten dung, overlaid by coarse stable litter. This protection not only saves the roots from being injured by the frost, but secures a vigorous growth during the next summer.

In the following spring, preparations should be early made for transplanting. This will be performed in March or April, just after the buds start, and before they are far advanced. Plants may remain in the seed bed for one, two and three years, but they seldom succeed when moved after that period. We think that, all things considered, the best time for the operation is when they are one year old, and here give directions based upon that opinion. The most suitable soil is a fresh, sandy loam, deep and mellow, but lying on a dry substratum. The situation should be open to the sun, and free from the injurious influences of trees or large shrubs. For a family of moderate size, a surface of eight or nine square rods is generally thought sufficiently large, as it can be made to afford one hundred shoots every day through the cutting season.

Spade it thoroughly to the depth of three feet, and intimately mix with it a large quantity of well rotted dung or sea-weed. It will be recollected that the natural asparagus grown on a poor, sandy beach, is a very different vegetable from that produced in a highly cultivated garden; indeed, the productiveness and sweetness of the shoots depend altogether upon the fertility of the soil. In addition to this application of dung, it will be a good way to add about fifty pounds of salt to a bed of the size above mentioned. It has been well observed by some writer, that this preparation of the ground in the outset, is of more importance than the after-management. After being thus spaded and manured, the plat may be laid out into beds four feet wide, with alleys of eighteen inches or two feet.

When the plants discover the first indications of growth, take them up carefully from the seed bed by means of a fork, and suffer them to be exposed to the air as little as possible. They may be placed in a small basket of sand, and covered with a mat. The delicate, fibrous roots are apt to get entangled if handled roughly, and thereby cause the loss of much time in effecting a separation without doing them injury. Stretch the line lengthwise of the bed, about one foot from the edge, and open with the spade a *V*-shaped trench, six or eight inches deep. The side next the line should be nearly perpendicular, against which the plants are to be set, at distances of twelve or fourteen inches, with the crowns about two inches below the surface. Draw the roots out regularly in the shape of a fan, and steady them in their places by a little dirt, until the trench can be filled up by the rake. After one row is planted, and the ground has been smoothly levelled, open a second trench in the same manner, a foot distant from the first. The bed will thus hold three rows of plants. It is a good way to place them in the quincuncial form, thus:—

```
*   *   *   *   *   *
  *   *   *   *   *
*   *   *   *   *   *
```

Rake the surface even, and bring all the small stones into the alleys, for removal in the wheelbarrow. In a dry season, water may be frequently applied with advantage. By an occasional use of the hoe, you will prevent the admission of weeds, which, in addition to their unsightly appearance, are of decided injury to the roots. Keep the edges of the bed trimmed even; and never tread upon it, as its narrow width renders that unnecessary. For economy of room, a few cabbages may be grown in the alleys; but lettuce and radish seed ought never to be sown among the asparagus plants, to rob the soil of what rightfully belongs to them alone.

At the approach of winter, when their natural season of growth is over, the tops will turn white, and they may then be cut down close to the ground. Care should be observed not to do this while they are at all green, because in that case the roots are likely to sprout again. The dead stalks, and all weeds—if any there be found, can either be gathered into a pile and burned, or else be taken to the compost heap or pig pen, to be subsequently returned to the ground in the shape of manure. The bed ought now to receive a thin top-dressing of good, rotten dung, about three inches thick, together with a covering of leaves, litter, or even a little rich soil. This is the only way to ensure a healthy growth of the roots in the coming year.

In March or April of the following spring, as soon as the frost leaves the ground, and before the buds are expected to start, remove the covering, and dig the surface of the bed with the fork, in order to mix the old manure with the soil, as well as to admit heat and air to the roots. The tines of the fork ought not to be inserted to a greater depth than three or four inches, lest the crowns of the roots be injured. This having been properly done, the next thing is to rake off the heavy clods and stones into the alleys. Owing to its marine character, the asparagus plant receives decided benefit from frequent and liberal applications of common salt. It is best applied at this season of the year, spread thinly upon the surface of the bed, and then raked under. A smaller quantity may be given some two or three times afterwards during the summer. Many gardeners recommend the use of brine of the strength of sea-water, to be sprinkled upon the ground every fortnight or three weeks through the growing season. There is but little danger of making the ground too rich; some caution must be observed, however, in the application of salt, as by its injudicious use several fine plantations are said to have been destroyed. In our own garden, all that we dare do, is to sprinkle on just enough to make the ground look white, as though a light snow had fallen.

This course of management for the spring and winter dressings, must be pursued annually so long as the bed remains. In summer, the only culture necessary is to keep the soil in good tilth. In dry seasons, a regular application of water at stated intervals will prove of decided benefit, securing a vigorous and uninterrupted growth. After the first year, the alleys should not be dug up by the spade or hoe, as they then contain a large quantity of the roots, injury to which would seriously affect the plants in the outside rows of the beds to which they belong. The foliage is sometimes attacked by beetles; the only remedy seems to be committing to the fire the parts which are affected. No portion of the crop ought to be gathered previous to the fourth season after the sowing of the seed. In the first three summers, the stalks must be allowed to grow up at will, in order that the roots may strengthen themselves, so as after that time to yield an annual supply of sprouts for the table. Cutting may commence in the fourth spring, when the shoots are about four inches high, the top buds being close and firm. Scrape away a little dirt from each shoot, and cut it off in a slanting direction, about three inches below the surface, by means of a narrow, sharp-pointed knife. Particular care must be taken not to wound the young buds, which are pushing themselves towards the light. Whenever, as will generally be the case with young plantations, the roots throw up shoots of an inferior size, the cutting season should be immediately discontinued; or, otherwise, the roots will be weakened, and rendered unfit for a generous crop in the succeeding spring. On no consideration whatever, should the cutting season be extended beyond the 20th of June. A healthy bed, under good management, will continue to bear abundantly for ten or twelve years, after which time the value of the crop generally declines, in quality as well as in quantity. Instances are recorded, however, of plantations continuing productive for half a century. Market gardeners are accustomed to take roots which are six or eight years old, and use them for forcing; so that to keep themselves constantly supplied with bearing plants, they are obliged to make a new bed every year. For small gardens, we should not recommend making a bed oftener than once in six years, or sooner than four years before it is intended to break up the old one.

Our plan required that we should give full directions for the culture of asparagus from the seed. We, however, advise the reader who is about starting a new garden, or trying asparagus for the first time, that he shall purchase two or three year old roots from a nurseryman. This will give him a crop one or two years sooner than he could obtain it from the seed. The mode of planting, and the subsequent cultivation, will be in every particular as above described.

Forcing.—With marketmen it is a matter of profit, and with amateurs of curiosity or rivalry, to produce asparagus out of its natural season; this must be accomplished by artificial heat. The first plantation may be made in the middle of autumn, and others every four weeks afterward until the middle of March; by which means, a continued supply of shoots can be obtained from December up to the time of the first cutting in the open ground. The process is simple and easily practised. The materials for the hot-bed should first undergo fermentation, that when put under a frame, the heat may be gentle and regular; because if it be at all violent, it is apt to bring the plants up weak and spindling. Dung may be advantageously mixed with ashes or tan, which mixture, by ensuring mildness and regularity in the heat, is better than dung alone. The soil should be a good, mellow loam, and about six inches deep. The gardener must not dream of putting in the roots, until the temperature of the bed is sufficiently reduced to prevent all danger of the mould being scorched. The maximum heat ought not to exceed 65°.

The best roots for planting are those from open air beds about six years old, and which are perfectly vigorous and healthy. Draw a little trench against one side of the frame, and set the roots therein about as near together as they will stand, with the crowns all at the same height. Another trench, about one inch distant from the first, is to be filled in the same manner; and so proceed until the whole frame be occupied, or the supply of plants be exhausted. In this way, a single sash frame will hold an almost incredible number of plants Then cover the whole with three inches of good soil, and apply water freely every three or four days. For the admission of fresh air, as well as for the escape of rank vapor, the glass should be raised an inch or two, whenever the weather will permit, and there is no danger of too great a reduction of heat in the bed. This is very important, and must on no account whatsoever be neglected. The proper temperature to be preserved, is a medium of 60°;—not below 50° at night, nor above 65° at any time. The heat can be revived, if necessary, by linings of fresh dung. In cold nights, the plants will require the protection of mats or coarse litter, laid upon the glass to exclude frost. In the course of two or three weeks, the shoots will be of a suitable size for use, and the roots will probably continue productive, for about one month. Cutting them with a knife is not advisable; the fingers can easily be pushed through the soil, so as to break off the shoot at the crown without injuring its neighbors.

For seed,—you must select some of the earliest and finest shoots,—those having large, close heads,—and allow them to run up without being cut. As some of the number will probably be unproductive, more must be left than at first would seem necessary to secure an abundance of seed. Support the stems by stakes, which, it may be worth while to inform some bunglers, need not be driven through the crowns of the roots. In autumn, when the berries are ripe, they should be stored in a dry place until wanted for sowing; unless the seed is to be sent away for sale, in which case the berries must be left several days in a vessel of water, for the pulp to decay, before the seed is washed out.

Use.—The esculent parts are the tender shoots, which are to be gathered soon after they peep above the surface of the bed. They are much esteemed on every table where they may be found, although not considered very nutritious. The plant possesses some diuretic qualities, which, it is said, render the shoots unfit for persons troubled with the diabetes, while of great benefit to such as are suffering from the gravel, or complaints of a kindred nature. Cobbett says, in his American Gardener, " Were I writing to Nova Scotians, I ought not to omit to give instructions as *to which end* of the asparagus the eater ought to use, for I know a gentlemen of that country, who being at New-York, on his first trip from home, began eating at the stem in place of the point."

To cook.—In the first place, cut off the tough, white part of the stalks, in such manner that they may be of nearly equal length. Put them into small bundles, and boil them from fifteen to twenty minutes according to their age. The addition of a quarter-teaspoonful of salaratus to three quarts of the water, will preserve the fresh, green color of the asparagus. A little salt should be put in the stew pan. Toast a large slice of bread, and lay it in the bottom of a vegetable dish. Then moisten the toast with a little water from the stew pan, and butter it. When the asparagus is taken up and drained, it is to be laid on the toast, and the strings removed. Serve with melted butter, and salt to the taste.

BALM.—*Melissa officinalis.*

A hardy perennial, having a fragrant smell, and a native of Switzerland. The name *Melissa* is from the Greek word for honey, which attracts large numbers of bees to the flowers. It is cultivated principally for medicinal purposes ; and only a few plants are required in a common-sized garden.

Culture.—It may be propagated by seed, by offsets of the roots, or by slips of the young shoots. The first two modes can be practised either in spring or in autumn, but slips are generally found to succeed best when they have been set out in the latter part of spring. Place them first in a shady border, where they may take root, and remove them to their final location in the following autumn. They should stand about ten inches from each other. The balm is best pleased with a poor, friable soil, and needs no manure. About the only attention required on the part of the gardener, is to prevent its extending itself too widely. The decayed leaves and stalks, however, ought to be cleared away, and the soil of the bed loosened by the hoe, at the close of each season.

Use.—Formerly, very extravagant notions were held, in relation to the medicinal virtues of the plant, but its importance is now rated much lower. By distillation it yields a fragrant oil, which, when diluted with water, proves grateful and beneficial in cases of fever, and to persons of a lax, debilitated habit. A strong infusion of the young shoots is also used for the same purposes. For drying, gather the stalks when the flowers are about to open, and when perfectly free from dew or moisture. Place them in the shade, or in an oven, where they may dry rapidly; and, after they become cool, press them into packages, to be covered with white paper, and hung away in a cool, dry apartment.

BASIL.—*Ocymum basilicum.*

There are two species of the basil, of which the *Sweet-scented* (*Ocymum basilicum,*) is most usually cultivated for culinary purposes. Though introduced as early as 1573, it has not been long used. It is a fragrant, aromatic annual, with an odor somewhat resembling that of cloves, and came originally from the East Indies.

CULTURE.—The plants require a fertile, mellow soil, which is free from the shade of trees or buildings. The seed may be sown in a warm, sheltered border, about the middle of April; or upon a small hot-bed, somewhere about the first of April; the plants to be removed to the open compartment in a month or six weeks afterwards. They ought to stand six or eight inches apart, in rows one foot distant from each other. Basil makes quite a pretty edging for the large beds. During the summer, the ground ought to be occasionally stirred with the hoe, and kept clean of weeds; by which trifling attention, the health and vigor of the plants will be greatly benefited. In dry weather, frequent sprinklings of water are found of advantage. Basil is rather tender, and liable to injury from early frosts, for which reason the winter supply ought to be cut in autumn, before the approach of cold weather. It can be tied in small bundles, and hung up in an airy garret to dry.

For seed,—let some of the healthiest looking plants remain uncut. The flowers open about August, and the seed will ripen before the middle of autumn.

USE.—Basil is considered an important pot-herb in the French cuisine. From their agreeable, spicy flavor, the young leaves are employed in many different kinds of highly seasoned dishes—such as soups and sauces. They are also put in salads, and the peculiar flavor of mock-turtle soup is chiefly owing to their presence. In England and this country, however, the plant does not maintain such a high reputation, and it cannot be considered a regular tenant of the kitchen garden.

BEAN.—*Phaseolus.*

Commonly called the Kidney, or French bean, in contradistinction to the English Horse bean, which is of quite inferior quality in this country. The botanical name is derived from the resemblance in the shape of the pods to a kind of ship, supposed to have been invented at Phaselis, a town of Pamphylia. It is considered to be a native of India. There are two species, viz: the Dwarf and the Pole, being named in accordance with their peculiar habits of growth. Each kind deserves a separate notice.

THE DWARF, OR BUSH BEAN.—*P. Vulgaris.*

Seedsmen enumerate many varieties, some of which are scarcely worth cultivation. Yet gardeners differ so much in their preferences, that it is almost impossible for us to present such a select list as will give satisfaction to every reader. In passing an opinion upon any selection of varieties, allowance must always be made for differences of soil and situation, as well as for other natural causes over which the cultivator can have no control. We believe the following kinds, named in nearly their order of succession for the table, to be the most valuable for small gardens:—the *Early Mohawk*,—the *Early Yellow Six Weeks*,—the *Early St. Valentine*,—the *China Red Eye*,—the *Rob Roy*,—the *Brown Valentine*,—and the *Royal White Kidney Dwarf.* Nearly all of these have synonyms; for instance, the *Brown Valentine* is known to be the Late Valentine,—the Refugee,—and the Thousand-to-one. The *Early Mohawk* is very hardy, and is generally planted for the earliest crop. A modern and but little known variety, is one called the *Turtle Soup;* it is considered superior to the ordinary bush beans, on account of the tenderness and excellent flavor of its pods, and the long time which they continue fit for use. It bids fair to supersede many of the old favorites.

Culture.—The Kidney bean prefers a light, rich soil, founded on a dry substratum; indeed, anything is better than a clay of a wet, tenacious character. For summer crops, it may be somewhat moist, but this quality is objectionable for both early and late sowings. Being originally a native of a warm climate, the seed is remarkably tender, and oftentimes, for the want of a proper soil, decays without germinating, or becomes a spindling and unfruitful plant. As the ground must be rich in order to yield abundantly, a good dose of well rotted manure should be applied broadcast, and spaded under, or else put in the drills at the time of sowing. The first course is much the best, and ought always to be followed where practicable.

Forcing—is often resorted to, for the earliest crop. The hot-bed is of moderate size, and covered with eight or ten inches of fine mould. After the rankness of the freshly prepared dung has escaped, and the heat becomes regular, the seed may be thinly sown in drills ten inches apart. The proper temperature to be observed is between 60° and 75° Fahr. Fresh air must, however, be admitted freely at all times when the weather will permit, while tepid water is to be applied in moderate quantities every two or three days. The most forward plants can, by the first of April, be removed to a warm, sheltered border, where the protection of hand-glasses or vine-shields is to be given them, at night and during cold days. They should be gradually accustomed to the change of locality, as well as to the absence of artificial heat, lest by a too sudden exposure to the chill air, both they and the cultivator's hopes be blasted at the same moment.

Planting in the open ground—may be commenced some time between the middle of April and the first part of May, after the ground has become warm, and the weather is apparently settled. The bean is very sensitive to cold, and the earliest sowing is frequently destroyed by late frosts. For a succession of crops, the sowing must be repeated every two or three weeks until the beginning of August. After that period, the cold frame, and subsequently the hot-bed, will be again necessary. For the early and late crops, a dry, sheltered border is desirable. In this way, the table can be kept constantly supplied for many months. Who that is acquainted with the merits of the bean as an esculent, will not be willing to make some extra exertion to secure so desirable a result?

Plant the seed one and a half inches deep, and two inches apart, in drills two feet asunder. One quart of seed will thus suffice for about two hundred and fifty feet of row. When the plants are three inches high, and again when about to flower, draw the earth carefully up around their stems; which protects the roots from the enervating effects of heat and drought. At all seasons of their growth, however, the soil ought to be kept, by the frequent use of the hoe, free from weeds, and open to the beneficial influences of the atmosphere.

THE POLE BEANS.—*P. limensis et multiflorus.*

Sometimes these are called Runners, or Climbers. Of the *Phaseolus limensis* there are two varieties which have a high and well deserved reputation for the table, viz: the *Green* and *White Limas.* The *Green* is preferable on account of size; but, as regards the certainty and uniformity of a crop, the *White* seems to have the advantage. They are both largely cultivated, especially in the vicinity of cities, where they will always meet with a ready sale, both when green and when dried for winter use. Of the *Phaseolus multiflorus*, which was carried from South America to England in 1633, there are the *Scarlet Runner*,—the *Dutch Case-knife*,—the *Carolina Sewee*, &c. These are all excellent of their kind, but in this country are generally ranked inferior to the popular *Limas*.

Culture.—As the pole beans are found even more tender than the dwarfs, planting in the open ground must be delayed still later, until all liability to rot, in consequence of cold, damp weather, shall have passed. Gardeners pursue many different modes of obtaining early plants. By some, the seed is put into small pots, which are set upon a hot-bed, and allowed to remain there until the stems are three inches high, when, with the balls of dirt attached, they are placed in a warm border. Others, however, put large sods upside down in a shallow frame, and, with the spade, cut them into small pieces like the squares of a chequer-board; upon each piece a single bean is planted, and removed to the open ground, as soon as the weather is settled and the stem is of sufficient size. Little advantage is gained by forwarding plants, because they are particularly liable to injury from a change of position. For the family gardener, we think it much the best policy to be patient until the earth becomes warm, and spring seems to have really opened.

The proper time for the first sowing, is somewhere between the first part and the middle of May. Should the season be remarkably early, perhaps the last week of April will be suitable. But the gardener must not be surprised, if untoward weather destroy both the first and second plantings. The soil should be mellow, rich, and in rather a warm situation. Lay the ground out in hills—say three feet apart each way,—as if for Indian corn, and put in the bottom of each a liberal supply of old dung or compost. They ought to be three or four inches above the average level. Plant five or six beans in a hill, and cover them about one inch deep. One quart of seed will supply in the neighborhood of three hundred hills. A curious fact is stated in relation to the *Limas*, viz: that the eye should always be put downward, as the seed rises out of the ground in that position; in defect of which, it often refuses to vegetate. Reduce the number of plants to three in a hill, and, if that number be wanting, sow again. When they are a few inches high, draw a little earth around them as a support. As soon as the runners start, it is time to set the poles, which may be ten or twelve feet high, and, for appearance' sake, ought to range accurately, and be of a nearly uniform height. Some of the runners will perhaps be a little wayward, and require being brought back to the poles. Use the hoe frequently; there is nothing like keeping the soil mellow and clean. We have often raised good crops in the hills with Indian corn, letting the vines run upon the stalks. Nipping off the ends of the shoots, when the first blossoms begin to drop, accelerates the growth of the pods.

For seed,—the varieties should be kept distinct, as they are very liable to intermixture. Either sow expressly for the purpose of raising seed, or else leave particular rows ungathered. An excellent mode is, when gathering the crop, to leave the best pods upon the bushes. Always select the earliest and finest looking, which, after being thoroughly ripened by the sun, are to be pulled with the vines, and left for several days in some dry place, that all their moisture may escape. Beat out the seed, and store it in a cool apartment.

USE.—As an esculent, the bean is wholesome and nutritious, well meriting the high favor in which it is universally held. In proportion to its weight, it gives more nutriment, and better supplies the place of animal food, than any of the ordinary vegetables. One of its most valuable qualities, is the ease with which it can be preserved for use in winter. In gathering for the kitchen, take those pods that are fleshy and tender, as being then in the highest perfection. Pull them carefully, so that the smaller ones may not be prejudiced in their growth. It must be the gardener's object, to render the vines as prolific and long-lived as possible.

To boil String Beans.—Take off the strings, and cut the beans into short pieces. Boil them with a little salt, from twenty to forty minutes, according to their age. A little salaratus in the pot, preserves their green color, and makes them more healthy. They ought to be quite tender, before being taken from the fire. Add salt and butter, and then carry immediately to the table.

Shell Beans—are cooked in the same way, either with or without the salaratus.

To bake White Beans.—Pick them over carefully, and at evening put them to soak in a slightly warm place. Put a quart of water to a pint of beans. The next morning, rinse them well in two or three waters, and boil them for ten or fifteen minutes; at the end of which time, take them up with a skimmer, and lay them in a baking dish. Put in the centre a piece of salt pork, having the rind scored, with the top just exposed; and then pour in cold water, so that it may be seen at the sides of the dish. Bake them in a hot oven for three hours; and the time may be extended to six hours with advantage.

For pickling,—gather the beans while small and tender. Keep them in salt and water, which should be changed every five or six days, until you have a sufficient quantity. Then scald them with hot salt and water, and, when they become cool, turn on hot vinegar, spiced with pepper-corns, mace, &c.

To preserve Lima Beans.—They may be dried on the floor of an airy garret, or put with layers of salt in a keg, to be covered tight, and kept in a cool place. Before being cooked, they should be soaked over night, and boiled with a little salaratus. They will then be as tender and palatable, as though just picked from the vines.

BEET.—*Beta.*

It would appear that the beet originated on the seacoast of southern Europe, where it may at the present time be found in a wild state. It was introduced into England by one of the Tradescants, about the year 1656, and was at first cultivated under the name of Beet-rave, or Beet-radish. The botanical name is said to have been derived, from the resemblance which the seed vessel, when swelling, bears to β (*Beta*) the second character of the Greek alphabet.

The genus *Beta* comprehends several biennial species, of which the principal are the *B. cicla*, and the *B. vulgaris*. The first named is cultivated for its large stalks, and the white, solid midrib of its succulent leaves. They are wholesome, with a pleasant, sweet taste. The green part of the leaves is boiled and eaten like spinach, while the stalks and midribs are dressed like asparagus. The principal variety is the *Swiss Chard*, or Sea-kale-beet. It produces abundantly, and is one of the chief vegetables of the agricultural laborers in Germany, France and Switzerland. We are in hopes to see it generally introduced into our gardens, as we believe it well worthy of attention. The second species, the *B. vulgaris*, is distinguished by a large, fleshy root, which is both palatable and nutritious. The varieties are numerous; those considered best are—the *Blood Turnip-rooted*, excellent for summer use; the *Early Long Blood*, which matures next in order, and is raised in large quantities for market, the *London Blood*, a new kind that is acquiring a good reputation; and the noted *Mangold Wurzel*, which, although principally used for farm animals, is when young and tender very good for the table.

Culture.—All tap-rooted vegetables require a rich, deep soil, and this seems particularly necessary for a successful growth of beets. As soon, therefore, as the ground is opened in spring, it should be spaded or trenched from a foot to eighteen inches deep, and enriched by a liberal supply of old manure. When danger of severe frost is over, the beds may be marked out into drills, sixteen or twenty inches apart, for the early crops. Scatter the seed rather thickly,—an ounce being sufficient for near one rod of ground,—and cover it about an inch deep. It is better to thin the plants when they stand too close together in the drills, than to be obliged to fill up vacant spaces by transplanting. The seed is most commonly steeped in warm water, for two or three days before the time of sowing, so as to soften the hard outer skin, and thereby facilitate the process of germination. If the soil be light and dry, press it down hard upon the seed, by means of a roller, or by walking upon a long board laid across the drills.

For the autumn and winter crops, sow later in the season,—say from the middle of May to the last of June,—as the produce will be found better suited for the table, and will keep better through the winter, than that of the early sowings Where the roots acquire their full growth before cold weather comes on, they soon lose their agreeable succulency, and oftentimes decay before the winter is half gone.

As soon as the plants are out of danger, their leaves being well advanced, they must be thinned out in the drill,—at first, to distances of four inches, and subsequently, if large roots be wanted, to distances of eight inches. If there be any vacant spaces in the rows, they ought to be filled at this time; although experience has shown that the beet succeeds best when not transplanted. The subsequent culture is simple, being merely to stir the ground often, and keep it free from weeds. Every hour's labor upon the bed will increase the quantity of the produce, and add greatly to its value for culinary purposes.

The roots ought to be taken up, as soon as vegetation is checked by the approach of frost. Dig them carefully, because they will bleed much, if broken or cut. After a few hours' exposure to the air, in order that any surplus moisture may be evaporated, they can be stored for winter use. Cut off the tops at least an inch above the crowns, and either feed them to the cattle, or put them in the compost heap. The roots may then be carried to the cellar, and piled up against the wall, with alternate layers of sand or dry earth; or they may be heaped up in the open air, with layers of earth, in the shape of a pyramid, or the roof of a house, and then covered with straw and earth for protection against frost,—a small hole being left at the top of the mound for the escape of steam, and a trench being dug around it to prevent water coming in contact with the roots.

For seed.—In the spring, plant out a few of the finest looking roots, such as are smooth and well-shaped, and, during the summer, keep them free from the company of weeds. It may be necessary to support the stems by tying them to stakes. Gather the seed as soon as it becomes ripe.

Use.—Apart from its value in an agricultural point of view, the beet root is considered indispensable on many tables. When of good size, it is tender, sweet and wholesome. It possesses some very slight medicinal qualities; and although very nourishing, if it be eaten in great quantity, is said to be injurious to the stomach. It can be substituted for malt in the manufacture of beer, while the white varieties are largely cultivated in France for the manufacture of sugar. The leaves grown on a rich soil, afford considerable pure nitre. For the table, the beet is used in a variety of ways. The young, tender tops are sometimes cooked in the same manner as spinach; while the root is put in salads, pickled in cold vinegar, or stewed with onions.

To pickle.—Do not cut or scrape the roots before boiling; which would cause the juice to run out, and render them insipid. It is only necessary to wash them clean. In summer, they will boil in about an hour; but, in winter, double that time will be required; allowance, of course, being always made for difference in size. After they have been boiled, cut them up in slices, and cover with cold spiced-vinegar.

BORAGE.—*Borago officinalis.*

Originally from Aleppo, this weed has become naturalized in many parts of the world. It grows about two feet high, with broad leaves, and handsome flowers. It was formerly much esteemed, but in most modern gardens has given way to more valuable plants.

Culture.—The most suitable soil is one that is both light and dry. It need not be very rich, because the pleasant flavor of the leaves and flowers would be injured by a rank luxuriance of growth. The seed may be sown in April, or, indeed, at almost any time during the spring and summer. Sow in shallow drills six inches apart, and afterwards thin out the plants to the same distances. After the operation of transplanting, water must be applied in moderate quantities until the roots become firmly established.

For Seed.—Some plants which have survived the winter, must be allowed to perfect themselves. Gather the stalks, and let the seed be perfectly dry before attempting to rub it out.

Use.—The tender leaves are in some places put in salads or cooked like spinach. The flowers are occasionally used to ornament a salad dish, or to flavor a cup of negus. In ancient times, many wonderful virtues were ascribed to borage, and, even now, by the ignorant it is ranked high in the list of medicinal herbs.

BORECOLE.—*Brassica oleracea*, var.

Borecole,—sometimes known under the name of Kale,—is

but one of the many varieties of the celebrated cabbage family. It seems to be distinguished by a large, open head, and generally by curled or wrinkled leaves. It has a peculiarly strong, hardy constitution. It is thought very valuable for cultivation in the Southern states, because it requires little or no protection during the winter months. The principal subvarieties are—the *Scotch Kale,*—the *Green Curled,*—the *Cæsarian Kale,*—and the *Thousand-headed Cabbage.*

Culture.—Sow the seed—one ounce of which will furnish four thousand plants, or about that number,—during the first part of May; but not earlier, unless the season be quite forward. Transplant in July into rich, mellow soil. For more particular directions, the reader is requested to refer to the article on Cabbage, which is cultivated in the same manner. For preservation in the open air through the cold weather, the plants should be set quite close together in a trench, with the earth drawn up to the lower leaves, and covered with straw or litter; when a head is wanted, it is only necessary to remove the covering, and cut off the stalk with a sharp knife, leaving the stump in the ground, where it will produce fine greens in the following spring.

For seed,—leave some of the best heads in the bed where grown, or else transplant, during open weather, into rows three feet apart each way. It is the nature of this family of vegetables to intermix freely, and run into hundreds of subvarieties; care must, therefore, be taken to prevent different kinds flowering at the same time in the vicinity of each other.

Use.—Borecole is considered very delicate, and is much improved by an exposure to the frost. The crown or head of the plant is cut so as to include the leaves, which do not exceed nine inches in length. It boils well, and proves very tender and sweet.

To cook Greens.—If not fresh and plump, they should be

soaked in salt and water for half an hour before cooking. Put them in boiling water, with a little salaratus to preserve their color. A little salt should also be added. Keep the water boiling briskly until they are quite tender.

BROCCOLI.—*Brassica oleracea*, var.

Another variety of cabbage, inferior to the delicate cauliflower only, which it much resembles in appearance, growth and flavor. It is supposed to have originated on the island of Cyprus, in the Mediterranean, and has been greatly improved by cultivation. The name by which it is generally known, is derived from the Italian language, and, indeed, we know that it was first carried to Great Britain from Italy. The several sub-varieties which have been produced by chance or intentional hybridization, differ greatly as to the color of their heads, some being yellow, while others are white, purple, etc. As broccoli can be raised more easily and with greater certainty than the cauliflower, it is becoming very popular, especially among small gardeners. The following kinds are considered among the best, viz.:—*Grange's Early Cauliflower*,—the *Early Purple Cape*,—and the *Early White Cape.*

Culture.—Market gardeners are accustomed to sow the seed in the latter part of summer, and, at the approach of winter, to set the plants in a cold frame for protection through the cold weather, in the manner directed for Cabbage. These plants are to be removed to the open ground in spring, and carefully cultivated; by which means, heads suitable for cooking are to be expected as early as the month of June.

It is most common in this latitude, however, to wait until April or May, according to the character of the season, before sowing the seed, one ounce of which yields about four thousand plants. In the Southern states, the summer frequently proves too hot for the early-planted broccoli to come to perfection, and there the seed can be sown about the middle of July, on shaded borders, to be watered occasionally, if the weather be dry. In about a month's time, the plants will be of a proper size for removal to a large bed.

The soil ought always to be mellow and rich, having an open exposure. Sow thinly in shallow drills, six inches apart, and, if the surface be light and dry, press it down compactly by means of the roller, or by walking over a board placed lengthwise of the bed. Should the weather continue dry, some delay in the vegetation of the seed will probably be experienced. The soil may then be sprinkled with water every two or three days until the plants appear, or it may be covered during the day time, with a thin layer of straw or light mats. In the latter case, the covering should be removed at an early hour in the evening, that the natural deposit of dew may not be interrupted. Transplanting can be performed in June or July, when each stem shows some five or six leaves. Set the plants out in rows, two feet apart each way. The work is best performed in dull, damp weather, and water ought to be given occasionally in moderate quantities until the roots become established, as well as subsequently during time of drought.

The after-culture consists in hoeing the ground frequently, and in the destruction of weeds as soon as they make their appearance. In the course of a fortnight or three weeks after transplanting, the earth should be drawn up to the stems in such manner as to form a kind of shallow basin around each. Broccoli will not flourish unless it receive considerable attention from the gardener. It is much annoyed, and oftentimes destroyed, by insects; the attacks of which must be guarded against by the use of snuff, charcoal, ashes, air-slacked lime, etc., sprinkled upon the plants when they are wet with dew or water from a watering pot. The earliest heads of the open-air sowing will be of a suitable size for the kitchen in September or October; and, in favorable seasons, a regular supply may be expected from that time until the coming of hard frost.

In the Southern states, the winter is mild enough for the plants to remain undisturbed in the open garden, where they will continue in bearing until April. In this part of the country, in the latitude of New-York, some protection is necessary. The plants are taken up, at the commencement of cold weather, and set in trenches, with the stems buried up to the lower leaves. A cold frame may be set over the ridges, or they can be enclosed by any rough box of boards, that has a gentle inclination of the roof sufficient to turn off rain. Boards or shutters may be used for the roof, instead of hot-bed sashes. When the frost becomes severe, throw some loose straw over the plants. In mild, pleasant days, the covering should be wholly or partially removed, for the admission of fresh air. In this way, fine heads can be gathered from time to time during the winter and spring. The protection ought to be gradually removed when the weather becomes warm. Or, the plants can be set out in a shed, or in a light, dry cellar, without the cold frame. Frozen heads should be covered up, so that they may thaw slowly, by which means their flavor will be less impaired.

For seed,—reserve a few of the best and earliest plants, and set them out in April. Water frequently, and when the head opens, remove all the shoots except four or five of the best, which will need support by a stake. The seed ripens in September, and ought to be perfectly dry before being beaten from the pods. American broccoli seed is sometimes in demand for exportation, but American gardeners generally make use of that which comes from England or France, while in England the Italian seed is preferred.

USE.—Broccoli is not only a very pleasant, but also a very wholesome, vegetable. It is prepared for the table in the same manner as the CAULIFLOWER, to which the reader will please refer.

BRUSSELS-SPROUTS.—*Brassica oleracea*, var.

Still another variety of the *Brassica* tribe, and by many cultivators known as the Thousand-headed Cabbage. The stem is erect, often four feet high, and having on the sides a great number of miniature cabbage heads, each being one or two inches in diameter, about the size of a large walnut. The top of the stem much resembles a late Savoy, from which, indeed, it is thought to have originated. It is greatly esteemed on the continent of Europe—particularly in Belgium, and is now attracting some attention in this country.

CULTURE.—The plants are raised from seed—an ounce being sufficient for about twelve square yards of ground,—to be sown in April or May, according to the earliness of the season. Transplanting is to be performed in June or July; the plants being set in rows, two feet apart each way. The leaves at the top of the stem are cut off, some ten or fifteen days before the sprouts are gathered. The other details of cultivation correspond so much to the management of CABBAGE, that, to avoid all unnecessary repetition, we refer the reader to that vegetable.

For seed,—cut off the top of the stem, and permit the flower-stalks to come from the little sprouts only. Great care is required to prevent intermixture with other varieties. Where this cannot be avoided, it is the best plan to purchase the yearly supply of seed from an honest seedsman.

USE.—The tops are said to be of very excellent flavor while the sprouts are eaten as winter greens. It is yet an unsettled question, whether the sprouts are improved by being touched with frost before they are gathered. They commence ripening in autumn, and continue in season for the table throughout the winter.

To boil.—Place the sprouts in a vessel of clear water, and let them remain for one hour. They ought to be washed clean from dirt and insects. Then boil them until they become quite soft, when they are to be drained, and stewed with cream or floured butter. Season with pepper and salt, or serve to the table with some kind of sauce.

BURNET.—*Poterium Sanguisorba.*

A hardy perennial, the young leaves of which taste and smell somewhat like cucumbers. It is not much cultivated, and only a few plants are required for the use of a common-sized family.

Culture.—Burnet grows upon the poorest class of soils which abound in calcareous matter. It may be propagated either by seed, or by partings of the roots. The seed is sown in early spring, soon after the frost leaves the ground, in drills about twelve inches apart, and not over half an inch deep. When the plants are three inches high, they must be thinned out to distances of eight or ten inches in the drill. The roots can be planted in autumn, in the bed where they are to remain, and water ought to be applied occasionally until they obtain a firm foothold. The hoe should be frequently used, to keep the weeds in subjection; and the stems of the plants are to be cut down, whenever a growth of young leaves is desired. At autumn, the decayed stalks should be removed, and the surface dressed with a little old manure. The bed must be renewed as frequently as once in every half dozen years.

For seed,—it is only necessary to permit a plant to throw up its flower-stalks. An abundance of seed will be matured in autumn.

USE.—On account of their warm, pleasant taste, the tender leaves are put in salads, soups and cool tankards. They are principally used by the French. We assure the reader, that there are many other plants more worthy of cultivation in a common family garden.

CABBAGE.—*Brassica oleracea*, var.

The history of the cabbage family forms one of the most interesting chapters in vegetable physiology. The several varieties of borecole, broccoli, Brussels-sprouts, cauliflower, and the common cabbage, are all derived, by difference of soil and cultivation, or chance intermixture, from the *Brassica oleracea* of Europe. Of all classes of culinary vegetables the *Brassica* genus seems to be the most ancient, as well as the most extensive. Dr. Lindley observes, that among nearly one thousand species scattered over the face of the world, all are harmless, and many highly useful. The *Brassica oleracea* is familiarly known in England by the name of Sea-colewort. It may be found growing on the cliffs in various parts of the southern coast, and few persons would suspect its having been the parent of so numerous and important a progeny. It bears but few leaves, weighs scarce half an ounce, and is far from being acceptable to the palate. Cabbage was a favorite vegetable with the Romans, and they probably introduced it into all those countries which they subjugated in war: in this way it might have been carried to Britain, whence it has been transmitted to America. Of the whole family, no member is more generally esteemed than the garden or field cabbage, which, without doubt, derived its name from the Latin word for head—*caput*. It is cultivated in large quantities in the neighborhood of cities, where it can be sold at such prices as to afford an ample profit. The varieties belonging to the garden are numerous, and of these the following may be considered a select list, viz:—the *Early Dwarf*,—the *Early*

York,—the *Early Battersea*,—the *Early Wellington*,—the *Early Vanack*,—the *Large York*,—the *Large Sugarloaf*,—the *Bergen*,—the *Drumhead*,—the *Curled Savoy*,—the *Drumhead Savoy*,—and the *Red Dutch*. The second named is among the best of the early kind, maturing early and having a very fine flavor; the eighth is esteemed for making sauer kraut; the ninth is extensively raised for exportation to a southern market; and the last is used for pickling purposes.

Culture.—Although the cabbage can be grown on any richly manured soil, yet a deep, mellow loam, inclining to clay, is to be preferred. The root is long, and needs a light, open subsoil. No vegetable is more benefited by a large supply of manure, because, as a general thing, "the richer the ground, the more luxuriant will be the growth, and earlier the crop." The situation ought to be free and open.

The time for sowing must always be regulated by the time when the crop is wanted. It has become common of late years to set out early plants in the spring, and the heads will be of a proper size for cutting, several days sooner than those from the first sowing in the open air. The best mode of obtaining these plants, is to sow the seed somewhere about the middle of September. One ounce of seed will yield from three to four thousand plants. The best varieties for this sowing are, the *Early* and *Large Yorks*, the *Battersea*, and the *Vanack*. The seed can be spread broadcast, or put in drills;—we prefer the latter plan, for its greater neatness and convenience of cultivation. If the weather be dry, the bed ought to be in rather a shaded situation, that the germs may not suffer from the hot sun. Level the surface, and press it down lightly by the spade or roller, or by walking upon a board. Give water in moderate quantities, in case the sowing shall not be followed by showers. Vegetation may be somewhat accelerated by a thin layer of straw. In about a week, the plants will make their appearance, when a little soot should be spread over them, to prevent the attacks of insects. The waterings may be continued every second or third evening during dry weather.

In the latter part of October, it will be necessary to remove the plants to their winter quarters. The best plan of protecting them is by a cold frame, which is nothing but a common hot-bed frame without heat,—it being set upon the bare ground, instead of upon a heap of dung. In the want of this, a cheap box can be made in a few minutes time, and at a very trifling expense. Take two boards, and set them up edgewise, six feet apart, in such manner that the north one shall be some six or seven inches higher than the other. By the addition of end boards, sloping down to the front side, you will have a frame six feet wide, and of any desired length. The boards can be supported in their places, by short posts driven firmly into the ground, and the earth should be banked up on the outside, to prevent the admission of water or frost. Set the plants quite thick in the frame or box, as the case may be, with the assistance of a small-pointed dibble. As soon as the weather becomes cold, cover them with plank or shutters, which are to be raised for the purpose of admitting light and air, on every clear, pleasant day, when there is no danger of hard frost. This is indispensable, for without such attention, the plants will prove of little value. When the depredations of mice or moles are discovered, it may be well to place a little arsenic, mixed with Indian meal, in some place where the trespassers will find it readily.

Another plan for protecting the plants through the winter, will find favor with some readers on account of its simplicity. It is often practiced by market gardeners. A piece of ground is thrown up into high ridges, about two feet apart, and running nearly east and west. By the middle of October, the plants are set out at distances of one foot from each other, on the south side of these ridges, so that they will be shielded from northerly blasts, while enjoying a full exposure to the sun.

When the weather is severely cold, straw, brush or corn-stalks, are to be laid across the ridges, and removed in the latter part of March, or the beginning of April. The ground is then to be gradually levelled by the hoe. In mild winters, this method succeeds very well, and the maturity of the crop is thereby hastened several days.

Where the seed has not been sown in autumn, and early plants are desired, they must be raised in the latter part of winter. A few can be brought forward in boxes, or pots, set upon the sill of a warm window; or, a large number can be forced on a small hot bed, with a moderate degree of heat—as described in the article on "Forcing Vegetation." Air is to be admitted, whenever the external temperature will permit; and the sashes may even be slightly opened in a mild night, so that the plants can get gradually hardened for their removal.

In spring, as soon as the weather becomes settled, transplanting may be commenced. Dig and manure the soil properly, and dibble holes for the reception of the plants. The rows may be from twelve to thirty inches apart, according to the varieties cultivated; the *Early York*, for instance, can be grown in rows only one foot distant from each other, while the large *Drumhead* requires at least double that space. Raise the plants carefully upon a trowel, and set them with the balls of earth attached, in the holes previously prepared. Put the largest plants by themselves, that the maturity of the crop may be regular, and that as soon as one part of the ground is cleared, it may be immediately appropriated to something else. When the plants are pulled by hand, or taken up by the spade, instead of the trowel, it must be done gently, to prevent the loss of the fibrous roots. We are accustomed to dip each root into a semi-fluid mass of cow-dung and water, that the dirt may adhere to it. After it is placed in the hole, the earth is to be brought up in close contact with it, by a dexterous thrust of the dibble, or a sharp-pointed shingle. Keep the soil well cultivated, and from time to time draw a little up around the stem.

For the main crop, which is intended for autumn and winter use, sow the seed at any time between the middle of April and the middle of May. The *Bergen*, the *Drumhead*, the *Curled Savoy*, the *Drumhead Savoy*, and the *Red Dutch*, are all good varieties for the purpose. The plants can be removed to their permanent location in six or eight weeks from the time of sowing. The operation ought to be performed just after the ground has been freshly stirred, and in damp, cloudy weather, when there is a probability of rain. In a dry time, a regular application of water, both before and after every removal, will much assist the roots in becoming established. In our own garden, we make use of the vine-shield, to prevent the tops being injured by the heat.

The cabbage is attacked by several kinds of vermin. When cultivated on the same spot for a number of years, the root is often found covered with little knobs; they are supposed to be caused by a burrowing grub, and the usual remedies are, a rotation of crops, deep tillage, and a change of manures. The beetle, or fly, devours young plants as they appear above ground, and so voracious is it, that the gardener not unfrequently finds himself obliged to repeat the sowing two or three times. Burning brush or straw upon the ground, immediately before sowing the seed, is a very good preventive. As soon as the plants appear, they can be dusted with soot, ashes, air-slacked lime, etc., when wet with dew, or water from a pot. Or, a hen having a brood of chickens, can be confined in the neighborhood of the bed, and the little chicks will destroy thousands of the agile insects.

The leaves are sometimes attacked by caterpillars, which must be picked off by hand; and are occasionally infested with aphides, or lice, which have a strong antipathy to soap suds. The cut-worm eats off the stem at the surface of the ground, and buries itself by the root, upon the appearance of the sun. Whenever a plant is found cut in this manner, search should be immediately made at the root, and the grub will generally be found there, enjoying a nap after its early breakfast. As a preventive, some gardeners wrap around each stem, at the time of its being transplanted, a piece of writing paper, or a burdock or walnut tree leaf; while others dip it into common fish oil, which gives it an odor somewhat disagreeable to vermin. The vine-shield proves an excellent protection, and has the further merit of advancing the crop. It must be the aim of the cultivator to hasten the growth of the plants as much as possible, in order that they may be the sooner out of danger. For more particular directions upon this important subject, reference must be made to the article called "DESTRUCTION OF VERMIN."

The after-culture is simple, but very essential. It consists in stirring the soil frequently with the hoe, that every weed may be checked in its growth, and that the plants may experience less inconvenience from drought. Every hour's labor with this effective implement, adds greatly to the value of the crop. The experiment of Curwen with cabbages, detailed on a previous page, is full of instruction to the gardener, showing what are the effects of keeping the surface open to atmospheric influences.

Cabbages are preserved through the winter in several different ways. They may be set in ridges, in some dry part oı the garden, with the dirt drawn up close to the lower leaves, and covered with straw, or a roof of coarse boards. The heads are cut off as wanted for use, while the stumps will, the next spring, produce fine greens for boiling. Or, the cabbages may be set head downwards in a trench, and covered with earth banked up like the roof of a house; they will be found, in spring, white, delicate and crispy. They will even grow while in their winter quarters, and the half-formed, almost worthless heads which were buried in autumn, get to be of quite a respectable size before they are disinterred. We know of no plan better than the one last mentioned. If heads are wanted during time of frost, they can be taken up with the assistance of the crowbar and spade.

For seed,—plant out, in spring, some of the finest heads, or even some of the best stumps, which will bear abundantly. It should be borne in mind, how liable to intermixture are all the members of the *Brassica* family, and that pure seed cannot be raised, if two or more varieties are suffered to bloom in the vicinity of each other. Support the stems by small stakes, and gather the seed before it has an opportunity to scatter itself upon the ground.

USE.—The merits of cabbage as an article of food are so conspicuous, that it is a universal favorite, especially among the laboring classes of the community. It is raised at a small expense, and may be had in season for a period of several months. It is much relished by many stomachs, but its use by persons of weak constitution, or quiet habits, is attended with bad effects. The modes in which it is prepared for the table are four, viz.: sliced raw, pickled, salted, and boiled; they vary much in respect to their wholesomeness and digestibility. The first, known as "cold slaugh," is simply raw cabbage, sliced thin, and eaten with cold vinegar. It forms a grateful addition to different meats.

To pickle.—The red cabbage is preferred for pickling purposes. Tear off the loose outside leaves, cut the heads into quarters, and lay the pieces in a keg, with a good sprinkling of salt upon each layer. After they have remained nearly a week, turn upon them hot spiced-vinegar; one ounce of mace, and one ounce of pepper-corns and cinnamon being put with a gallon of the vinegar. To make the cabbage tender, the vinegar should be drawn off, and returned scalding hot, at least half a dozen times.

Sauer Kraut—is much eaten by our German population, and by them considered very wholesome. The soundest heads are selected, and sliced fine. A layer, six inches deep, is put at the bottom of the barrel, sprinkled with a handful of salt, and rammed down by a heavy pestle. When the barrel is filled by these successive layers, a cover is laid on the cabbage, and loaded with heavy stones. In four or five days' time, all fermentation will have subsided, and the kraut is then fit for use. It is eaten cold, or warmed, with the addition of a little vinegar.

To boil.—Remove the outer leaves, and cut the head into quarters. Boil them in the same pot with a piece of corned-beef, or by themselves with a little salt in the water. Do not take them up until they become quite tender. Dr. Paris has suggested that the water be changed once, in order to extract the essential oil, which is so offensive to the nostrils, and is, moreover, believed to be somewhat hurtful to the system.

Capsicum.—*See* PEPPER.

CARDOON.—*Cynara cardunculus.*

This hardy perennial is a species of artichoke, a native of Candia, and found growing wild in the southern part of France. The stem rises to the height of four or five feet, and the leaves spread out widely. It was introduced into England in the year 1658, about a century later than the artichoke. It is thought highly of, in various places on the continent of Europe, but has not been extensively received into favor either in England or in this country.

Culture.—A light, rich, deep and mellow loam is best adapted to the wants of this vegetable. The situation ought to be open, and free from the influences of trees. The seed—one ounce being allotted for six hundred plants,—is sown in the latter part of April, and covered about half an inch deep. When the plants become strong, thin them out in the bed to distances of five inches, that they may have ample room to strengthen themselves for the process of transplanting, which is to be performed in six or eight weeks after the date of sowing.

In setting them out in their final quarters, it is well to trim off the loose leaves, and to shorten the roots. Put them in rows, four feet apart each way. Water must be applied abundantly, not only at this time, but afterwards until the roots become firmly established. The ground should be kept mellow, and free from weeds, by the occasional use of the hoe. By the commencement of October, the leaves will be of a suitable size for blanching. Select a dry day, and, after pulling off those on the outside which are decayed, gather up the remainder in a regularly shaped bunch, and wind around it matting or hay-bands for about two-thirds of its height above the ground. Then draw the earth up around this covering, so carefully that none may reach the ribs of the leaves, to cause them to decay. The plants can be taken up as wanted, whenever they become sufficiently blanched, and may be kept in perfection through the winter by a simple covering of dry litter.

For seed,—permit a few plants to remain unblanched, and guard them against the effects of frost, by a covering of litter or mats. The flowers will open in the following July.

USE.—The edible parts are the stalks and midribs of the leaves, after they have been blanched in the manner above described. They are used either in the form of a salad, or stewed, or put into soups. They are not thought very nutritious, and are chiefly valued on the table as making a variety of dishes.

CARROT.—*Daucus carota.*

Believed to have been introduced into Europe from the island of Crete. It was carried to England by the Flemish refugees, during the reign of Elizabeth, and the leaves were then used by ladies in their head-dresses at evening parties

The root of the wild carrot is white and small, as well as dry and strong-flavored; which fact illustrates the remarkable improvement that has been effected in our common esculents, by cultivation for a long series of years. It is now, with justice, considered one of the most important root crops of both the farm and the garden. The best varieties are thought to be the following:—the *Early Horn*, decidedly the earliest, but smaller than, and not as profitable as, the *Long Orange*, which is, therefore, best adapted for the main crop. There are also several other kinds worthy of notice; among the principal of which, are—the *Altringham*,—and the *Long Surrey.*

Culture.—The most favorable soil for the carrot is a rich and mellow sandy loam. It should be spaded at least two feet deep, and finely pulverized. If not thus prepared, the roots will be found short and forked, instead of long and cylindrical. Should the ground not have been left in good condition by the previous crop, the autumn is the best time for the application of manure, especially if it be rank and unfermented. The space allotted for the bed ought to be dug over roughly, so as to court the action of the frost, and the dung buried beneath the bottom spit; by which means, the soil will become sweet and mellow by spring, and the roots will descend to the substratum in search of nutriment, instead of throwing out a mass of fibres near the surface.

For the early crop, sow in a warm, sheltered border, as soon in March or April as the state of the ground will permit. An ounce of seed is generally thought sufficient for a bed containing two rods. Take a clear, calm day for the labor, in order to secure an even distribution of the seeds, which are very light and liable to be blown away. As they are covered with hairs, causing them to cling together, they should be briskly rubbed between the palms, and mixed with dry sand, so as to separate them as much as possible. Sow rather thinly in drills one foot apart. In dry weather, it is advisable to press the seeds into close contact with the soil, by the roller, or by walking upon a board laid across the drills. Cover about half an inch deep.

The sowing of the main crop, intended to be drawn by the first of November, and stored for winter use, can be delayed until the middle or latter part of May.

The drills ought to be kept free from weeds, and the plants, when one or two inches high, to be thinned out to distances of four inches. Where full-sized roots are desired, these intervals should be of six or eight inches. To be grown in perfection, the carrot should not be closely crowded. Keep the soil in good tilth by the frequent use of the hoe. About the most effective implement for weeding or thinning out a drill, is the gardener's own hand. Careful treatment in the early stage of their growth, will have a marked effect upon the health of the plants; indeed, we consider an hour at this period worth more than a whole day at any subsequent season.

In the latter part of October, the crop having attained maturity, the leaves will change color. The roots may then be taken up, on any dry, pleasant day, with care to avoid breaking or injuring them. Cut off the tops about an inch above the crowns. After the roots have been exposed to the sun for a few hours, that some of the surplus moisture may escape, they can be stored for winter use. They keep well when piled in layers of sand in a dry cellar or shed, or upon the open ground, in a large heap, to be covered with straw, and a foot of earth on the outside. They are tolerably hardy, and but little difficulty will be experienced in their preservation.

For seed,—set out, in spring, a few of the largest and best-shaped roots, about two feet distant from each other, the crowns being buried a few inches below the surface. As soon as the flower-heads become brown, the seed ought to be gathered, before it has a chance to get scattered upon the ground, or injured by stormy weather. Gather from the finest heads only, because their seed will produce the most vigorous plants. Dry it well before attempting to thresh it out.

USE.—The carrot contains about six times as much nutriment as the potato, and is by physicians considered wholesome. It is, however, difficult of digestion when imperfectly boiled. It is prepared for the table in several different ways, such as boiled plain, in a pudding, in soups, stews, etc. Its value in an agricultural point of view is well known. As it yields considerable spirit, it is somewhat employed in the distillery; but, we believe that every effort to extract sugar has proved unsuccessful. When boiled, it makes an excellent poultice for foul and cancerous ulcers. A pretty ornament for the mantel-piece of the parlor in winter, is obtained by taking a thin slice from the crown of a root, and placing it in a shallow vessel of water; the leaves will soon start, and form an elegant, radiated tuft, which is very pleasing at that season of the year.

To boil.—Wash the carrots, and, if they are of large size, split them in two. Lay the pieces in a stew-pan with the flat side down, and turn on sufficient boiling water to cover them. Boil until quite tender, when they may be peeled, and afterwards buttered.

Carrot Pie.—Scrape the carrots, boil them soft, and strain through a sieve. To one pint of the pulp, put three pints of milk, six beaten eggs, two table-spoonfuls of melted butter, the juice of half a lemon, with the grated rind of a whole one. Sweeten to the taste, and bake in a deep plate without an upper crust.

To color Butter.—We have for a long time used carrots in our dairy to color winter butter. For eight pounds of butter, grate a common sized root into cold water. After the pulp has remained fifteen minutes, strain it, and add the water to the cream before churning. The color of the butter will be like that made in summer, while the flavor will not be at all injured.

CAULIFLOWER.—*Brassica oleracea*, var.

"Of all the flowers in the garden," said Dr. Johnson, "I like the cauliflower best." It is the most curious, as well as the most delicately flavored, of the numerous varieties of the cabbage family. The white flower buds form a large, firm head, surrounded by long, green leaves,—being somewhat like a "giant rose, wrapped in a green surtout." Its history is not so well known as that of some other plants less valuable in the culinary department. On its being introduced into England from the island of Cyprus, about the beginning of the seventeenth century, much attention was paid to its culture, by which means its appearance and character have been greatly improved. In our own country, it is much less known than its merits deserve. To show what an enormous size it can be made to attain under skilful management, we mention a single plant raised in the garden of the late Hon. Peter C. Brooks, Medford, Mass. The bare flower measured thirty-eight inches in circumference, and weighed six pounds and five ounces. Its culture is attended with not a little anxiety and trouble, but not by any means sufficient to discourage an enterprising man from the labor. It is not one of the fancy vegetables, and we think it ought to occupy a prominent place in every garden that is worthy of the name. There are two sub-varieties, viz.:—the *Early*,—and the *Late*, or *Large*,—which will afford a succession of crops.

Culture.—For the early crop, the seed—one ounce of which will afford between three and four thousand plants,—should be sown in the middle of September, in the manner directed for Cabbage. If the weather be dry, a little straw kept upon the bed until the seed has sprouted, and, subsequently, an occasional watering, will prove of great advantage. When the plants have acquired a height of two or three inches, they must be thinned out to distances of four inches, so that they may acquire a good, strong growth before cold weather. About the first of October, a piece of ground is to be selected for the cold frame. It ought to be in a warm, sheltered situation, spaded deep, and heavily manured. After being laid into a bed of suitable size, the surface should be finely pulverized and raked smooth. In the course of a week, the frame is to be placed over this bed, with a bank of earth upon the outside, in order to prevent sudden alterations of temperature within. When the ground becomes settled, take up the plants from the seed bed, by means of a trowel, and set them in the frame about four inches asunder. Give a gentle sprinkling of water, but do not attempt putting on the sashes or shutters until the weather actually demands it. The longer it can be delayed with safety, the stronger and healthier will be the plants. During very severe weather, the further protection of mats or straw will be necessary; but, to prevent a weak, spindling growth, air must be freely given in every clear day. There is much more danger of injury from close confinement, than from a moderately low temperature.

Where such accommodations cannot be afforded, and early plants are desired, recourse must be had to a hot-bed, made somewhere about the beginning of February. Should they come up too thick, they ought to be thinned out to distances of four inches, and the surplus ones can, if desired, be set in another bed. The leading direction for the management of the frame, is simply to keep the heat at such a degree that the stems and leaves will have a bright green color. To effect this, a good supply of light and fresh air are required at all times when the weather will admit of the sashes being raised.

In the middle of spring, or as soon as the gardener deems it prudent, preparations must be made for removing a portion of these early plants from the cold frame, or hot-bed, to the open ground. The soil should be rich and mellow. In order to secure a succession of crops, two beds may be selected; one having a warm, southern exposure, with shelter on the north-west, and the other in the open compartment. In taking the plants from the frame, some of the very best ought be left standing, in rows about eighteen inches apart each way. By the protection of mats in cold days and nights, together with extra care in their cultivation, these will come to maturity much earlier than those which are removed. The trowel is a very valuable implement for the work of transplanting, as the roots can be taken up with slight injury. The balls of earth may be set out at distances of eighteen or twenty inches. If the plants in the bed having the southern aspect, are covered with hand-glasses, flower-pots, vine-shields, or even common wooden boxes, during cool, frosty weather, in maturing they will succeed those left in the frame, and be several days in advance of those in the open compartment. By a little management like this, the cauliflower season can be much extended, and a result so desirable is well worth the gardener's serious attention.

In case the reader cannot raise plants in autumn or winter, and is unable to obtain them from some more fortunate neighbor, or a nurseryman, he must be content with a late crop. The seed is to be sown from about the middle of April to the beginning of May, and the plants, when four or five inches high, are to be set out like cabbages, in rows two feet apart each way. From unfavorable weather, the crop is somewhat uncertain.

The hills for the cauliflower ought to be hollowed upon the top, like a shallow cup or basin, that they may be better able to collect moisture. The thorough and frequent use of the hoe is very essential. When the season is dry, the plants need artificial watering at least every other day. They ought not to suffer from the drought,—a circumstance that will be indicated by a drooping of the leaves, reminding the gardener of his negligence. The head, which it will be remembered is the edible part, and esteemed only for its tenderness and delicacy, can be finely blanched by bending over the leaves, or tying them loosely together with a string. Where the whole crop threatens to come to maturity at the same time, a portion may be retarded by the same method. In every season, the cultivator must carefully guard against the extremes of heat and cold, as well as of drought and moisture.

Late plants, which at the approach of cold weather have no appearance of blossoming, are sometimes removed to a warm cellar, where they will perfect themselves as if in the open ground, and continue in season throughout the greater part of winter. The operation is best performed on a damp, cloudy day, and the roots should be taken up with large lumps of dirt attached. The heads will gradually acquire a good size, and be equally good with those taken from the hot-bed.

For seed.—Set out, in spring, some of the finest-looking heads,—the flower-buds of which are firm and close. Support the stems, and gather the best seed as it ripens. As with all the members of the *Brassica* family, particular care must be taken to prevent intermixture. We would refer the reader to our article on "SAVING SEED," to be found in the first part of the book, for some valuable hints on this subject.

USE.—We have already quoted the remark of Dr. Johnson about the cauliflower. As far as our own opinion may be worth anything, we do not hesitate to place this in the very front rank of culinary vegetables. Nothing is more inviting to our palate than a good head, which is brought to the table well cooked and properly seasoned. It is wholesome and nourishing, especially for invalids, and makes a very ornamental dish.

To boil.—The head should be cut with most of the surrounding leaves attached, which are to be trimmed off when the time comes for cooking. Let it lie half an hour in salt and water, and then boil it in fresh water for fifteen or twenty minutes, until a fork will easily enter the stem. Milk and water are better than water alone. Serve with sauce, gravy, or melted butter.

To pickle.—Place the heads in a keg, and sprinkle them liberally with salt. Let them remain thus for about a week, when you may turn over them scalding hot vinegar, prepared with one ounce of mace, one ounce of peppercorns, and one ounce of cloves to every gallon. Draw off the vinegar, and return it scalding hot, several times until the heads become tender.

CELERIAC.—*Apium rapaceum.*

Frequently called the Turnip-rooted Celery, to which order of plants it belongs. It is much esteemed in Germany, but is not often found in American gardens.

Culture.—Sow the seed, in drills ten inches apart, at different times during the spring months, in order to obtain a succession of crops. The seed germinates slowly, and in dry weather, ought to receive a moderate application of water every evening until the plants become established. Keep the ground light, and free from weeds. When the plants are six inches high, they can be removed to their final quarters. The soil of this bed should be mellow and fertile, and laid off into rows sixteen inches apart each way. At this time, and subsequently during dry weather, water is to be given freely at least every other day,—the quantity to be increased with the growth of the roots. When the plants are nearly full grown, it is customary to earth up the bulbs to the height of four or five inches. In about a month, they will be found sufficiently blanched for use. They may be preserved in sand through the winter.

For seed.—See the directions given for Celery.

Use.—The roots may be boiled tender, cut into thin slices,

and put in soup or meat pies. Or, after being scraped and sliced, they may be boiled very tender, and then stewed, for four or five minutes, in just milk enough to cover them; after which they are to be buttered and seasoned with salt.

CELERY.—*Apium graveolens.*

No vegetable noticed in this volume has been more strikingly improved by cultivation, than our common garden celery. It seems to have been derived from a rank, worthless weed, known by the name of Smallage, which is found growing in marshy places, and on the banks of ditches, in Great Britain. The two plants are very dissimilar in their general appearance and habits, and while one is a favorite on the table of every epicure, the other is shunned as poisonous and disagreeable to the taste. The long, crisp stalks, and the mild, delicate flavor of the improved celery, remind the gardener how much has been done, and how much can hereafter be done, in his occupation, by skill and perseverance. Every such fact should stimulate him to increased diligence and enterprise. There are several varieties, the best of which are, probably,—the *White Solid,*—and the *Red Solid.* Many other kinds to be found in catalogues, are highly recommended for their monstrous size; a quality that seems to depend altogether upon a favorable soil and unremitted attention.

Culture.—The celery prefers a soil that is deep, light, moist, and rich in vegetable mould, but not rank from the application of fresh dung. The situation ought to be open, and free from the influence of trees.

Early plants are often raised on a small hot-bed, made somewhere about the first of March. Only enough heat is required, to bring them forward to a suitable size for removal to the open ground, as soon as the weather will permit. For this reason, the heap of dung need not be over eighteen or twenty-four inches in height, and the depth of mould should be just sufficient to prevent injury to the roots by the heat and rank steam. Water is to be applied in moderate quantities, shade given during the middle of the day, and air admitted freely in all pleasant weather. When the plants are four inches high, remove them to a bed of rich soil having a warm situation. Here they are to be set in rows, four or five inches apart each way. They should be watered and shaded as before, and at night receive the protection of mats or cold frames until all danger of frost be over. In this place, they will acquire size and strength for their final removal.

The principal sowing may be delayed until the first fortnight of April. The best position for the seed bed is a warm, sheltered border, but having a northern aspect so as to be free from the powerful effects of the noon-day sun. The ground should be finely pulverized, as the seed is so small that one ounce will afford ten thousand plants. We prefer sowing in drills six inches apart, and perhaps one quarter of an inch deep. In very dry weather, it is advisable to give a little water both before and after germination commences. When the plants are three or four inches high, they are to be thinned out to four inches apart in the row, and those pulled up to be set in another bed at the same distances. Water should be given until the roots become established.

Preparations for transplanting the early crops into trenches, must be made in the beginning of June, at the time when the leaves are about eight inches in height. The removal of the principal crop may be delayed some four or five weeks later. As before remarked, the celery prefers a rich soil, with an open exposure. The trenches should be at least two and a half feet apart, ten inches wide, and fifteen inches deep. That they may be straight, it is a good way to stretch the line, and to mark out the sides by thrusting down the spade, previous to digging the earth, which is thrown equally on either hand. In the bottom of each trench is to be placed four inches of well rotted dung, together with about four inches of good loam, the whole being intimately mixed by the spade. The plants are carefully taken up from the nursery beds, and have their roots and leaves trimmed, besides being divested of loose, straggling leaves and side shoots. They are then set six inches apart, in a row through the middle of each trench. Where they have been taken up by the trowel, with balls of earth attached, they seldom fail to do well. The work is most successful when performed in an evening, or in a damp, cloudy day. A bountiful supply of water should now be given, and, subsequently, from time to time until the roots become accustomed to the change of location. During the day, in order to prevent injury by the hot sun, the trenches must be covered, or rather shaded, by boards, brush or corn-stalks; the gardener being careful to remove everything of the kind upon the approach of evening, that the regular deposite of dew may not be interrupted.

The soil ought to be often stirred by a small hoe, or a sharp-pointed stick. When the plants have attained a height of ten or twelve inches, it will be time to commence "earthing up," as it is called. On a dry day, when the leaves are free from moisture, they are to be gathered together in the left hand, and held in an upright position, while the right one is engaged in drawing some of the fine soil up against them. At first, this ridge must be slight, and have the top rather hollowed, so as to catch the rain. The dirt should be rendered very fine before it is brought in contact with the stems, and drawn up in such a manner, that none gets upon the centre shoots to cause decay. This process is to be repeated every ten days or fortnight while the plants continue growing, and the quantity of dirt drawn up at a time to be gradually increased, until only about six inches of the leaves are exposed above the ridge. The stalks will be good for the table, when blanched to the height of twenty inches. With the crop intended for winter and spring use, the "earthing up" process must be commenced rather later in the season, because, when performed in extreme hot weather, premature decay is apt to follow. In taking up the crop, dig with the spade quite down to the roots, so that the stalks can be raised without being broken, which would much diminish the beauty of their appearance upon the table.

Celery may be kept in the open air through the winter, by having boards, nailed together like the roof of a house, placed over the trenches. Another way, is to take it up, when frosty weather sets in, and put it in a pit in some dry, elevated part of the garden. It is placed in rows about three inches apart, with the tops of the leaves just above the surface, and covered with a thick layer of straw to keep out frost, and a roof of old boards to shed the rain. A large bank of earth should be on the outside. By removing the straw, the stalks can be dug up with ease, at any time when they may be wanted for use. The plants are sometimes packed in a box of sand, and kept in the cellar; they will continue good and fresh for several weeks, but afterwards become wilted, losing that delightful crispness for which they are esteemed.

For seed.—The cultivator must either leave a few of the best plants—those which are solid and of a middling size,—in the place where grown, or set them out in the spring, in rows two feet apart each way. The loose, hanging leaves and side shoots, should be previously removed. The seed-stalks, if not supported by stakes, will be likely to suffer injury from violent winds. Water may be applied with advantage after the flowers have opened, at least as often as every second or third evening. The seed ought to be perfectly ripe before being gathered, and be stored in a cool, dry apartment.

Use.—The celery is a grateful addition to the winter table. Its tender, sweet and crispy stalks are general favorites. They are eaten as a salad, or simply with salt, or used in soups, stews, and sauces. They should always be freed from sand and dirt, before being carried to the dining-room. In Italy, the unblanched leaves, or seeds when bruised, are considered excellent for flavoring soups.

Celery sauce, for boiled fowls, &c.—Wash the stalks, and cut them into thin slices about two inches long. Stew them till tender, in a little weak gravy or water. Season with powdered mace, pepper and salt. Then add the juice of a lemon, and thicken with a piece of butter which has been kneaded in flour.

To stew.—Strip off the outer leaves of six heads, and cut the blanched parts of the stalks into lengths of about four inches. Stew the pieces in broth until they become quite tender, when you may add two table-spoonfuls of cream, together with a lump of floured butter. Season to the taste with salt, pepper, and nutmeg, and let the whole simmer gently for a few moments.

CHERVIL.—*Scandix cerefolium.*

An annual, much esteemed by the Dutch and French. It is a native of southern Europe, and in its appearance somewhat resembles parsley. In ancient times, it was thought to possess many extraordinary qualities, and was diligently sought after by the illiterate herb-doctor. In this country, it is seldom an inmate of the kitchen garden.

Culture.—The most favorable soil for chervil, is one of average fertility, light, and mouldy, with a free exposure. The seed is sown in autumn, soon after it ripens, or at almost any time in the following spring. It is to be barely covered, in drills about eight inches apart. Press down the surface of the bed, and, in dry weather, give it a gentle sprinkling of water. When the plants show themselves, they are to be thinned out to distances of eight inches in the drill. The leaves are fit for gathering, as soon as they are three inches high, and by being cut down close, the stems will soon sprout again. The ground ought at all times to be kept free from weeds.

For seed,—some of the plants must be suffered to grow up without being cut. They will ripen their seed in the early part of summer. Keep it in paper bags through the winter.

Use.—Apart from its medicinal properties, chervil has something of a reputation in the kitchen. Having a warm, aromatic taste, the young leaves are extensively used by Europeans in salads and soups. Two hundred years ago, it was written, "Chervil should be eaten with oil and vinegar, being first boiled, which is very good for old people that are dull and without courage: it rejoiceth and comforteth the heart, and increaseth the strength." Its influence upon the mental and physical faculties, is now rated at a much lower degree. There are many other plants which are quite as valuable as this for seasoning dishes, and are certainly much more worthy of cultivation.

CHIVE.—*Allium schœnoprasum.*

This is a hardy perennial of Great Britain, there found growing in meadows and pastures. It is a member of the onion family. The roots are bulbous, while the leaves are awl-shaped, and produced in small tufts or bunches. The flowers are white, tinged with purple. Only a few plants are required for a family of moderate size.

Culture.—The chive will flourish in nearly every kind of soil, but prefers that which is light and rich. It may be easily propagated by offsets from the roots, in spring or autumn, put in rows ten inches apart each way. The leaves and flowers make quite an ornamental appearance, and, therefore, are well adapted for the edgings of beds. The only cultivation necessary, is to prevent their becoming choked with weeds. When the leaves are wanted for use, they should be cut down close to the ground, and they will shortly be succeeded by a new growth. After the tops change color in autumn, the bulbs may be taken up, and stored as a substitute for the onion.

USE.—The chive has a mixed flavor of the leek and the onion. It has the great advantage of earliness in spring. The tops, when green, are used for seasoning soups, omelettes, salads, etc. Many poultry breeders are accustomed to chop the leaves into very small pieces, to be mixed with the food of young chickens, as a real or fancied preventive of disease. The bulbs are sometimes used like onions.

CORN (INDIAN).—*See* INDIAN CORN.

CORN SALAD.—*Fedia olitoria.*

This annual, a native of Europe, is also known by the names of Fetticus and Lamb's lettuce. The term corn salad is probably derived from the circumstance of its being found wild in corn-fields, while the more popular English title of lamb's lettuce arises from its being a favorite food for young lambs. It is a pleasant herb, and is valuable for its earliness. The first dish placed upon the table, in the olden times, was a red herring set in a corn salad.

CULTURE.—Sow the seed somewhere about the middle of September, soon after it ripens, in drills six inches apart, on a bed of mellow, rich soil, having an open situation. The seed ought to be fresh, and one ounce will be found sufficient for two rods of ground. The drills should be very shallow, not more than one quarter of an inch deep. In dry weather, the soil must be pressed into close contact with the seed, and an occasional sprinkling of water will materially hasten vegetation. The plants may be thinned out to distances of four inches in the row, and ought at all times to be kept free from the evil companionship of weeds. Late in autumn, the bed can be covered with a slight layer of straw, or any other stuff that will afford protection from frost. Should the weather prove mild, the leaves will be in season until the next spring. The sowing can be repeated at the beginning of March, and again about the first of August, or as much oftener as desired ; but it is believed, that these three beds, if of any reasonable size, will be quite sufficient for the wants of a single family.

For seed,—it is only necessary to permit some of the plants to throw up their seed-stalks, a very few of which will produce enough for the cultivator's own wants.

Use.—Corn salad has a mild, pleasant taste, and is much esteemed in England. The tops are commonly eaten while young and tender, in the form of a salad ; but in France, it is sometimes dressed like spinach. In the summer season, the whole plant may be gathered, but, during the spring and winter months, only the outer leaves.

CRESS.—*Lepidium sativum.*

A small salad herb, of which the principal variety is familiarly known as *Pepper-grass.* It proves a hardy annual, and has been cultivated in England for over three hundred years; having been brought from Persia, or Cyprus, as is supposed, about the year 1548.

Culture.—For the first crops, recourse must be had to a gentle hot-bed, built in the latter part of winter. The heat must be sufficient to bring the plants forward for cutting in a few hours' time, without the growth being so rapid as to deprive them of their agreeable flavor. As soon as the weather will permit in March, seed may be sown in the open ground, in some warm, sheltered border. One ounce is allowed to a bed four feet square. The surface soil should be finely pulverized, and laid out into shallow drills six inches apart. The seed is to be barely covered, and pressed down by the spade or a board.

This open air sowing can be repeated every week or fortnight, until the arrival of cold weather. In a dry time, the bed ought either to be in a shaded situation, or to be protected from the effects of a midday sun by a thin covering of brush or straw. It ought also to receive occasional applications of water. When the season is cold, an old hot-bed frame may be called into requisition, or reliance placed upon straw and mats. The leaves are in perfection, when two or three inches high, and it is best to cut them down close to the ground. By merely taking off the tops, the roots will be induced to sprout again, but the second growth is inferior to the first.

For seed,—a few rows may be left uncut, or a sowing can be made in spring, especially for that purpose. The flower-stalks will ripen in autumn.

Use.—The leaves of cress, when young and tender, have a sharp taste, that is peculiarly agreeable. They are most usually put in salads, together with chervil, lettuce, mustard, and plants of the like character.

Cress (Indian).—*See* INDIAN CRESS.

Cress (Water).—*See* WATER CRESS.

CUCUMBER.—*Cucumis sativus.*

This fruit is distinguished for its great antiquity and general dissemination. We are told in the Mosaic history, that the Israelites had enjoyed it while they were in Egypt, and murmured at its loss during their journeyings through the wilderness. Even at this day, it forms a principal article of food in many countries of the east. It is supposed to have been introduced into Europe from some part of the Levant. It was highly esteemed by the Romans, and they cultivated it with great skill and success. The Emperor Tiberius had it in season throughout the whole year, by the employment of artificial heat. In England, it has ever been a great favorite, and large tracts are annually devoted to its production for market. The poet Cowper invoked his muse, to sing the praises of "the prickly and green-coated gourd," and has given us in verse an account of its growth in the winter months, which, for minuteness of detail, is worthy of the professed gardener.

The fruit is pleasant and agreeable to the taste; and "as cool as a cucumber," has become an every-day expression of well understood meaning. Physicians, however, maintain that it has little nutritious value, and we all know that its use by persons of a delicate constitution, is frequently attended with unpleasant effects. There is a good deal of rivalry about obtaining early crops, and perhaps we should say, a good deal of interest, as they command extraordinary prices when exposed in market. It is said, that in the London fruit-stalls, a dozen cucumbers will be sold in March for a guinea, while in August they will not bring more than a penny. There are many varieties, among the choicest of which we enumerate—the *Early Short Prickly*,—the *Long Prickly*,—and the *Long Early Frame*. The list is small, but very select, including those kinds best adapted to the wants of small cultivators. The last one of the three, as its name implies, is most usually grown in the hot-bed. Some English varieties, like the *Manchester Prize* and the *Nepal*, have been made to attain an enormous size, being perhaps two feet in length, and weighing twelve pounds each. The cucumber flourishes in every part of the United States, and its popularity among all classes will be a sufficient apology for the extended notice given it here.

Culture.—As far as soil is concerned, it seems best pleased

with a light, fresh loam; yet it will grow vigorously, and yield an abundance of fruit, in almost any spot of average fertility, provided it have a good supply of heat and moisture. As we remarked above, it is an object with many to employ artificial heat, so as to bring the crop to maturity in the winter season. This is rather a delicate process, attended with considerable expense and numerous discouragements; but, if successfully carried through, it speaks loudly of one's skill and enterprise. Most family gardeners for whom this little work is designed, are content with setting out early plants in the spring, and sheltering them under hand-glasses; by which means, they will obtain fruit several days sooner than those, who wait until the weather becomes mild enough for the seed to be sown in the open ground. Our plan requires that we should describe each of these three modes; and, first, of

The Hot-bed.—For all general directions upon the construction and management of the hot-bed, the reader is referred to the article on "FORCING VEGETATION," to be found in a previous part of the volume. We remind him, however, that the dung he uses should be of good quality, without too large a proportion of litter. It should lie in a conical-shaped heap for ten days or a fortnight, being turned over every three or four days, in such manner that all portions of it may be equally exposed to the atmosphere. When its rankness shall have escaped, the straw assuming a brown color, it is to be immediately made into a bed between three and four feet high, in some sheltered corner of the grounds. The different courses of dung must be beaten down gently with the fork, while the sides are occasionally combed to insure regularity of shape.

After the dung has been carried up to a proper height, the frame and sashes are to be placed, and the sashes kept close for a couple of days, to draw up the heat. The size of the bed depends, upon whether it may be intended merely for the production of young plants, that are to be removed to another frame in which they may perfect themselves. As a general thing, they succeed best when transplanted, and, in that case, the first bed should be a small one, and the second of the largest dimensions, as being required to afford a great and long-continued warmth during the coldest part of the year. The next thing necessary, is to let the steam that now fills the frame, escape by raising the north end of the sashes for a few inches. This is done by the insertion of wedges. In the course of a week, the dung will be in a proper state for the reception of the mold. If the bed be designed for nothing more than raising plants, the dirt is spread over the surface to the depth of five or six inches; but, otherwise, it need not be deeper than three inches, except under the centre of each sash, where it is drawn up into a little hillock, eight inches high, and a foot in diameter. In three days afterward, examine the soil, and, if it appear caked or burned by the heat, it must be renewed, or the seeds cannot be sown with safety.

When the seedlings are to be transplanted, it is best to sow in small pots which are plunged in the mould; if to remain, then the seed should be put on the tops of the little hillocks; but in neither case is it to be buried more than half an inch deep. Indeed, it is always a good way to have a few in pots, to supply any deficiencies that may occur in the hillocks. At night, as well as during any tempestuous weather, the glass ought to be covered with mats, straw or litter, to prevent a violent reduction of the temperature within the frame. It should range between 65° and 85°,—not being below 65° at any time. The seeds germinate quickly, and when the plants are in the rough leaf, their number is to be reduced to three in each pot or hillock. Let them have plenty of light, and admit fresh air at every favorable opportunity, by tilting the sashes at the back of the frame. Tepid water should be applied to the soil whenever it appears dry: the most suitable time of day for doing it is about noon. Guano-water is sometimes used with the best results. If the plants suffer from the heat of midday, a little straw, or a thin mat, spread upon the glass, will be found of great benefit. When their rough leaves attain a breadth of two or three inches, they are fit for being removed to the fruiting-bed,—which is of large size, and has a hillock raised under each sash. Set them out carefully, with the balls of earth unbroken, and keep the glass closed until the following morning. Of course, care must be taken that the heat be not too violent, and that the plants do not droop under the influence of the sun. A little water given at this time, will be gladly received by the roots; and as soon as they become established, the depth of the soil is to be gradually increased, until the surface is level with the tops of the hillocks.

To strengthen the vine, as well as to cause the early development of fruit, it is usual to "stop" the main stem, by pinching off the point, as soon as four leaves are formed. Should the growth of the lateral branches be too luxuriant, they must be stopped in the same manner. They ought to be spread over the ground, so that they may not interfere with one another, and that all the foliage shall be equally exposed to the light. The temperature of the bed should now range between 75° and 95°, but on no account to be suffered to fall below 70°. Where the heat of the bed has decreased, linings must be applied to the sides successively, and banked on the outside with earth. Give water in moderate quantities, every two or three days: and admit air freely whenever the weather is clear and pleasant. Flowers may be expected in four or five weeks from the time of sowing the seed. It is necessary to assist nature in the impregnation of the fruit, by gently twirling the male flowers over the females, which are distinguished by a solid swelling at the base. Without this care, the value of the crop would be much depreciated. Cowper speaks of the

"Golden flowers,
Blown on the summit of th' apparent fruit.

These have their sexes! and, when summer shines,
The bee transports the fertilizing meal
From flower to flower, and e'en the breathing air
Wafts the rich prize to its appointed use.
Not so when winter scowls. Assistant art
Then acts in Nature's office, brings to pass
The glad espousals, and ensures the crop."

Fruit may be cut in fifteen or twenty days afterward, and where the good quality of the produce is considered of more importance than its quantity, it is well to reduce it in the early stages of its growth. Should the heat of the bed again decline, so as to be insufficient for the perfection of the crop, the old linings are to be taken away, and be replaced by fresh dung. This, as a matter of course, is not so essential in the months of March and April, as in the middle of winter. The length of the whole process varies from eight to twelve weeks, according to the time of year. The same poet well describes the difficulties which the gardener has to encounter, although some of our enthusiastic friends may think the statement too highly colored:—

"Ye little know the cares,
The vigilance, the labor, and the skill,
That day and night are exercised, and hang
Upon the ticklish balance of suspense,
That ye may garnish your profuse regales
With summer fruits brought forth by wintry suns.
Ten thousand dangers lie in wait to thwart
The process. Heat and cold, and wind, and steam,
Moisture and drought, mice, worms, and swarming flies,
Minute as dust, and numberless, oft work
Dire disappointment, that admits no cure,
And which no care can obviate. It were long—
Too long, to tell th' expedients and the shifts,
Which he that fights a season so severe

Devises, while he guards his tender trust,
And oft at last in vain."

A small hot-bed is often used for obtaining early plants to be removed to the open ground. The seed is sown in pots of earth, or in small pieces of turf, so that the roots may suffer as little injury as possible from being transplanted. Every cheap and practical method of hastening the maturity of the crop, is worthy of consideration.

The Hand-Glass is useful in forwarding plants. And for small cultivators, we think it more important than the hot-bed. In the beginning of April, a small hole, say eighteen inches deep, and as wide as the glass to be employed, should be dug on a warm border having a southern exposure. Put in fourteen or fifteen inches of active manure, and cover that with six inches of fine, rich soil, on which the seeds are to be sown. Place a hand-glass over the hill, and, during cold days or nights, give the additional protection of a mat, or a layer of long litter. While it is desirable to preserve a high temperature below the glass, fresh air must be admitted, in such quantities and at such times as will secure a vigorous growth, together with a strong, healthy green color in the plants. As the season advances, they ought to be gradually hardened, in order that they may not suffer serious inconvenience from the entire removal of the glass. The proper regulation of this matter will require a good deal of judgment, lest the tender vines experience a fatal check, from the want of that shelter under which they have been coaxed into a premature existence.

Hand-glasses are also valuable in the protection of early plants raised on a hot-bed, or in a warm kitchen window and removed to the open ground before the weather becomes settled. We have found the vine-shield a very cheap and efficient substitute; although it may be considered inferior to the regular hand-glass.

Sowing in the open air may be performed in the latter part of

April, or any time during the month of May, according to the character of the season. Plants of very early sowings are apt to be cut off by a late frost. Nevertheless, it will be for one's interest to get the seed into the ground as soon as it can be done with safety. The first labor will be to mark out the hills at regular distances ; perhaps, five feet apart each way will be sufficient, but to allow six feet is much the better plan. They should be dug out to the depth of twelve or fifteen inches, with about the same diameter, and be partly filled with well rotted dung, or a compost of hen-dung, overlaid by some rich, mellow loam. Sow five or six seeds in each ; at which rate, one ounce of seed will plant near two hundred hills.

The attacks of the striped cucumber-bug, the flea, and other vermin, may be somewhat guarded against, by the use of wood-ashes, tobacco-dust, road-dust, charcoal-dust, air-slacked lime, soot, or the offensive solution of hen-dung. The war, on the part of the gardener, should be diligently prosecuted, by which means only can he expect a suitable reward for his labor. The vine-shield is a valuable assistant, for besides preventing the ravages of the vermin, it greatly hastens the growth of the plants. When they have attained such a size that they are no longer in danger, the number in each hill should be reduced to three, and still later in the season to two. The ground may be occasionally watered at evening in dry weather, with decided advantage, and the hoe ought to be used so often as to keep the surface open, and prevent the encroachments of weeds. Some persons are accustomed to put a layer of straw under the vines, some three or four inches in depth, that they may suffer less injury from continued wet weather, and that the soil may be less affected by drought.

Cucumbers intended for pickling purposes, should be planted sometime during the first fortnight of July. In the bearing season, the vines ought to be examined daily, and, in order to secure greater productiveness, be relieved of the fruit as soon as it acquires a proper size.

For seed,—select some of the best fruit, and permit it to remain on the vine until it turns yellow. Then cut it off, and let it be exposed to the sun for some two or three weeks, at the end of which time the seed may be washed from the pulp, and spread out to dry. It will continue good for years, and, in fact, is to a certain extent improved by age.

USE.—Cucumbers are not remarkably wholesome, and to persons of weak constitution are positively injurious. However prepared for the table, they ought always to be eaten with great moderation. The expressed juice is sometimes employed as a cosmetic, and it enters into the composition of several French pomades.

To be eaten raw,—they should be freshly picked, and placed in a dish of clear, cold water. About fifteen minutes before they are wanted, pare and slice them into another dish of water. Just before carrying them to the table, drain off the water, sprinkle them with salt and pepper, and cover with good vinegar.

To stew.—Cut several large cucumbers into thick slices, flour them well, and fry them in butter; then put them into a saucepan, together with a tea-cupful of gravy, and season with salt and Cayenne pepper. Let them stew slowly for an hour, when they may be served hot.

To pickle.—The best cucumbers for this purpose are small, green, tender and free from blemishes; and they must be removed from the vines, as soon as they acquire a proper size. Immediately after being picked, they should be put in a vessel of boiling water, and allowed to remain in it for four or five hours. Then put them in cold vinegar, with alum and salt in the proportion of a table-spoonful of the first, and a tea-cupful of the second, to every gallon. When the time for pickling arrives, turn off the vinegar, and scald it. After being skimmed clear it should be turned back upon the cucumbers when hot.

They will be greatly improved by the addition of a few pepper-corns. The vinegar will require to be drawn off, and returned scalding hot, several times; if it prove weak, it ought to be thrown away, and fresh procured.

CURRANT.—*Ribes.*

We are not acquainted with any fruit which is more generally disseminated through the northern states, than the one now under notice. In some sections, it would be a difficult matter to find a respectable farm house that is without a few currant bushes, either disposed along the path which leads to the front door, or planted by the fence of the vegetable garden. It is true, that in nine cases out of ten they receive little or no cultivation,—being seldom relieved of the old, barren wood, and not manured from one year's end to another; still the good wife places a high estimate upon the fruit, and would not willingly be deprived of it. There are many reasons by which to account for this, such as the hardy character of the shrub, its free growth, and great productiveness, in addition to the excellent qualities of the fruit, both when freshly picked, and in its preserved state.

There are several species to be found growing wild in this country, but those of our gardens came originally from the northern parts of Europe and Asia, and are largely indebted to the skill of the Dutch horticulturists. In Siberia, the berry of the black species, the *R. nigrum*, frequently attains the size of a hazle-nut. Botanists aver that the white currant, which by some has been considered a distinct species, the *R. album*, is nothing but a variety of the red species, the *R. rubrum*. When the shrub is found in its natural state, the berry is either black or red, of small size and poor flavor. The name of the fruit is said to have been derived, from the resemblance of the berries to the little Corinth grapes or raisins, which have long been known in commerce as currants—the word evidently being a corruption of Corinth.

It seems strange that so little attention should be paid to the selection of the best varieties for culture, when they can be obtained so easily, and at such a trifling cost. They are not only more profitable than the common kinds, in a pecuniary point of view, but their fruit is infinitely superior for domestic uses. Of the popular red species, the following varieties may be considered chiefly worthy of notice, viz.:—the *Red Dutch,*—*May's Victoria,*—and *Knight's Sweet Red.* Of the white variety, the *White Dutch,* and the *White Grape* are undoubtedly the best sorts for a garden. The *Champagne* is of a light pink color, between the *Red* and *White Dutch;* it is acid, and cultivated by many as a curiosity. Of the black species, the *Common Black* is much inferior to the *Black Naples.*

CULTURE.—An idea appears to have become prevalent, that currant bushes require neither high culture, nor attention of any kind. They are generally choked with grass and weeds, of a stunted, inferior growth, full of dead wood, and producing fruit of the poorest description. Experience has demonstrated, however, that no inmate of the garden can be more improved by a rich soil, and careful cultivation.

New bushes are easily obtained by planting cuttings of the last year's growth. They should be taken from the most vigorous shoots, and with a sharp knife, so as to leave no rough or jagged edges to the bark. They ought to be about ten or twelve inches in length, and, when they are to be trained as standards, to have the buds on the lower half smoothly cut out, in order to prevent the appearance of troublesome suckers. Plant the cuttings, after being thus prepared, about six inches deep, and at least two feet apart, in early spring, or just before winter sets in.

It is best to have them in rather a shaded situation, so that they will not suffer from the heat of noonday. The application of a little water at intervals, will encourage the speedy formation of roots. In the second spring thereafter, remove the bushes to the spot in the garden where they are to stand permanently. They are sometimes placed in the border, but more commonly on the sides of the principal walks. They will thrive in almost every soil, although they have a decided preference for one that is strong, rich, deep and somewhat moist. They succeed well in a free, open exposure; but, to secure their general health, a partially shaded location is undoubtedly best. The gardener should, however, have bushes in both situations, as those having the full benefit of the sun's rays will ripen their fruit earliest in the season, but it will be smaller and less delicately flavored than that which has been perfected in the shade. They are to be set out in rows, four feet apart each way.

It has become common of late years, to recommend training currant bushes in the shape of trees, with the main stems running up from twelve to thirty-six inches high, before the side shoots are permitted to branch out. These standards have a very respectable appearance, and are rather more easily cultivated than the shrubs, where suckers are allowed to grow up at will. But, Mr. Cole, a distinguished authority on the subject, says that if they are permitted to sucker moderately, under a regular system of pruning, they will be longer lived, and produce more abundantly, than where the whole nourishment of the top passes through a single channel.

Nevertheless, the shape of the bush is not of as much importance as the other details of management. A due regard to pruning is very necessary to the production of fruit, which is borne mostly by two-year old wood. In some leisure hour of autumn or winter, all the old and stinted branches should be removed, and the shoots of the preceding year's growth shortened some five or six inches. By such a course, the sap, instead of being wasted upon barren wood, is confined within a small compass, and is permitted to form short, fertile spurs. Care must be taken to prevent too dense a growth; the branches should be few, spreading out widely, and not crossing or interfering with one another, so as to admit the sun and air to every leaf.

When there is a convenient opportunity in the latter part of summer, the soil ought to be enriched by the addition of a little good manure, dug in among the roots. Omitting this until winter, or the following spring, has been aptly compared to cramming an animal with food just before it is slaughtered. The roots require their food whilst they are getting in readiness for the next summer's crop, and not after their growth is suspended for the season. At all times of the year, the soil should be kept light and free of weeds, so that the roots may have no cause to complain of inattention on that score. Fruit of the very finest quality may be expected, attractive for its size, rich color, and delicious flavor. It can easily be kept on the bushes until the middle of autumn, by covering it with mats, cloths, or anything to shield it from the sun. Should the reader be disposed to think such particular care in the cultivation of the currant unnecessary, we advise him to manage at least one bush in the manner above described, while he permits the remainder of the plantation to take care of itself in the good old-fashioned way; and, if we mistake not, he will ere long be convinced of the justice of our remarks. The borer, which in some districts occasions a good deal of injury, is produced by a blue-black moth appearing about the middle of June. Every stem that is affected should be burned. As a preventive, apply to the bushes, before the season of the moths, lye or potash-water, or some other offensive wash. Various insects and worms that annoy the foliage may be repelled by the application of lime, or whale oil soap-suds.

Use.—The reputation of the currant has long been established as one of the most wholesome and grateful of fruits for the dessert. The cool, acid flavor is peculiarly agreeable in the summer season, and has led to several different preparations of the fruit for winter use. Before they get to be fully ripe, currants are stewed for tarts or puddings, either alone, or together with some other green fruit. The expressed juice is made into shrub, wine and jelly. The shrub makes a pleasant summer drink; the wine was formerly very popular among our agricultural community; while the jelly is an indispensable accompaniment to many dishes. The fruit of the black species is chiefly used for making a jam, which is thought valuable as a remedy for various disorders of the throat. The young leaves have been dried, and used as a substitute for green tea, from which, it is said, that it can scarcely be distinguished. All kinds of currants are much esteemed in cases of sickness, for quenching thirst, and having a cooling influence upon the stomach.

To preserve the green fruit.—Pick it when fully grown, dry the surface well without shrivelling, and cork it tight in glass bottles,—covering the cork with sealing wax. Then bury the bottles to the neck, in a box of sand or earth placed in a cool cellar. The fruit may thus be kept for almost any length of time, in as good condition as when gathered from the bushes.

Currant Pudding.—Put a layer of pastry in a dish, fill it with ripe currants, and cover them with a top crust. Boil for one hour, at the end of which time you are to remove the top crust, for the purpose of putting in butter, sugar, nutmeg and cloves. The pudding is to be eaten with hard sauce.

Currant Shrub.—To one pint of strained currant juice, put one pound of sugar. Boil together gently for eight or ten minutes, and then set the syrup in a place where it will cool. When lukewarm, add to every pint a wine-glassful of French brandy. Bottle tight, and keep in a cool apartment. A little of the shrub, mixed with water, makes a very refreshing drink for hot weather.

Currant Jelly.—The best way of extracting the juice, is to put the ripe fruit into a glass or earthern jar, which is suspended in a kettle of boiling water, and cook it partially. Then put it into a flannel bag, and let the juice strain through without squeezing. To every quart add two and a half pounds of white sugar, with the beaten white of an egg. Boil the syrup very gently, skimming it all the while until it becomes clear and thick. The proper time for taking it from the fire, will be indicated by its dropping in a solid lump to the bottom of a tumbler of cold water. Fill the glasses, and let the jelly be exposed to the sun for a few days, as it will thereby be much improved. There are a great number of receipts for making currant jelly, and this one is believed to be among the very best.

Currant Wine.—Gather the ripe fruit, when it is perfectly dry, and extract the juice by pressure, or in the manner above indicated. For every gallon of juice, allow one gallon of water and three pounds of good, clean sugar. Dissolve the sugar in the water, and, after removing all scum which may rise, add the liquid to the currant juice. Mix them well together in a keg or cask, but do not close it tight until fermentation has ceased, which will not be under a week. Then add one gill of French brandy to every two gallons of the liquor, and close the cask tight. In three or four weeks, the wine will be fit for bottling. In six months' time, it will be good for use, but its quality is improved by age.

DILL.—*Anethum graveolens.*

Dill is a hardy biennial, and a native of Spain and Portugal. It somewhat resembles the common fennel, but is smaller, and has a less agreeable odor. It is mentioned in the original Greek of St. Matthew's gospel, but has been translated *anise,* which is an entirely different plant. A bed containing twelve square feet is quite large enough for any family.

Culture.—The plants must be raised from seed,—one half ounce of which will be sufficient for a bed of the size above mentioned. Sow in drills one foot apart, and cover about one third of an inch deep This is best done in autumn, soon after the seed ripens, because it is then not only more likely to germinate, but it produces stronger plants, than where sown in the following April. The soil must be kept light, and free from weeds. A little water will greatly assist the vegetation of the seed. When the plants have attained a growth of three or four weeks, they must be thinned out in the drill to distances of at least ten inches; or otherwise, they will be rendered weak and spindling. The leaves may be gathered as they are wanted for use.

For seed,—the stalks shall be suffered to run up unchecked. The seed-vessels should be picked as soon as they are fully ripened, and before they have a chance to waste their contents upon the ground. This caution is seldom necessary, however, for such are the habits of the plant, that a bed, once made, will perpetuate itself.

Use.—The seeds and leaves of dill, on account of their warm, aromatic taste, are much used in pickles, and frequently to give zest to soups and sauces. The seeds are well known to have some medicinal virtues; yielding a volatile oil and a distilled water, which are excellent carminatives.

EGG-PLANT.—*Solanum melongena.*

Having been brought from Africa, this plant is known to many cultivators as the Guinea Squash; but, its most common name is derived from the resemblance which the partly-grown fruit of the *white* variety bears to a pullet's egg. We cannot call it a popular vegetable, although it appears to be gradually working itself into favor. Its history is somewhat like that of the tomato, which was little regarded at first, but has acquired for itself a deservedly high reputation. The peculiar taste of the fruit, even when cooked in the most approved manner, is very disagreeable to some persons; and by many gardeners it is raised more for its ornamental appearance in their grounds, than for any particular value which they may attach to it in the culinary department. By others, however, it is esteemed as a great delicacy. It is now well known in the markets of cities, for which it is cultivated in large gardens situated in the vicinity. Even if it be desirable on no other account, it helps make a variety upon a table. Of the several sorts commonly grown, the *Long Purple* has such valuable qualities as recommend it in particular for family use. But there are other kinds,—like the *Smooth-stemmed Purple*, and the *Prickly-stemmed Purple*,—which are respectively worthy of notice.

CULTURE.—Where earliness is an object, the seed may be sown in a small hot-bed, at the very commencement of spring. One ounce of seed will afford between three and four thousand plants. The heat of the bed need not be very powerful,—only sufficient to bring the plants forward for their removal to the open ground by the first of May. It is with them as with all other vegetables started under glass by artificial warmth,—their growth should be so regular and moderate, as to give the leaves a healthy, green color, instead of a pale, sickly yellow. Apply water in small quantities, at all times when the earth appears dry. The sashes may be kept closed until the young plants have fairly made their appearance, after which, air ought to be admitted freely at midday. In all severe weather, as well as at night, a slight additional protection of litter or mats is necessary, to prevent too great a reduction of the temperature within the frame.

When the plants are about three inches high, they must be thinned out to distances of three or four inches; and those which are pulled, can be set in small pots, to be plunged up to the rim in the mold of another bed. They should be removed to a warm border, where the soil is rich and mellow, somewhere about the middle of May, or earlier in the month if the season be sufficiently mild. They would suffer not a little from being exposed to a late frost, or even continued cool weather. Put them in rows, two and a half feet apart each way, so that they can have ample room for the development of their leaves. Water them abundantly at the time of transplanting, and for a few days afterward shelter them at noonday from the hot sun. The after-culture is simply to make a good use of the hoe, keeping the soil light and clean. When the stems are a foot high, they need the support of a little earth drawn up around them. Fruit may be expected in July or August.

For a crop to mature later in the season, or where early plants cannot be obtained from a hot-bed, the seed may be sown about the end of April. The bed should be in a warm, sheltered situation, protected from cold winds, and having a fine, fertile soil. The plants may be removed to their final location some five or six weeks afterwards, either at evening, or on a damp, cloudy day.

USE.—As we have already remarked, the fruit of the egg-plant is not held in general esteem. Like the tomato, which is seldom relished at first, it will, after a few trials, be thought very palatable. We know, from personal observation, that its excellence depends altogether upon the manner in which it may be cooked. It is used in soups, and stews, but is commonly cut into thin slices and fried, for which we give the following

Receipt.—The fruit contains an acrid juice, which ought to be removed before cooking. For this purpose, pile up the slices on a plate, with layers of salt, and raise one side of the plate, so that the juice may run off without affecting the taste of the lower slice. After remaining so for about half an hour, they should be well washed in fresh water, and then fried quite brown in batter.

ENDIVE.—*Cichorium endivia.*

Originally of eastern Asia, the endive has been known in Europe since the sixteenth century. It is a hardy annual, and was introduced into Great Britain about the year 1548. In several countries of Europe it is much esteemed, particularly in France,—where it is prepared for the table in many different ways. It is there thought to be very wholesome and nutritious. There are three varieties, viz.:—the *Green Curled*,—the *White Curled*,—and the *Broad-leaved Batavian*. As to their respective merits;—the *Green Curled*, which is considered excellent for salads, is also the hardiest, and, therefore, the best adapted for the main crop; the *White Curled*, on account of its tenderness, is better suited for summer and autumn use; while the *Batavian* is thought preferable to either of the others, for soups and stews.

CULTURE.—The endive is best pleased with an open situation, and a soil which is deep and mellow, dry and rich. That it should be both deep and mellow, is necessary as much for the accommodation of the long roots, as to secure thorough drainage, without which the plants cannot flourish. This last particular is so important for those plants which stand out through the winter, that some cultivators even go to the expense of founding the bed upon a substratum of stones and small blocks of wood.

The principal season for committing the seed to the ground, is between the first and fifteenth of July. Small sowings may be made from time to time, during the two previous months, but the plants will mostly run to stalks, without attaining a vigorous growth for blanching. Towards the first of August, a final sowing can be made for late winter and spring supplies.

After the soil has been thoroughly spaded, open small drills lengthwise of the bed, one foot apart, and about four inches deep. Then sow the seed—one ounce of which may be expected to yield five thousand plants,—in the bottom of the drills, and cover it thinly. It is advisable, during dry weather, to give a little water now and then until the plants become firmly established. When they have attained a height of two inches, thin them out in the drills so that they may stand twelve inches apart. Or, where another bed is wanted, this first thinning should be only partial, and the strongest plants be allowed to remain until they are five or six inches high, when they are to be removed to trenches, and set twelve inches apart therein. Water must be applied in a moderate quantity at the time of transplanting, and the application repeated every evening, as long as any danger exists of the roots being injured by the heat or protracted drought. The ground is to be kept open and free from weeds, at all times during the growing season.

When the plants are about ten inches high, and appear perfectly healthy, the process of blanching may be commenced. Select a dry afternoon, when the leaves are free from moisture,—which would cause them to decay, or otherwise injure their appearance,—and gather them together in a close bunch, around which matting is to be wound several times, bringing it to a point at the top in such a manner as will prevent the admission of rain. Finally, some earth is to be drawn up against the plant, in order to save it from being broken down by the wind. To avoid the trouble of tying up each plant separately in this way, some gardeners cover them with inverted pots, or a roof, formed by two boards set at right angles, placed lengthwise of the trenches, and banked with mold to exclude the light. In the hot season, tying up is considered much the better plan; but, at other times, covering the plants preserves while it blanches them. If the weather continue warm and dry, the blanching will be effected in a week or ten days; but, if otherwise, not under a fortnight or three weeks. The plant should be taken up soon after the process is completed, or it will rot, particularly during a long rain.

The reader will, of course, inqure how the plants are to be protected through the winter. They may be taken up about the beginning of November, each set in a ball of dirt, and placed in a box of sand, in a cellar or shed, where they will continue in a tolerably good state for a month or six weeks. But the best mode, however, is to take them all up at that time, and plant them, six or eight inches apart, on a bank of light earth, sloping to the south. This bank is to be sheltered by a cold frame and shutters, or by bent hoops and mats. The additional protection of leaves or litter, may be required during rigorous weather, but on every mild, pleasant day, air must be admitted freely, in order to prevent the appearance of disease among the plants. Blanch them as wanted for use, in the manner above described, with the precaution not to tie them up when in a frozen state.

For seed,—allot some of the most healthy and perfect plants that remain in spring, and set them out, eighteen inches apart, on the south side of a fence. Or, you can sow the seed in April, and remove the plants to another bed, as soon as they are five or six inches high. The flower-stems ought to be supported by stakes, and the seed-vessels to be gathered as they successively ripen. Lay them on a cloth, where they can get perfectly dry before being threshed.

USE.—The endive is cultivated for its head of leaves, which, after being blanched to deprive them of a certain bitter taste, are used in several different forms. The French eat them raw, stewed, boiled, fried and pickled; but they are most commonly dressed in the form of a salad. When boiled, they are said to be an effectual remedy for the jaundice. They never disagree with the stomach, but, on the contrary, are considered cool and refreshing. The root, when roasted and ground, is said to be good mixed with coffee, giving it a fragrant taste, and greatly increasing its exhilarating qualities.

ESCALOT, OR ESCHALOT.—*See* SHALLOT.

FENNEL.—*Anethum fœniculum.*

A well known aromatic perennial. It is a native of Italy, and has become a tenant of most European gardens. The stem is tall, bearing umbels of small, yellow flowers. By domestication, the seeds lose their acrid properties, and acquire an agreeable flavor, which makes them a popular medicine with the poor.

CULTURE.—The fennel will be found to flourish in almost any kind of soil, although it appears to be longest lived upon a dry formation. It is by no means particular in regard to the exposure. Sow the seed in autumn, soon after it is ripened, or early in the following spring. One quarter of an ounce will be enough for a piece of ground containing twelve square feet. Sow in shallow drills, one foot apart, and cover about one third of an inch deep. When the plants are three inches high, thin them out in the drill to distances of ten inches. Or, a plantation can be made with the offsets of old roots, in spring, summer or autumn. Water should be freely applied every other day, until it is ascertained that they have taken a firm foothold. One advantage of making such a plantation is, that it comes into immediate bearing. No cultivation will be necessary, other than the occasional use of the hoe. To prevent the plants going to seed, the stems should be cut down as often as they manifest a disposition to flower, and this will cause a young growth of leaves. The fennel is always inclined to perpetuate itself, and when a bed is once formed, it will remain in good order for many years; indeed, such are the habits of the plant, that it may be advisable not to permit the formation of seed, unless it be wanted for some particular purpose.

For seed,—allow some of the best stalks to run up and flower. They will bear abundantly in autumn. Put it in paper bags, and keep in a cool, dry apartment.

USE.—Fennel is highly prized in European kitchens, but as yet it has attained little popularity in this country. The young stalks are used in salads, soups and fish sauces, as well as for a garnish to dishes. The Italians blanch them like celery, by which means their strong taste is destroyed, and they are then eaten with oil, pepper and vinegar. The seeds are employed in medicine as a carminative.

GARLIC.—*Allium sativum.*

Garlic is a hardy perennial, found growing naturally in Sicily and some other parts of southern Europe which border on the Mediterranean. It belongs to the *Allium* family, and is, therefore, nearly connected with the common onion. The botanical term is said to be derived from the Celtic *all*, which signified hot or burning. Garlic has been extensively cultivated for domestic purposes, for at least three hundred years, having been introduced into England in 1548. The root is a compound bulb, consisting of a dozen or more small bulbs, called cloves, which are enveloped in a single membrane; the stem runs to the height of about two feet; while the leaves are long and narrow. The whole plant has a powerful fetid odor, and a sharp, acrid taste, which are very unpleasant to those persons who are unaccustomed to them. It seems to have been worshipped by some nations—as, for example, the Egyptians; and detested by others—as by the ancient Greeks. We cannot say that it is much esteemed either in this country or in England. It is not common in family gardens.

Culture.—It is propagated by the cloves, or sub-divisions of the bulbous root. Although very hardy, and grown easily on almost every kind of soil, still it has a preference for one that is dry, mellow, and rich—but not rank from the recent addition of fresh dung. Little preparation is necessary. Set the cloves, in early spring, in rows about six inches apart each way, and to the depth of two inches. As the root end should in every case be downward, the best method of planting, is to take a clove between the thumb and forefinger, and push it gently into the soil.

The after-culture is simply to keep the surface open and clean. Some of the bulbs may be drawn from time to time as they are wanted for use, yet the principal part of the crop intended for preservation through the winter, should be allowed to remain until it has come to maturity. This will be indicated by the leaves turning yellow, and, in the middle states, occurs generally about the beginning of August. In harvesting, pull up the bulbs by the stalks, and let them lie exposed to the sun for a few hours; after which, they may be tied in bundles, and put away in a cool, airy apartment for safe keeping. They can be preserved until the following spring, without any difficulty.

Use.—Several valuable and curious properties are ascribed to this plant. In some countries, it is used extensively as a seasoning for food;—thus, among all classes of society in the southern parts of Europe, it enters into the composition of nearly every dish for the table. In England and the United States, however, it is by no means a favorite, as its strong, nauseating smell is repulsive to our more *refined* taste. Garlic is, likewise, celebrated for its medicinal virtues. It forms an excellent expectorant, and has been administered in a great variety of diseases, such as hysteria, obstructions, dropsy, cutaneous eruptions, deafness, etc. The juice is said to be the best cement known for mending broken glass and china.

GOOSEBERRY.—*Ribes grossularia.*

England seems peculiarly adapted, by the coolness and moisture of its climate, to the successful culture of this fine fruit. In Lancashire and the adjoining counties, there are annual meetings of the gooseberry growers, at which prizes, ranging in value from ten shillings to as many pounds sterling, are awarded among the exhibitors. It is true, that the size and weight of the berry are, as a general thing, considered of greater importance by the judges, than its excellence for culinary purposes. An account of each meeting, giving full descriptions of the prize sorts, is afterwards published in a small volume called "The Manchester Gooseberry Book." In its wild state, as found in the northern part of Europe, the berry is half an inch in diameter, and weighs only one quarter of an ounce; but under the influence of high culture, it has in some cases attained a diameter of two inches, with a weight of one ounce and a half. Such is the effect of horticultural exhibitions.

Although thus successful in Great Britain, the foreign gooseberry, owing to the difference in climate, cannot be naturalized in the southern part of Europe, or of the United States. Indeed, the crop often fails in what are called the northern states. We have several native varieties, which undoubtedly might be made worthy of attention, as being better suited to our long, oppressively hot summers, than any which could be imported from England. A result so desirable should lead to the thorough investigation of the subject by our intelligent gardeners. We believe that nothing but skill and perseverance is required, to accomplish as much in this country, as has been already accomplished by the humble cottagers of Lancashire.

The number of varieties which have been produced in England, is really surprising; of the thousands raised from seed, the catalogue of the London Horticultural Society enumerates one hundred and forty-nine that are worthy of notice; while Lindley gives a list of over seven hundred which have been distinguished at various times by prizes. The following sorts are certainly among the very best:—of the reds, the *Crown Bob*,—the *Red Warrington*,—*Houghton's Seedling*,——and the *Champagne*;—of the yellows, the *Early Sulphur*,—*Gorton's Viper*,—the *Yellow Champagne*,—and the *Golden Fleece*;—of the greens, *Parkinson's Laurel*,—the *Green Walnut*,—the *Jolly Tar*,—and the *Jolly Angler*;—and, finally, of the whites, the *Whitesmith*,—*Wellington's Glory*,—the *Bright Venus*,—and *Crompton's Queen of Sheba*. The difficulty of making any selection like the above, will be readily appreciated by the reader.

Culture.—New varieties are raised from seed, but the old established sorts are propagated by cuttings, in much the same way as the currant. These cuttings are taken in autumn, just before the leaves fall, or as soon as the frost is out of the ground in spring, from the strongest and straightest shoots of the last season's growth. They should be of healthy appearance, and about twelve inches long. If you propose training them as standards, you must cut out, with a sharp knife, all the buds, except three or four at the upper end, in order to prevent the appearance of troublesome suckers around the main stem. Experience has shown, however, that the bushes will be longer lived, and much more productive, when permitted to sucker moderately, than if the whole support of the top be drawn through a single channel. By a judicious system of pruning, the bearing wood will be frequently renewed, and the sap will not be wasted upon that which has become old and barren. The cuttings should be inserted about half their length, in a bed of rich, moist soil, situated on the north side of a fence, or in some shaded spot. The dirt is to be firmly pressed around them, and again in the following spring, if they appear to have been at all lifted by the frost.

In the second year after, they will probably have become so well rooted that they may then be removed to their final location. Being exceedingly sensitive to heat and drought, they require a soil which is at once deep and moist. It ought to be subsoiled or trenched, before they are taken from the nursery bed. Richness is also an essential requisite, and, in addition to a liberal application of dung at the outset, a generous top-dressing should be dug in around the roots in every succeeding autumn. The situation must be open, and away from the injurious influences of trees. It has been said on good authority, that when the bushes are planted near a white-washed fence, they are not so liable to suffer from the mildew, as they would be in an open compartment. Transplant during any mild, pleasant weather in autumn or spring. To prevent their shade affecting vegetables grown in their neighborhood, it is a good plan to put them on the sides of the principal paths, or in a border that is not wanted for other purposes. Let them stand in rows, between three and four feet apart. The ground should always be kept in good tilth,—light and porous, as well as free from weeds and grass.

Thorough pruning is considered very essential to the successful growth of the gooseberry. It is best performed in autumn, when the leaves have fallen, and the position of the branches is thereby better exposed, or at any time during the winter and spring, before the buds get to be much swollen. The rules to be followed in pruning, are learned only from personal observation or experience; and we can but suggest a few leading hints, the application of which must, in every case, be governed by sound judgment and discretion. Old and unproductive wood should first be removed, as that absorbs sap without rendering any equivalent; while the young shoots are to be shortened and reduced in number, so as to admit the light and air freely to every leaf,—without which the perfection of the fruit cannot be expected. With a little practice in the use of the knife, this winter pruning can be so performed as to give the bushes a very neat appearance, and to secure an abundant crop in the coming season. At the same time, the ground ought to receive a generous application of manure, to ensure its fertility, and add to the security of the plants against disease.

The "mildew," as it is termed, proves the most serious obstacle to be encountered by the American gardener. It does not exist in the cool climate of England, and is only occasionally known in the extreme northern parts of our own country. But, in the middle states, as we go towards the south, we find the crop very uncertain. When partly grown, it suddenly becomes coated with a grey mildew or scurf, which in a short time destroys its value. The berries should be picked as soon as may be after the appearance of the disease, and either used in the cultivator's own kitchen, or carried to market. How is this obstacle to be overcome? Being local and confined to particular districts, it never can be entirely. All remedies that have been proposed, are partial in their effects. High culture—or, keeping the soil rich and in good tilth, accompanied by a judicious system of pruning,—is most important. Wood ashes are sometimes sifted on the leaves, while lime and sulphur are dug into the soil. The most efficient remedy is covering the ground with a layer, ten or twelve inches in thickness, of salt hay or sea-weed. In places where these cannot be procured, litter or straw can be used in their stead, by being sprinkled with small quantities of fine salt or brine. Spent tan around the bushes is good to prevent the attacks of the destructive caterpillar.

USE.—The fruit is deservedly held in high esteem for culinary purposes. In fact, its name is derived from the circumstance of its having been in olden times considered an indispensable accompaniment to a green goose. In its unripe state, early in the season, it is made into sauces, tarts, pies, puddings, etc.; while, when fully matured, some of the choice varieties are very acceptable for dessert, and make good preserves. In every form it is wholesome, as well as pleasant to the taste. It makes a very excellent wine, which is said to be so near equal to Champagne, that it often passes for that among inexperienced judges.

To preserve green gooseberries.—Fill a bottle with the green fruit, and let it stand a few minutes in a vessel of boiling water. Cork and seal it immediately after being taken from the water, and keep it in a cool cellar, with the neck downward.

Gooseberry Pie.—Pick the heads and stems from unripe gooseberries, and rub them with a towel for the purpose of cleaning them. Fill a dish with them, and add a little water, together with sufficient brown sugar to correct their acidity. Cover with puff paste, and bake for upwards of an hour. Some persons stew the fruit in sugar before putting it in the plates, so that it requires less baking.

GRAPE.—*Vitis.*

Scripture abounds in allusions to the vine. The excellence of its fruit, and the unrivalled beverage which can be made therefrom, led to its cultivation in the earliest ages of antiquity. By a figurative mode of expression, it was known as the type of plenty and the symbol of happiness. Thus, in the description of the peaceful and flourishing state of the kingdom of Israel under Solomon, we find it recorded that "Judah and Israel dwelt safely, every man under his vine and under his fig tree, from Dan even to Beersheba." And it was a curse pronounced upon the same people for their disobedience, that they "should plant vineyards and dress them, but they should neither drink of the wine, nor gather the grapes, for the worms should eat them." The ingratitude, unprofitableness and idolatry of the Jewish Church, are represented as a vineyard yielding the disappointed proprietor only wild and poisonous fruit; while its ruin is set forth under the simile of a vineyard laid waste. Two of the most beautiful parables left for our instruction by Jesus Christ, are drawn from the appearance and culture of the same plant. In one, He represents Himself as the son of the Lord of the vineyard, sent to collect the fruits thereof; and in the other, as the true Vine, His people being the branches, and His Father the Husbandman.

A distinguished writer upon the management of the grape, speaks in the following enthusiastic language:—"Of all the productions of the vegetable world, which the skill and ingenuity of man have rendered conducive to his comfort, and to the enlargement of his sphere of enjoyments, and the increase of his pleasurable gratifications, the vine stands forward as pre-eminently conspicuous. Its quickness of growth,—the great age to which it will live, so great, indeed, as to be unknown,—its almost total exemption from all those adverse contingencies which blight and diminish the produce of other fruit-bearing trees,—its astonishing vegetative powers,—its wonderful fertility,—and its delicious fruit, applicable to so many purposes, and agreeable to all palates, in all its varied shapes,—combine to mark it out as one of the greatest blessings bestowed by Providence to promote the comfort and enjoyments of the human race."

The grapes of the old world are all descended from the *Vitis vinifera* of Persia, but the natives of this country are distinct species, which have been greatly improved by domestication. The foreign kinds are not suited to this climate, and can be grown with success only under glass. The best native varieties are—the *Isabella*,—the *Catawba*,—the *Bland*,—the *Ohio*,—and the *Elsinburgh*. The first two are placed by general consent at the head of the list, and their good qualities are such as to recommend them in particular to the favorable notice of the farmer and small gardener. Common and popular as they are, we cannot but wish that they were even more so. We would that every cultivator of the soil, however humble may be his position in society, should be able, in the language of Holy Writ, to "sit under his own vine," and to be gratified by its fruit. No man who has a yard of ground, with a naked fence, or the side of a building, at his disposal, should be without this source of pleasure and comfort. It can be obtained from a nurseryman at the cost of a few shillings, and the expense of its subsequent cultivation is too trifling to be thought of for a moment. Its management, which proves a bugbear to so many, is but little more difficult than the management of a turnip patch, or a hill of Indian corn. We shall offer a few hints upon the subject, and refer the reader who wishes farther information, to the numerous excellent treatises which may be found in the bookstores.

Culture.—In the propagation of the old varieties, we have succeeded best by making *layers* of young wood, some time during the month of June. The shoots are bent down into little trenches, where they are confined by forked sticks, and covered with a little mellow earth. The occasional application of water while the weather continues dry, will induce the speedy formation of roots. In the latter part of autumn, the stem connected with the parent stalk may be cut, so that the new vine can be removed to any place where it is intended to remain. Propagation by *cuttings* is more easy, but less certain. They should be about a foot long each, having three buds, and planted in a sloping direction, with one end just above the surface. Early spring is the proper time for the operation, and the soil ought to be rich and mellow, as well as in rather a shaded locality. As the vines are apt to bleed when cut in spring, take off the cuttings in autumn, and keep them through the winter in the cellar, covered by a little light soil. Making use of *eyes* is a favorite method, especially for scarce varieties. In February or March, take some of the last year's shoots, and cut them into pieces two inches long, with an eye in the middle of each. Split them, and plant the halves containing the eyes under glass, or in a warm window. Cover them about half an inch deep, and be sure that the eye is uppermost. The vines can be removed to the open garden, as soon as they acquire sufficient size to bear transplanting.

The next thought will be regarding the situation. In vineyards, it is customary to tie the vines up to large stakes, which are set in rows, eight feet apart each way. In gardens, they are placed by the fence, or by an upright trellis not over eight feet high. They are often permitted to run up the sides of buildings, which are thereby relieved of their unseemly nakedness. The best native grapes we have ever tasted, were picked from a vine that completely covers the south side of a dwelling-house, where it has borne enormous quantities of fruit for many years past, and bids fair to be as productive for many years to come. The situation ought to be neither in a valley, nor on a high, bleak hill; a moderate elevation, such as we have in another place recommended for the general wants of a garden, is most suitable. The exposure should be open, for although the shade of trees or buildings may induce luxuriance of growth, yet the crop will be smaller and more uncertain than where it has the full benefit of light and air. The best soil is one which is at the same time "dry and light, deep and rich." A dry substratum is so essential to the prosperity of some varieties, that where they are cultivated, gardeners frequently take the trouble to make an artificial bed of bones, blocks of wood, and stones, at the depth of two or three feet below the surface.

A certain degree of fertility in the soil is necessary to the health and continued productiveness of the vine. To use a homely comparison, the vine is somewhat like a cow which is fastened in her stall, and can get nothing to eat except what her master puts before her. If she be regularly fed, and with food suited to her wants, she will keep in good condition, or perhaps even improve in flesh, and will yield a generous return of milk. If she be neglected at times, or be not allowed a reasonable supply of hay and roots, the quantity of her milk gradually decreases, while her bones seem disposed to force their way through the skin that covers them. If she be altogether neglected, her death is a natural consequence; but, on the contrary, if her owner should feed her too liberally, she would soon become so fleshy as to be unfit for the pail. It is so with the vine. The roots must have a proper supply of nutriment given them, or they cannot maintain a luxuriant growth of foliage, and mature a crop that is valuable alike for its size and the excellence of its flavor. When they have exhausted the soil within their reach, they are like the cow tied to an empty manger. But should they be fed injudiciously, with food not adapted to their wants, or at unseasonable times, the fruit will be found of inferior quality.

The conclusion is obvious;—the cultivator, after having in the first place selected a favorable soil, and spaded it deeply, must afterwards give it regular applications of manure, in order to ensure its fertility and the vigor of the vine. Animal excrements applied in large quantities, are known to affect the rich flavor of the fruit, and sometimes to cause the loss of the crop. They should, therefore, be composted, or else given frequently, and in small doses. Ashes, bone-dust and soap-suds from the wash-room, are very excellent fertilizers. Yet, nothing is so good for the purpose, as the annual trimmings buried near the roots, as they will decay, and furnish all that is required for a new growth. This important fact was discovered by certain poor peasants, who were unable to purchase manure. We have for a long time been in the habit of applying soap-suds to the roots on washing days, and a solution of whale oil soap on one or two other days of each week, during the summer season. It is only by the pursuit of such a liberal policy that we can hope for our reward.

Although in its wild state the grape vine attains a prodigious size, the stem being perhaps three feet in circumference, and the branches two hundred feet long,—it is well known that when under cultivation, a judicious system of pruning is conducive to its general health and productiveness

When suffered to extend its foliage according to its own pleasure, but little dependence can be placed upon realizing either profit or satisfaction from its fruit. While all persons are ready to admit the value,—nay, the actual necessity,—of such pruning, there is much uncertainty in regard to the best mode of doing it. Thus Buist has aptly remarked, that "frequently so great a mystery is thrown around these simple attentions, that the timid are afraid even to touch the vine with the knife; while others, whose boldness goes farther than their knowledge, cut right and left with considerable dexterity, feeling satisfied if they show that the wood is at least cut off." Pruning is so intimately connected with the manner of training the branches, that we shall explain our ideas concerning both, by following the growth of the vine from the time it leaves the nursery until it comes into bearing.

When it is planted by the trellis, cut it down to the lower two buds or eyes, which may be permitted to form one shoot in the coming season. Train this shoot in a perpendicular direction, but, at the approach of winter, cut it down to four buds. In the second summer, train up two shoots in the shape of the letter Y, but at autumn take them down, and extend them horizontally along the lower rail as far as desired. Three or four feet on either side of the main stem is probably far enough, and a single vine will then occupy from six to eight feet of the trellis. In the third year, four upright branches shall be grown from the horizontal arms, at equal distances apart, and stopped as soon as they reach the upper rail. In the fourth season, a few bunches of fruit can be allowed to perfect themselves, just so that the cultivator may be encouraged, and feel that he is actually reaping some of the benefits of his industry. It is not advisable, however, to try the roots too severely, or they will be less able to yield generously in subsequent years. They are still young, and must be permitted to strengthen themselves. In the autumn, they shall be cut down to the first bud from the horizontal arms. Four shoots of the summer's growth are to remain to perfect fruit in the fifth season, at the end of which they will be cut down in the same manner, to make room for the four new branches, which have sprung up in place of those cut down a year previous. And so the gardener must proceed from year to year, cutting out the old wood which has just done bearing, and leaving young shoots to produce the next crop.

This long explanation will be better understood by reference to the accompanying Fig. 23, which represents the vine at the end of the fourth year. The main stem is indicated

Fig. 23.

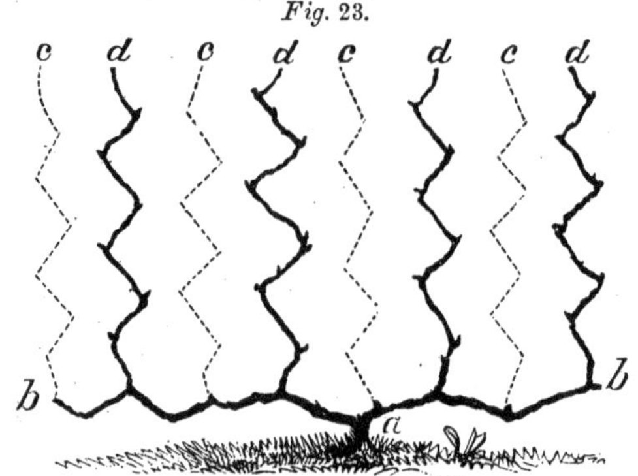

by the letter *a*; *b b* are the horizontal arms; *c c c c* are places occupied by the four upright shoots which bore fruit and have been cut down; and *d d d d* are the four branches of the summer's growth, which are expected to bear in the coming season. This is called the "renewal system," and is, undoubtedly, the one best adapted for open air culture, because the circulation of the sap is principally through young, vigorous wood, rendering the whole plant healthy and productive. The fruit is larger and better than where the "spur system" is followed, although not so abundant. The most suitable time for pruning is in November, but the general practice is to delay the operation until the mild days of February or March, about a month before the buds are likely to commence swelling. At midsummer, instead of pulling off leaves and cutting away good-sized branches, as is so common, it will be only necessary to pinch off the ends of the shoots, and, perhaps, to remove feeble laterals, that the whole strength of the roots may be expended upon the perfection of the fruit. It is a great piece of folly to strip the vine of its leaves, in order to expose the berries to the sun, for every schoolboy knows that the foliage of a plant is intended by nature to digest the sap, which then descends to impart vigor to the whole system. Should too large a quantity of fruit be set, it ought to be reduced early in the season; and this is particularly necessary with young vines, lest the imperfectly established roots become exhausted by overbearing.

The devastations of various insects may in a measure be prevented, by means of large open-mouthed bottles, that are half filled with sweetened vinegar and water, and then hung up in different parts of the trellises. Lice that gather upon the ends of the tender shoots to suck out the juices, should be dipped into a weak solution of whale oil soap. Caterpillars and worms are to be picked off by hand. The enemy most to be dreaded is the rose bug, of which we have given a short description in the article upon the "DESTRUCTION OF VERMIN." The only chance of saving the crop, is to go round among the vines, several times a day during the season of that insect, and quietly knock every trespasser into a cup of water or turpentine. Endeavor thus to "secure indemnity for the past, and security for the future." Every measure of this kind must be prosecuted diligently, and commenced as soon as the danger is discovered, or there can be little hope of a crop.

USE.—Who needs to be told what an addition to the dessert, is a dish of fine grapes just picked from the vines? As a fruit, they can scarcely be surpassed for richness of flavor; and they are, moreover, wholesome for the stomach, as well as palatable to the taste. Their use in particular cases of disease, such as severe dysentery and pulmonary complaints, has been attended with the most beneficial effects. When dried, they are called raisins, and, in that form, are used extensively for the dessert and in various prepared dishes. The fermented juice, or wine, has a world-wide reputation. In its pure state, it is, undoubtedly, a very healthy and refreshing liquor; but, experience has long since shown, that even its moderate use may result in the most melancholy consequences. The temperance movement is a noble one, deserving the support of every honest and intelligent citizen.

To preserve grapes through the winter.—Procure a tight cask or barrel, and at the bottom put a layer of bran, which has been thoroughly dried in an oven. Upon this place a layer of grapes, gathered before they have become "dead ripe," as it is termed. They should be perfectly dry, and carefully cleaned, by means of a light brush, of dirt, cobwebs and insects. Then put on a second course of dried bran, then one of grapes, and in this way fill up the barrel with layers of bran and grapes alternately. Take good care that the bunches are not crowded closely together, and that the top layer shall be of bran. Head up the barrel very tight, to exclude the air as completely as possible. Thus packed, grapes have been kept in a first-rate state of preservation for nine months, or a year. When they are taken up, their flavor will be much improved, by cutting off the hardened end of the stems, and putting them for a few moments in sweet wine.

HOP.—*Humulus lupulus.*

Mesue, a celebrated Arabian physician, who died about the year 846, makes mention of the hop vine in his works; and, indeed, it seems to have been cultivated for an unknown period. It did not attract attention in England, however, until somewhere about the year 1525, when the Reformation was in progress, as appears by the following doggerel:—

> "Hops, heresy, pickerel and beer,
> Were brought into England in one year."

And its value was at first so little understood, that in 1528 the Parliament was requested to prohibit its use, as an unwholesome weed which would spoil the taste of beer. Public attention was attracted to the subject, and in less than half a century afterward, a little work, called "A Perfecte Platforme of a Hoppe Garden," was published by Reynold Scott; which gave, in addition to a full description of the appearance and uses of the plant, curiously minute instructions for its propagation and management. This book has become exceedingly rare, and is much prized by antiquarians. The number of acres in Great Britain devoted to the culture of the hop has steadily increased; in the year 1837, they amounted to over fifty-six thousand, but, in 1846, the number fell to fifty-two thousand. The duties paid during the latter year exceeded four hundred and forty-three thousand pounds sterling, or near two and a quarter millions of dollars. These few statistics show the dignity and importance of the hop in an agricultural point of view. In this country, it is raised to a certain extent for exportation, while nearly every garden contains a few vines for family use, two facts which will justify the admission of the present article in a work of this character.

The hop belongs to the same family as the hemp and nettle. It is a native of Europe, Siberia, and North America, and may be found growing spontaneously on the banks and intervals of many of our large rivers. The root is perennial, giving out several herbaceous climbers; the fruit is a sort of cone, composed of membranous scales, each of which envelopes a single seed.

Culture.—The whole process, from the time of planting to the preparation of the crop for market, requires much experience and many precautions. The vine is tender, and the produce somewhat uncertain,—varying in quantity and quality, according to the season and management. The most favorable soil is a deep, sandy loam, lying upon a dry substratum. Instances are recorded of the roots having been traced to the depth of more than ten feet, which is certainly a good reason for giving them plenty of room in which to extend themselves. The soil ought to be finely pulverized, and made rich, if not naturally so, by the liberal application of well rotted dung. As regards exposure, the bed should be protected from severe northerly winds, perhaps situated on a gentle declivity towards the south-east.

The best mode of obtaining roots for a new plantation, is in early spring, to take a hoe and draw the earth from the old stools. Then cut off as many of the last summer's shoots as you deem necessary for your purpose. They should be about eighteen inches long, and are usually known as "trimmings." In making a large plantation, the ground is to be laid into parallel rows six feet apart, and holes for the reception of the roots marked out at the same distances from each other in the rows. These holes may be two feet square, and one foot deep, to be filled with good compost, or with the soil itself, if it be sufficiently rich, after having been spaded fine and light. Three roots shall be allotted for each hole, and they are to be placed in this position. They may be covered about six inches deep. A short stake should be placed in the centre of each hill. The soil is carefully cultivated during the first year, and at intervals a little is drawn up around the stems. The runners will probably climb the poles without assistance, but should any be disposed to wander, bring them back,

Fig. 24.

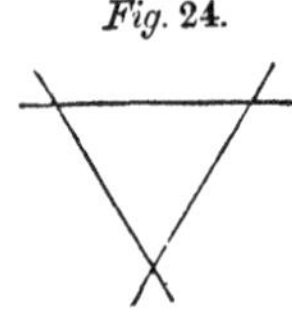

and fasten them with twine or bass. In autumn, a little compost may be thrown upon the stools, to prevent their suffering from frost during the winter.

In the second spring, the hills are to be examined, in order to cut off the last year's shoots and suckers, nearly close to the main roots. The trimmings can be dressed for the table like asparagus, forming a very wholesome dish. A little rotten manure or compost ought to be placed within reach of the roots, in order to secure their vigorous growth. The dirt is then levelled over them to the depth of ten inches, and two poles, fourteen or eighteen feet high, are set firmly in each hill. Thorough cultivation with the hoe,—or plough, in the case of a large plantation,—should by no means be neglected, while every care is taken to keep the runners upon the poles. This course of treatment is to be pursued annually.

The vines will commence bearing in the second or third season, according to circumstances. Select for this purpose only such shoots as are strong and healthy, while the earliest ones, generally weak and feeble, are buried in the hill to become food for the others. Be careful not to overload the poles, nor to lessen the crop by having too many vines growing from a single hill. The time of harvesting is about the first of September, being six or eight weeks after the flowers have expanded. They are in perfection when of a fine straw color, turning to a brown, and should be immediately gathered; because, if suffered to get too ripe, they lose many of their good qualities. In gathering the crop, the poles are taken down, and the stems cut off three feet above the ground, that the roots may not be injured by bleeding. The poles are then laid upon a wooden box, or "bin," about nine feet long, three feet wide, and two and a half feet high, which is surrounded by women and children, who take off the hops by hand. The labor ought not to be commenced in the morning until the dew is off, lest the flowers be rendered musty, or deprived of their fragrance. This is usually a festive season in hop-producing countries.

The work must be performed in pleasant weather, and it leads to the congregation of the young of both sexes, who beguile their time with humor and sport. Travellers in England tell some laughable stories of the practical jokes which are occasionally played by the pickers upon the incautious spectator, or even upon one another. As many love matches are formed, and life-long friendships commenced, at these social gatherings, as at our apple-bees, donation-visits, or quilting-parties.

The most important part of the management of hops, is the curing, or drying, of them. This is done in a kiln, where they ought to be carried within three or four hours after being picked. They are spread out evenly, and allowed to remain unmoved, until they have become perfectly dry by a moderate, steady heat. The details of this process would consume too much space for insertion in such a small volume, and as we do not intend our remarks for a large cultivator, we will refer him for farther information to standard treatises. With the small gardener who raises a few vines for the use of his own family, it is only necessary to spread the hops out upon paper or a cloth, and to let them remain until they are quite free from moisture, when they can be put away in paper bags.

USE.—We have already mentioned, that the young shoots and suckers are by some persons considered a good substitute for asparagus. The vines, however, are cultivated for the flowers, the principal use of which is to give strength and permanence to beer. They impart an agreeable, although bitter and aromatic, flavor, besides preventing the too rapid progress of fermentation. They are good for making family yeast, and also have valuable medicinal qualities. A pillow filled with them is often thought excellent to induce sleep, when other expedients have failed.

To make Yeast.—Boil one handful of hops, and two of wheat bran, in two quarts of water, for twenty minutes; then strain off the water, and, while it is boiling hot, stir in wheat or rye flour, till it becomes a thick batter; let it stand until it is about blood warm, when you are to add a half pint of good yeast, together with a tablespoonful of molasses, and mix the whole well together. In summer, put the yeast in a cool place, but, in a warm one in the winter season. As soon as it becomes light and frothy, it is fit for use. Put it in a large, open-mouthed jar, and do not cork tightly for twelve hours or so, when it will have done working. It will keep ten or twelve days.

HORSE-RADISH.—*Cochlearia armoracia.*

From a fancied resemblance in the shape of the leaves, being rather hollow, to an old-fashioned spoon called *cochlear*, is said to have been derived the botanical name of the horse-radish. It is a cruciferous plant, inhabiting the temperate parts of Europe, in moist situations. The stem is herbaceous, bearing small, white flowers. The root is cylindrical, penetrating very deeply into the ground, and, when fresh, possesses a pungent taste and odor, which are highly esteemed upon the dinner table. Of late years, it has been very extensively cultivated for pickling purposes, and a few plants are considered indispensable in every common-sized family garden.

Culture.—The horse-radish delights in a deep, sandy loam, which is moldy, rich and somewhat moist. The banks of a water-course, where the roots will not suffer from drought in summer, nor be liable to inundation during the winter, is a very eligible situation. The exposure should be free and open, as the roots never attain a large size when grown on poor land, or beneath the drip of trees. It is a good way to spade the ground intended for the bed, to the depth of two or three feet, in the previous autumn, and to turn under a good quantity of well rotted dung or decayed vegetable matter. The plantation can be made in March or November, as most convenient.

The horse-radish is propagated by sets, or small pieces of the old root, two inches long, and each having two buds or eyes. Any part—either the main root itself, or its offsets,—will answer, but those sets which prove most successful are taken from the top or crown. The most expeditious mode of planting, and perhaps the best one, is by means of the dibble. After the ground has been properly prepared, by being spaded, manured and levelled, holes, sixteen inches deep, should be made by the dibble, in rows eighteen inches apart, and at the distance of one foot from each other in the rows. The holes ought to be smooth, and large at the bottom, so that the set can be at least fourteen or fifteen inches below the surface; to secure this, an old spade handle, or a blunt stick, either of which will very readily penetrate the mellow soil, is better than a sharp-pointed dibble.

When the sets are dropped into their appointed places, the holes are to be filled with loose earth; and the bed is to be smoothly raked over, for a sowing of lettuce, radish, or some other crop which will be removed early in the season, before it can prove injurious to the horse-radish. The mold ought to lie as loose and light as possible; and, for this reason, the gardener should avoid treading on it, after the sets are planted. They will soon start, and show their leaves above ground. Their subsequent growth can be much invigorated by occasional waterings with liquid manure. The only cultivation required, is to keep the bed free of weeds, as well as, in autumn, to clear off the decayed leaves and rubbish.

The roots will have attained a suitable size for use, by the second autumn after planting. In taking up the crop, a trench must be dug alongside the outer row of the bed, and the roots cut so as to leave a small piece to grow in the following season. But, it is decidedly the best plan to make a new plantation every year, because the roots become tough, bitter, and less profitable for market, as they advance in age. In addition to all that, the reader will recollect that an alternation of crops is to be pursued whenever practicable, and that of right no vegetable should be grown twice successively upon the same spot. When the old bed is to be destroyed, great care must be observed to dig up all the lateral roots, as the smallest of them will vegetate. The first trench is to be filled with the dirt taken from the second one, which is dug alongside the next row of roots, and the whole plantation to be managed in the same way. The winter's supply can be stored in the cellar, in a box of damp sand or earth.

USE.—As a condiment for the table, the horse-radish is much esteemed. The roots should be used only when fresh and sprightly; they are then said to assist digestion. They are scraped into shreds, and covered with vinegar, to be eaten with roast meats, fish, etc. Thus pickled, and preserved in tightly-stopped bottles, they are yearly brought to market in large quantities. Moreover, the horse-radish has several medicinal virtues, it being a stimulant, and useful in cases of hoarseness, rheumatism, palsy, etc.

HYSSOP.—*Hyssopus officinalis.*

Hyssop is a perennial, of hardy habit, from the south of Europe. It is often mentioned in Scripture, and is cultivated in gardens mainly for its medicinal properties. The leaves and flowers have a sharp, warm taste, while the whole plant is possessed of a strong, fragrant smell.

CULTURE.—It likes a light, dry soil, because, if its growth be too luxuriant, it will become tender, and lose its aromatic properties. New plants are obtained from seed, slips, cuttings of the branches, or from divisions of the old roots. The first mode is much the easiest. Sow the seed somewhere about the middle of spring, in drills six inches apart, and not deeper than half an inch. Thin the plants, when three or four inches high, to distances of twelve inches in the drill. Cuttings of the old stalks are to be taken off in the middle of spring, and slips of the young shoots somewhere about midsummer. The divisions of the roots can be set out in either spring or autumn, as may be most convenient. They ought all to be planted in a shaded locality, and upon a fine, mellow soil, where they will become firmly rooted by October; and they are then to be removed to their permanent location. Water should be given, not only at the time of planting, and at every removal, but also twice or thrice a week during hot weather until they become well established. Keep the ground mellow and clean, by frequent hoeings. In spring and autumn, dress the surface of the bed with the rake, and remove all the dead branches.

USE.—Hyssop is but little valued for culinary purposes, although the powdered leaves are occasionally put with cold salad herbs. The whole plant, however, has something of a reputation for its medicinal virtues, being used in several disorders of the lungs. The branches should be gathered on a dry, pleasant day, and kept in a cool garret.

INDIAN CORN.—*Zea mays.*

Perhaps no early vegetable is in greater demand at the market of a city than good green corn. It seems to be a favorite among all classes, and the first supply of the season is eagerly bought up at a high price. Much of that which is annually exposed for sale is of a very poor quality, and it seems strange to us that gardeners are willing to cultivate the second-rate varieties, when the choicest are so easily procured. It costs no more to raise a delicious Virgalieu, that actually melts in the mouth, than a hard, indigestible choke-pear; nor is it more difficult to raise the excellent *Sugar*-corn, than the kind usually grown in the field. We would recommend the following varieties for the kitchen;—the *Extra Early*, and the *Eight-rowed Sugar*. The first named is remarkable for its earliness and fine flavor, and yet, for the main crop, it can scarcely be called equal to the latter. A new kind by the name of *Stowell's Sugar*, which has been brought into notice within a few months, is spoken of very highly by those who have tried it. If the husks are suffered to remain on the ears, the grains will continue milky and in a good condition for boiling, for several months after being plucked. This property will render it a very desirable sort, for those who relish a dish of green corn in midwinter.

Culture.—Any common garden soil that is rich, dry and mellow, will be found adapted to the wants of this cereal. But its principal characteristic should be fertility, because the plant is a gross feeder, and requires considerable nourishment to perfect its large stalks, leaves and ears. It would be folly in any person to expect a good crop from a poor half-starved soil. The first planting should be as soon as the season becomes sufficiently mild, and have the benefit of a warm, sheltered situation. To keep the table supplied for a long time, the planting must be repeated at intervals of a fortnight or three weeks until the middle of summer.

After the ground has been ploughed or spaded, it is to be marked out in cross rows four feet apart each way. In the bottom of each hill is to be put a shovelful of old dung or compost, and that to be covered with a little mellow dirt. The seed should have been soaked for at least twelve hours in a solution of saltpetre, or in simple warm water, to arouse the dormant germ, and then rolled in plaster of Paris. Five or six of these kernels are not too many for one hill, as the number of the plants can easily be reduced. The proper depth of covering for the seed, is about two inches; if too much mold be drawn upon the hill, the stalks become enfeebled, and decay before they are able to reach the surface.

When the plants have made their appearance, and acquired a height of two or three inches, it will be time to enter upon the duties of after-culture. With the hoe, the soil in the hills is loosened ; and such weeds as cannot be reached by that implement, without risk of injuring the corn, must be pulled by the thumb and forefinger. The number of plants in a hill can be reduced to three, either at this, or at the next, hoeing. Three stalks will bear as much, and possibly more, than the whole half dozen. Putting a pint of ashes, or a gill of poudrette, around the roots at this time, will secure a quick and abundant growth of ears.

In the course of two or three weeks, the plants will again make urgent calls upon the gardener's attention. They ought not to be neglected any longer than need be, or a diminished product will surely be the result. After they have once got fairly under way, they will, in a measure, take care of themselves, requiring only an occasional hour's labor, to keep the soil light, and to eradicate weeds. Where the plantation is extensive, the use of the hoe alone is too laborious, and the assistance of the plough or cultivator will be required. There is nothing like keeping the ground mellow, and open to atmospheric influences. We have previously shown its especial value in times of drought, when field crops that receive only occasional attention, are almost burned up by the heat. The old-fashioned practice of raising high hills has fallen into disrepute, except on very moist land ;—it is only necessary to draw a little mold around the stems when they are about a foot high, to steady them against the wind. As soon as the kernels are well developed upon the ear, it is fit for cooking. When the stalks are stripped, they can be cut close to the ground, and given to the cows, for which they prove an excellent summer feed.

For seed,—only the best ears from the most productive stalks should be gathered. By pursuing this course for a number of years, the character of the variety can be much improved. At any rate, there will be no chance for its degenerating. For the early crops, the earliest ears must be selected. When they are fully ripened, braid the husks together, with the ears hanging out like a string of onions, and hang them up in a cool, dry place.

USE.—The following receipts are recommended to the housekeeper. She ought not to be content with corn in its green state alone; but, every season, endeavor to preserve a quantity for winter use in the shape of succotash.

To boil.—Green corn is sweetest when boiled upon the cob, from fifteen to thirty minutes, according to its age. Some persons do not strip off the inner husks, until after the corn has been boiled, thinking that its rich flavor is thereby better retained. The kernels can be cut off by a knife, and seasoned with butter, pepper and salt, or carried to the table untouched. None but the over-fastidious will object to eating them directly from the cob.

Green Corn Pudding.—To three teacupfuls of grated corn, add two quarts of milk, eight eggs, two teaspoonfuls of salt, one half teacupful of melted butter, together with a little nutmeg. Bake for one hour, and eat with sauce.

Green Corn Oysters.—To one pint of grated corn, add one well-beaten egg, one teacupful of flour, one half teacupful of butter, with salt and pepper to the taste. Mix them well together. A tablespoonful dropped into lard, will make a cake of the size of an oyster. Fry to a light brown, and when cooked, moisten it with cream or butter

To dry for winter use.—After the ears have been boiled, the kernels are to be cut off by a knife, or shelled by running the prong of a fork along the base of the grain. Spread them upon a cloth in a shaded, airy place, but carry into the house at nightfall. They will require several days to become perfectly dried, when they are to be put away in cloth bags. The ravages of mice must be carefully guarded against.

Succotash.—Put three quarts of cold water to one half pound of salt pork, and place them upon the fire. Cut three quarts of green corn from the cobs, which are to be boiled with the pork, as they add much to the richness of the mixture. When the pork has boiled for half an hour, take out the cobs, and put in their place one quart of freshly-gathered shell beans. After they have boiled fifteen minutes, add the three quarts of corn, and let the whole boil for another fifteen minutes. Then turn it out into a dish, and add five or six large spoonfuls of butter, together with sugar, salt and pepper to your taste. If the liquor have boiled away, it will be necessary to add a little more water before taking it from the fire. In winter, the dried corn must be soaked over night, and not added to the pot until the beans become tender.

INDIAN CRESS.—*Tropæolum majus.*

Generally known as the Nasturtium. It is a native of South America, and is distinguished for its brilliant show of orange and crimson-colored flowers. It was carried to England in the sixteenth century. Being a good climber, it is useful in covering a trellis or lattice as a screen, and for its gay dress is often made a tenant of the flower garden. The value of its seeds for pickling, and of the tops for salads, entitle it to a place among other family vegetables.

Culture.—Indian cress will grow on almost any soil, and in nearly every situation; but it flourishes best on a fresh, mellow loam, having an open exposure. Where the ground is very rich and strong, the vine will be luxuriant, while the crop proves small, and of inferior character. Sow the seed in the middle of spring, about three or four inches apart in a single row, along a fence or trellis. Cover the seed three quarters of an inch deep. The plants are afterward to be thinned to stand about one foot apart in the row. The runners soon manifest a disposition for climbing, and at first, they may need a little assistance in fastening themselves upon the trellis. Where they have been sown in an open compartment, they ought to be supported by stakes or brushwood. The occasional application of water in continued dry weather, is of great advantage,—strengthening the plants, improving their appearance, and increasing their powers of productiveness. Other than this, they require little attention. Flowers will open in or about the month of July, and the fruit is to be picked as soon as it acquires full size, before it loses its fresh, green color.

For seed,—let the fruit remain upon the vines until quite ripe, and avoid storing before it becomes dry and hard.

USE.—The leaves and flowers have a sprightly taste that is pleasant in salads. They are also often used as a garnish, and sometimes as a remedy for weakness or pain in the stomach. The fruit is excellent for pickling. Immediately after being gathered, it is put in salt and water, which must be changed once in three or four days, and there kept until a sufficient quantity is collected. The salt and water is then drawn off, and replaced by hot vinegar.

JERUSALEM ARTICHOKE.—*Helianthus tuberosus.*

A small sunflower, bearing nutritious tubers, for which it is cultivated. It is a hardy perennial of Brazil, and was first carried to England in the year 1617, where it soon became exceedingly popular as an esculent, being thought much superior to the potato. Loudon says that the name Jerusalem is a corruption of the Italian word for sunflower—*girasole.* Its name of artichoke is probably derived from a resemblance in the taste of its roots to the "bottoms" of that plant. The stalks are large, and frequently attain the height of ten feet. The roots are produced in great quantity,—the crops sometimes exceeding two thousand bushels per acre. During the past few years, they have been much extolled for agricultural purposes, and, indeed, they would seem better suited for the farmer than for the kitchen gardener.

CULTURE.—The Jerusalem artichoke is not very particular in regard to soil or situation; it is, however, best pleased with a light and moist loam, having a free exposure. It requires little attention, and is so much inclined to perpetuate itself, that it may even become a nuisance in a small garden. It is propagated in the same manner as the potato, by sets of the large-sized tubers. Plant them in March or April, according to the forwardness of the season, in drills three feet apart, and at distances of twelve or fifteen inches in the drill. Cover the sets about three inches deep. Be exceeding careful to guard against the intrusion of weeds. Keep the soil light, and draw a little around the stems for their support. The tubers can be taken up as wanted for use, during the months of September and October, but in November they are to be raised for preservation through the winter, in sand or earth. The smallest piece left in the ground, proves troublesome by vegetating in the following spring. The crop may, however, remain where grown, as it does not suffer from the frost.

USE.—In an agricultural point of view, this plant deserves a high position. It is exceedingly hardy, bearing exposure to the severe weather of winter without injury;—it can be grown upon poor soil, without the addition of much manure;—it requires little attention;—and is distinguished by great productiveness. The stalks make very good fodder, if cut before the flowers have fully opened; while the tubers are thought particularly valuable for cows, sheep and store pigs. When prepared plain for the table, the roots form rather a second-rate dish. After having been boiled soft or tender, they are to be peeled, and then stewed with wine and butter. By many persons, they are then considered nutritious and possessed of a good flavor.

KALE.—*See* BORECOLE and SEA-KALE.

LAVENDER.—*Lavandula spica.*

Johnson says that the botanic name of this plant, *Lavandula*, is derived from the Latin word *lavo*, to wash, in allusion to the use formerly made of its distilled water in the baths. It is a hardy under-shrub, a native of the south of Europe, and has been cultivated in England since the year 1568. It is distinguished for its aromatic and stimulating properties. To its general dissemination in some parts of Europe, has been attributed the excellence of the honey there made by bees.

CULTURE.—It can be grown with the greatest success in a poor, gravelly soil. In a rich garden, it loses much of the fragrance for which it is esteemed, while becoming tender and less able to withstand the severity of winter. This is by no means peculiar to the lavender plant, for it has long been remarked in the cultivation of other aromatic herbs, that in proportion to their luxuriance of growth, are their hardiness and flavor diminished. The situation should be free and exposed. When having the full benefit of the sun, the plant sometimes contains one-fourth part of its weight in camphor. Propagation is easily accomplished, in spring, by slips and cuttings of the young branches, about six inches long. The lower half of each should be stripped of leaves, before its insertion to that depth in a shaded border. They are to be planted in rows, nine inches apart each way. A little water may be given every other evening, to encourage the formation of roots. In autumn, or the succeeding spring, the plants can be safely removed to their permanent location, in rows two feet apart each way. The only culture necessary is to keep the soil clean, and to remove the dead branches at the close of the season. The flowers ought to be gathered when they are in the greatest perfection. The bed will last a long time.

USE.—The delightful fragrance of the leaves and flowers is well known, and has led to the preparation of the distilled water, the tincture, and the volatile oil. In addition to their value as a perfume, they are ranked among the stimulants and carminatives of medicine. The flower-spikes are frequently put in little paper bags, to be laid among linen in drawers.

LEEK.—*Allium porrum.*

The leek is a member of the onion family, and has been cultivated from time immemorial. It has always been regarded with particular favor by the Egyptians, who eat it raw with their bread, or as a sauce for meats. It is frequently associated with the name of St. David, the patron saint of Wales, for the reason that Welshmen are accustomed to sport leeks in their hats upon his festival, the first of March. This is a very ancient custom, and we find frequent mention of it in the old writers. Some persons have thought that it commemorates the introduction of the plant into that country by St. David; but more probably, as Shakspeare says, in his Henry the Fifth, it is "worn as a memorable trophy of predeceased valor." According to "an antient tradition," in a celebrated victory of the Welsh over the Saxons, in the sixth century, the former, under the prelate's directions, were distinguished by leeks which they gathered near the battle ground. As he was supposed to have power to work miracles, it is not strange that their glorious success should have been attributed to this cause. Whatever may be the origin of the custom, it would be quite as remarkable, to find a Welshman without his leek on the first of March, as it would to discover a genuine Hibernian without a shamrock in his buttonhole, on St. Patrick's day. For certain purposes the leek is preferred to the onion. The varieties most worthy of cultivation, and perhaps of equal excellence, are—the *London*,—and the *Scotch*.

Culture.—Sow the seed in March or April, as soon as the ground becomes open, and the weather settled. One ounce of seed will yield between two and three thousand plants. Select for the bed a warm, sheltered border, and sow in drills, three quarters of an inch deep, and eight inches apart. When the plants have become established, they ought to be thinned out to distances of about two inches in the drill. Frequent and thorough hoeing is of the first importance, while an occasional application of water during a dry time, proves of great benefit. As soon as the seedlings acquire a height of eight or nine inches, they are fit for transplanting.

The leek is best suited with a mellow loam, which has been deeply dug, and made rich by the application of old dung or compost. The subsoil should be dry, and the exposure rather open. Make shallow trenches across the bed, one foot distant from each other, for the reception of the plants, which are to be drawn from the seed bed, either during showery weather, or after the soil has been rendered yielding by the application of water. Some should be allowed to remain at the distances of six inches asunder in the drill. Shorten the extremities of the tops and roots of those which are taken up, and insert them in the trenches, by means of the dibble, eight inches apart. They ought to be inserted just so deep, that the centre leaves and buds shall not be covered with earth.

In dry weather, give water freely ; and, at all times, during the season of their growth, make good use of the hoe. The soil must be kept mellow, and, every now and then, a little should be drawn up around the stems. Some gardeners cut off the tops of the leaves, at intervals perhaps of three weeks or a month, in order to increase the size of the roots. A portion of the crop can be raised as wanted for use, by the beginning or the middle of autumn. The plants will stand the winter well ; but, on the approach of hard frost, it is customary to store in sand a quantity sufficient for the wants of the family until the ground opens.

For seed.—Remove some of the best plants, in spring, to a warm, sheltered border. The flower-stems should be supported by stakes, or tied to the fence, to prevent their being broken down by the wind. Cut the heads when they turn brown, with a portion of the stems attached, by which they are to be tied together in bundles of three or four, for convenience in hanging them up to dry. When the seed becomes perfectly hardened, it can be beaten out at any convenient time.

USE.—From its mild, agreeable taste, as well as on account of its hardiness, the leek is by many preferred to the onion. The whole plant is used in various ways, such as being boiled plain to be eaten with meat, in soups, stews, etc.

LETTUCE.—*Lactuca sativa.*

Lettuce is a hardy annual of which the original country seems to be unknown. It has been found wild in many different parts of the world, and was first cultivated in England about the year 1562. It is divided into two families, called the Cos and the Cabbage lettuces. The first—distinguished by an upright growth,—was introduced from the island of Cos; and the second,—the habits of which are somewhat indicated by its name,—from Egypt. Our climate is not altogether favorable to the Cos family; or, at least, we find the other one much more thrifty and worthy of cultivation. For the information of the curious reader, it is well to state, that the botanical term *Lactuca* is derived from *lac,* the Latin word for milk, in allusion to the milky juice which exudes from the stem when broken. This juice, when the plants are young, contains but a small quantity of the narcotic principle; but it gradually acquires a strong, bitter taste, and becomes notably sedative. This property seems to have been known at a very early period, and a lettuce supper was thought highly conducive to repose. The varieties and sub-varieties are numerous, and, as is usual in such cases, a very few include the leading merits of the whole.

The best soil for lettuce, is, undoubtedly, a mellow loam, deep, rich, and founded upon a dry substratum. It should be fertile, and if not so naturally, must be supplied with a good quantity of old dung, some time previous to the sowing of the seed. This is better done in autumn, than in the spring.

CULTURE.—By the exercise of a little forethought, the family gardener can keep his table supplied with lettuce throughout the year, at a very trifling expense. To have early plants for spring use, the first sowing must be made either in the previous autumn, or else in the latter part of winter upon a hotbed. The first plan we consider decidedly the best, as the plants are hardier, and better able to bear removal to the open ground, than those obtained by artificial heat.

This sowing may be between the first and the middle of September, upon a bed of light, rich soil, having the benefit of shade at midday. The best varieties are,—the *Large Greenhead*,—the *Brown Dutch*,—and the *Early Cabbage*,—together with such others as are capable of standing severe winter weather. From nine to twelve thousand plants have been raised from a single ounce of seed. Sow rather thinly in drills eight inches apart; cover the seed lightly, and, in a dry time, press the surface of the bed, by patting it with the spade, or by walking upon a board. When the plants crowd one another in the drill, thin them out to distances of two or three inches, allowing them just sufficient space to secure a good, stocky growth before cold weather sets in. Such as are pulled, can be set out in another place,—perhaps on the spot to be enclosed by the cold frame. The soil should be kept light and clean.

In the latter part of October, the plants are to be furnished with their winter protection. Some of the hardy varieties which are intended for early crops, can be set out, one foot apart, upon the south side of ridges, that will be covered with straw during severe weather. The principal part, however, should be removed to the cold frame or box, and there dibbled as closely as they will stand, without interfering with one another. The covering, be it of glass or plain boards, must be often opened in mild, pleasant days, for the admission of fresh air. Look out for the attacks of earth worms and slugs; dusting the leaves with soot is somewhat of a preventive. Or, instead of using a cold frame, the seed bed can be covered with mats placed over bent hoops. Whatever may be the plan adopted, do not omit regular ventilation in all pleasant weather.

Where the sowing was not made in autumn, according to the above directions, and early plants are wanted, they must be obtained from a small hot-bed, built in the latter part of winter. No great amount of heat is required, but care should be taken to prevent any bad consequences from the want of pure air. For general directions upon the formation and management of hot-beds, the reader must refer to our article on "Forcing Vegetation."

Taking it for granted that the gardener is supplied with plants, which have been safely kept through the inclement season, let us follow their subsequent growth. At the moment that frost leaves the ground, a small number ought to be transplanted to a very warm border, having the full benefit of the sun's rays, and protected from cold winds on the north side. They will for some length of time require the friendly shelter of hand-glasses, until they become gradually accustomed to the change of quarters, and until the progress of the season permits their exposure with impunity. A second, third, or fourth removal of these plants can be made in the same way, at intervals of seven or eight days. By such a course, a great advantage will be obtained in the regular maturity of the crop.

The first spring sowing in the open compartment, should take place as soon as the weather and ground will permit,—

perhaps between the middle and beginning of March. For the bed select a warm border in a sheltered situation, and mark out the drills twelve inches apart. The varieties well adapted for this sowing, are—the *Brown Dutch*,—the *Early Cabbage*,—and the *Drumhead*. Sow thinly, and, in dry weather, press the earth in close contact with the seed. When the plants are two inches high, they are to be thinned out to distances of four inches in the drill, and those which are pulled can be easily inserted in another bed. At this time, transplanting can be practised successfully, but, when the season is further advanced, they seldom head well if removed from the seed bed. When they are four or five inches high, they should be so thinned as to stand one foot apart each way. Water ought to be given freely at every removal performed in a dry day, and regularly afterwards until the roots are established. The hoe must be used frequently between the drills, not only for the purpose of eradicating weeds, but also for the sake of keeping the surface soil light and porous.

Another sowing can be made about a month later, and a third in August for the late autumn crop. The best varieties are the *Indian*, the *Royal Cabbage*, and such others as are able to withstand the intense heat of summer. Sow in drills, at the same distance apart as before, and thinly, so as to avoid transplanting. It will be recollected that lettuce seldom does well, when transplanted in warm weather.

The winter crop is to be sown in the latter part of September. The *Early Cabbage* is an excellent kind for this purpose. In the following month, when the weather becomes cold, the plants are to be removed to a hot-bed, or the forcing-pit. The mold should be some eight or ten inches below the glass. Take the roots up very carefully by means of the trowel, and set the balls of earth in rows, nine inches apart each way. Water ought to be given in moderate quantities from time to time through the winter, and the sashes shaded at midday until the roots have taken hold. Air is to be ad-

17*

mitted freely in all pleasant weather, while in a severe frost the protection of mats upon the glass, as well as of a bank of earth around the frame, will be necessary. Decayed leaves must be removed as soon as they are discovered. Good heads for eating may be obtained in December, and through the remainder of the winter.

In this climate, the Cos lettuces are far from being as successful as in Europe. They can be sown in autumn, and protected through the inclement season, to be transplanted into the open ground in spring. They are blanched by being tied up like the endive, a week or ten days before wanted for use.

For seed,—select some of the best plants of the autumn or spring sowings. Put them in rows, eighteen inches apart each way, and do not omit to keep the varieties separate. Where two or more kinds are suffered to blossom in the vicinity of each other, a mongrel will surely be the result. Support the flower-stems by stakes, and gather the branches as the seed ripens, instead of waiting for a large portion to be wasted on the ground. That borne by stalks which have run up prematurely, cannot be depended upon. Place the branches on a cloth, or a large newspaper, spread in the shade, and let them get perfectly dry before you attempt to thresh out the seed.

USE.—Lettuce may be considered as belonging to the very best class of salads, and perhaps it is superior to all others. It possesses a mild, agreeable taste, while it is wholesome and easy of digestion. It is also sometimes used in soups. It is largely cultivated for the extraction of its narcotic properties, which are somewhat similar to those of opium, but have not the constipating effects of that drug. The stalk is cut just before the flower is ready to open, and the crust which forms upon the top is carefully gathered. The stalk is cut again and again, until the milky juice ceases to exude.

To dress a Salad.—This seems to be a convenient place for giving directions how to dress a salad, which is a general name for certain vegetables, such as lettuce, endive and mustard, prepared so as to be eaten raw. They should be well washed, and cut into small pieces. An egg is boiled hard, and, when it becomes cold, the yolk is to be taken out, and broken on a plate. Then put with it, a large teaspoonful of cold water, and near a teaspoonful of salt. Rub all this together, by means of a spoon or fork, till the egg is a thick paste, free from lumps. Next, add and mix a tablespoonful of salad oil, or cold melted butter; and after this, add at least one tablespoonful of good vinegar. When these are all well mixed, the dressing is made, and is either to be put immediately with the salad, or be sent to the table in a separate dish. The top of the salad may be ornamented with small pieces of the white of the egg, and slices of pickled beet.

MARIGOLD.—*Calendula officinalis.*

An annual, with bright yellow flowers, sometimes called the Pot Marigold. It is a native of southern Europe. Only a few plants are required by a common-sized family.

Culture.—Sow the seed in drills, ten inches apart, either in the autumn of the year in which it ripened, or in the following spring. Select for the bed a soil that is light, dry, having a free exposure, and poor rather than rich. When the plants are two inches high, thin them out to a foot apart in the drill. Those which are pulled can be set out in another bed, to receive regular applications of water until the roots have become established. Gather the flowers at the time they are in full bloom, and dry them in the shade before storing for winter use.

For seed,—select none but the finest-looking heads.

Use.—The marigold was formerly somewhat esteemed in broths, soups, stews, etc., but now it is little regarded. Many medicinal virtues have been ascribed to an infusion of the leaves, particularly in agues. The flowers yield a distilled water, a kind of vinegar, and a conserve.

MARJORAM.—*Origanum.*

A well known family of aromatic herbs. The botanic name is derived from *oros*, a mountain, and *ganos*, joy ; meaning "the delight of the mountain," in allusion to the natural situation of the plants. There are as many as eight species, all having numerous varieties. We shall notice only two, viz.: the Sweet, or Summer, (*O. marjorana,*) and the Winter,—or Bastard, (*O. heracleoticum.*) They both prefer a dry, mellow, moderately rich soil, in an open situation.

The Sweet Marjoram (*O. marjorana,*) is a native of Portugal, and is propagated by seed. Sow in very shallow drills, eight inches apart, somewhere about the middle of spring. Cover the seed regularly, and not deeper than half an inch. Thin the plants to distances of six inches in the drill. The surplus ones can be transplanted into another bed, water being given until the roots become firm. Keep the ground light and free from weeds.

For seed,—it is only necessary to let a few of the healthiest plants remain uncut, and to gather the seed as it ripens.

The Winter Marjoram (*O. heracleoticum,*) is a hardy perennial, a native of Greece. The general appearance of the plant is much like that of the sweet marjoram. It is propagated by divisions of the roots, or slips of the branches. They are to be set in rows, one foot apart each way, by the middle of spring. They must be sheltered at noonday when the sun is powerful, and receive an application of water, at least every other evening, until they are well established. The bed should have an autumnal dressing ;—the decayed branches being removed, the surface dug over, and covered with a very little rich mold. The hoe must be used frequently, so as to keep the soil light and clean.

Use.—Both species of marjoram are aromatics, having a warm, pleasant taste. They are much employed in seasoning soups and broths, and are thought to be serviceable in complaints arising from a disordered state of the nerves. In the season of their growth, the tops can be gathered as wanted for use; but, for a winter supply, delay cutting them until the flowers are about to expand. Tie the stalks together in small bundles, and hang them in a shaded place to dry. Keep in a cool, dry apartment.

MELON.—*Cucumis melo.*

Among the most delicious of fruits, the common, or musk, melon holds a conspicuous position. It has been cultivated in hot climates for seemingly time immemorial, for which reason it is difficult to ascertain its native country, although botanists generally agree upon Persia. It was brought into Europe by the Romans, and by them disseminated wherever they carried their arms. Every reader will admit the richness of its flavor, that proves so tempting to the palate; while its wholesomeness may be understood from the fact, that in southern Europe, during its season, it makes a principal part of the food of the lower classes. It is very easily raised in some parts of this country, and immense quantities are yearly exposed for sale in the markets of our chief cities. The plant on which it is borne, is a trailing annual, propagated by seed. The varieties are, as might be expected, numerous; yet, comparatively few are worthy of the gardener's attention. The *Musk*,—the *Nutmeg*,—the *Netted Citron*,—the *Green-fleshed*,—and the *Canteloup*, are among the best. In this connexion it may well be remarked, that, whatever be the variety chosen, fine fruit cannot be obtained without the exercise of considerable care and skill.

CULTURE.—The preparation of the soil is certainly of the first importance. We prefer a loam which is dry and mellow, rich and deep. It is customary to add some powerful manures, such as strong dung, guano, hen-dung, or an active compost. Nearly all of the amelioraters that have been proposed, are objectionable to our mind, because producing a luxuriant growth of vine, at the expense of that flavor and juiciness for which the fruit is alone esteemed. The cultivator must then seek in his land fertility, rather than rankness. Perhaps, a well mixed compost of equal parts of loam and rotten dung, will answer the purpose.

Melons in family gardens are most usually grown in the open air. Those persons who can well afford the time and money required, may resort to

Forcing.—To avoid repetition, we refer the reader to the article on "FORCING VEGETATION," as well as to the CUCUMBER, for an account of the process of building a hot-bed. In the following directions, we shall aim to be as brief as possible. The plants are to be raised on a small bed, in midwinter. After the mold has been put on, and become warmed under a close sash, the seeds are to be sown in small pots, which can be raised in the holes whenever the heat is too violent. The sowing should be repeated in four or five days, to avoid all chance of disappointment. Ventilation must be given at noonday, and also when the steam collects upon the glass, with care not to reduce the temperature within too suddenly. At night, and when the sun shines powerfully, the glass is to be covered with mats, according to the coldness of the weather. Tepid water ought to be applied to the roots, at such times as the soil appears dry and hard.

In the course of a month, the plants will be of a good size for their removal to the fruiting-bed, constructed like the other with the exception of being much larger, and having a mound or hillock under each sash. Those in pots can be transplanted most easily in the following way;—reverse the pot, with the stem of the plant between the fingers, and strike against its side with a small stick, so as to loosen the ball of dirt, which is then to be set in the middle of a hillock. Not more than two healthy plants should be allotted to one sash. To strengthen them, and promote the growth of fertile runners, the main stem should be pinched off, at the second joint, and the laterals at the sixth joint—when they proceed so far without showing fruit. While it is desirable to maintain the heat of the bed, every opportunity for ventilation must be seized. The medium degree of temperature is 65° until the fruit sets, and subsequently 75°. At first, care is to be taken to prevent the injurious effects of a violent heat, by substituting fresh mold in place of that which becomes caked, as well as by making large holes in the pile of dung. Linings will be needed in the latter part of the process, so that the plants shall not be checked by the decrease of artificial warmth. An occasional application of tepid water should be given whenever the earth appears parched, but with care not to wet the foliage. The quantity must be small, and given less frequently, as the plants approach maturity, for too much moisture is apt to injure the crop. The glasses ought to be shaded at midday, and not deprived of their nocturnal covering until all danger of frost be over.

It is well to assist impregnation in the manner directed for the CUCUMBER. Decayed leaves ought to be removed as soon as discovered. The fruit should be frequently examined, in order to pick off that which is imperfect, and to reduce the crop when it appears too large for one vine to mature. Many are accustomed to place straw or blackened shingles under the melons, and to turn the fruit twice or thrice a week, to prevent the lower side becoming disfigured. The time of maturity will be indicated by a fragrant smell, together with a crack or indentation near the stem.

The principal difference between the hot bed culture of the

melon and the cucumber is, that the first named requires a higher temperature, and more fresh air, but less moisture.

In the open ground.—As a matter of course, it is very desirable to have early plants,—particularly on account of their being less liable to fall a prey to the striped bug. The cheapest and most convenient mode of obtaining them, is to plant the seeds upon small sods, and to start them into life under glass. In the latter part of April, or earlier according to the forwardness of the season, take a hot-bed frame, and place it on the ground in a warm, sheltered position, having a good exposure to the sun. Then procure some clean, mellow turf, and cut it, with the spade, into pieces of a regular size, each about six inches square. Put these in the bottom of the frame, with the grass side down. Spread rich loam upon them to the depth of an inch or two, and plant half a dozen seeds in each. Keep the sash closed in all cold or unfavorable weather, and, as soon as the plants are an inch high, reduce their number just one half, so as to leave but three in a square. Admit the air freely on every pleasant day, in order to secure a strong, healthy growth; and, as they advance in size, take off the sash altogether, that they may be hardened for removal to the open compartment. Take each square up separately on a spade or trowel, and put it in the centre of a hill previously prepared for its reception. Give the plants a gentle watering, and they will suffer little from the change of quarters. The seeds vegetate finely in the grass sods, which decay and furnish considerable nourishment to the roots. The frame not only prevents the depredations of insects, but also guards the plants against the bad effects of cold winds in their early growth. The crop is brought forward much sooner than that from the first sowing in the open air; while the gardener avoids all the cost and trouble of a regular hot-bed.

Early in the month of May, preparations are to be made for sowing in the open compartment. The ground is first to be properly dug and manured, and then to be marked out into hills six feet apart each way. For each one a hole should be dug to the depth of fifteen inches, and of as many inches in diameter. About twelve inches of compost, or well rotted dung, are to be put at the bottom of the hole, and thoroughly incorporated with three inches of good, mellow loam. More of this loam is then to be thrown on, until the top of the hill shall be some four or five inches above the surface of the ground. Nine or ten seeds are to be planted on the top, at the depth of half an inch; and, at this rate, one ounce of seed will supply over one hundred hills.

We are accustomed to cover the plants, as soon as they appear above ground, with vine-shields; by which means, they will not only be protected from the attacks of insects, but will also be materially quickened in their growth. When the vine-shields are elsewhere in use, we depend upon the solution of hen-dung, whale oil soap, or some other of those remedies that we have mentioned in the article upon the "DESTRUCTION OF VERMIN." Without some precautionary measures, we should probably be obliged to make a second, or perhaps a third, sowing. The number of plants in a hill ought not to be over three, as they will bear a greater crop than a dozen crowded into so small a space. It is advisable to keep the soil light and free from weeds, and occasionally to draw a little up around the stems for their support. If they appear too luxuriant, and disposed to run to vine, it may be well to pinch off the extremities of the shoots, which strengthens the roots, and causes the early development of fruit-bearing laterals. The ground should be evenly covered with the foliage, so that every leaf may have a fair exposure to the light. Keep the fruit from being injured by lying on the ground. Putting slates or blackened shingles under it will hasten its maturity, by attracting the sun's rays. It loses much of its luscious flavor, by being suffered to become dead ripe before being picked.

Seed—ought to be saved from none but the best fruit.

Wash them from the pulp in a vessel of clean water, and skim off all the light ones that float on the surface. Dry the rest, and keep them in small paper bags. It should always be borne in mind, that where the different members of the cucumber family and their many varieties are grown in close companionship, intermixture and degeneracy must unavoidably follow. Keep them as far apart as the limits of your territory will admit. The seed will continue good for several years.

USE.—It has long been understood, that as a palatable and wholesome article of food, the melon maintains a high rank among fruits. It is generally eaten with sugar, salt or pepper, but in France it is also served up as a sauce for boiled meats. We add the following receipt for making

Mangoes.—The melons should be picked late in the season. Cut a small, square hole in the side of each, and take out the seeds. Wash the melons clean, and soak them for three or four days in salt and water. Then sprinkle them on the inside with powdered cloves, pepper and nutmeg; and fill them with cinnamon, string beans, mustard seed, small strips of horse-radish, etc. Insert the small pieces that were cut out a few days previous, and keep them in their places by strips of cloth. Then put the melons in a stone jar, which is to be kept closely covered, and turn scalding hot vinegar over them.

MELON, (WATER).—*See* WATER-MELON.

MINT.—*Mentha.*

According to the poets, a daughter of Cocytus, called Minthe, was transformed into mint by Proserpine in a fit of jealousy. This is one of the small herbs of which the Jewish law did not require tithes, but the Pharisees were desirous of distinguishing themselves by a "tithe of mint, anise and cummin," while they omitted the weightier matters of judgment, mercy and faith. The genus is extensive, comprising about sixty species. Those cultivated in gardens are,—the Penny-royal, (*M. pulegium*) ;—the Peppermint, (*M. piperita*) ;—and the Spear-mint, (*M. viridis.*)

Culture.—The species mentioned above are all cultivated in the same way. They are best pleased with a fertile and moist soil, of rather a tenacious character. Propagation is easily effected by slips or cuttings of the stalks, and by offsets or divisions of old roots, planted in rows nine inches apart each way, somewhere about the middle of spring. If the operation be not performed in cloudy weather, or when there is a prospect of rain, water should be given plentifully at the time. The ground must be kept quite mellow, and free from weeds, or, otherwise, the plants will be likely to receive a serious check in their growth. The tops are to be cut for drying, as soon as the flower-buds open, and on a pleasant day, because if cut in damp weather, the leaves will turn black. They are to be dried in a shady place, or in front of a fire; and either hung up in bundles, or powdered and kept in tightly-corked bottles. When the tops become too old for use, they may not be cut down until October, when the bed should receive a small top-dressing of dung or rich soil. A plantation will continue in bearing for five or six seasons, but to ensure a full supply, a new one ought to be made every three years.

Use.—The green and dry leaves of the spear-mint are used in salads, soups and sauces, as well as in that popular American drink, the mint julep. Pennyroyal is occasionally employed in cooking; while the distilled waters of the peppermint, both simple and spiritious, are much esteemed for their medicinal virtues. They all partake of the tonic and stimulating properties found in labiate plants, and have a warm, aromatic taste.

Mint Sauce.—After washing the leaves and chopping them up in very small pieces, put them with vinegar and sugar.

MUSHROOM.—*Agaricus campestris.*

The genus *Agaricus* is undoubtedly the most extensive in the whole vegetable kingdom. Some of the species are much esteemed for food, while others possess very deleterious qualities. The one cultivated in gardens is thus described by Loudon;—"The mushroom is a well known native vegetable, springing up in open pastures in August and September. It is most readily distinguished, when of middle size, by its fine pink or flesh-colored gills and pleasant smell; in a more advanced stage, the gills become of a chocolate color, and it is then more apt to be confounded with other kinds of dubious quality; but that species which most nearly resembles it, is slimy to the touch, and destitute of the fine odor, having rather a disagreeable smell: further, the noxious kind grows in woods, or on the margins of woods, while the true mushroom springs up chiefly in open pastures, and should be gathered only in such places."

Culture.—This branch of gardening is gradually becoming better understood. The mushroom has long been cultivated in Europe for culinary purposes, but in this country it is not by any means extensively known. In the outskirts of New-York, we have noticed many large beds and houses devoted exclusively to its production, for sale at market or at French eating-houses. The process is so simple, that we consider the attention of the family gardener may well be drawn to the subject.

The mushroom is propagated by spawn, which resembles pieces of fine white thread, and is collected in old pastures, or other places where the fungi abound. The following is the mode practised by seedsmen of making spawn for sale:—A quantity of fresh horse-dung, mixed with short litter, is composted with one third part of cow-dung, and a small portion of good loam. This compost is cut up into bricks, which are to be set on edge, and frequently turned, until they become half dry. Then a couple of holes are to be made in each, by means of the dibble, and in each hole is to be put a piece of spawn as large as a walnut. When the bricks are dry, they shall be piled upon a layer of dry horse-dung, six inches thick, and covered with sufficient fresh dung to produce a gentle heat through the whole. As soon as the spawn has spread itself through the bricks, the process is ended, and they may be stored in a dry place, where they will preserve their vegetative powers for many years.

Beds for the culture of mushrooms are constructed in several different ways. Sometimes they are in the open air, when they require a covering of boards to prevent injury from cold or wet weather; at other times, in boxes or baskets, in pits or frames, in sheds or moderately warm cellars; and again, in mushroom houses. The latter are decidedly the best, when the necessary expense may be justified. They are sheds built in a dry place, ten feet wide, and of any length desired. A walk runs through the centre, so as to accommodate a bed on each side of four feet in width.

In the first place, it is necessary to procure a sufficient quantity of good horse-dung, and make it up into a heap, which must be turned frequently to induce regular fermentation. In a fortnight all the rankness will probably have escaped, when it will be time to build the bed. The dung should be well shaken by the fork, and built up with perpendicular sides to the height of twelve inches, and then gradually drawn to the centre like the roof of a building. In a mushroom house, the beds should be three feet high on the back side, sloping towards the walk. Every forkful is to be well beaten into its place, so that the sides of the bed be even and firm. Cover the dung with long straw or litter, in order to exclude frost and prevent the escape of the volatile gases.

In the course of ten days, or a fortnight, the temperature will be sufficiently reduced, and the covering is to be removed in order that one inch of fine loam may be laid upon the dung. On this plant the spawn, which has been broken into pieces of the size of a walnut, in rows six inches apart each way. Put on a second inch of mold, which, after being beaten smooth by the spade, must be protected by the covering of straw. Where the bed is in the open air, it will need mats during stormy weather. Guard against the extremes of heat and cold, and of drought and moisture. A medium temperature is probably somewhere about 60°. The covering of straw must vary in thickness from three to twenty-four inches, according to circumstances. When the mold appears too dry, a gentle application of tepid water should be given in the morning; in summer, this may be necessary every other day, but in winter perhaps once a month. After each watering, the covering ought not to be replaced for some fifty or sixty minutes.

If the operation be successful, young mushrooms may be expected in about five or six weeks after the date of spawning, although, from a variety of causes, the time is frequently much longer. Where the bed has been kept too hot and moist, the spawn may have been destroyed; but, in many cases, it requires only a little extra warmth, or a gentle sprinkling of water, to produce a generous crop. In gathering mushrooms, after the straw has been removed, each one is drawn up by a gentle twist of the fingers, and the hole is then filled with earth. A knife ought never to be employed, because the stumps left in the ground become nurseries of maggots, which prove very destructive to the succeeding growth.

USE.—Mushrooms are considered a great delicacy by epicures. They are boiled, stewed, pickled, or dried. When reduced to powder, and kept in close bottles, they are very useful at those seasons when they cannot be gathered fresh. The catsup sold in stores is *said* to be made from the juice of mushrooms, seasoned with salt and spices.

To stew Mushrooms.—Cut off the lower part of the stems, which are apt to have an earthy taste. Peel the other parts and put them into a saucepan, with only enough water to prevent their burning to the bottom. Add a little salt, and shake the dish occasionally. They should be stewed slowly until quite tender, when just before taking up, add also butter and pepper, with spices and wine if desired. Serve on buttered toast.

To pickle Mushrooms.—They must first be peeled, and stewed in a very little water,—the pan being shaken occasionally. Take them up when tender, and put them in scalding hot vinegar, which is spiced with mace, cloves and peppercorns. Add a little salt before bottling.

Mushroom Catsup.—Put the fresh mushrooms in a deep dish, and upon each layer sprinkle a little salt. After they have remained thus for several days, mash them fine, and to each quart add one tablespoonful of black pepper, and one quarter teaspoonful of cloves. Put the whole into a stone jar, which is set in a vessel of boiling water, and let them boil for two hours. At the end of that time, the juice is to be strained without pressure, and boiled for fifteen minutes, all scum that rises being carefully removed. When the catsup is well settled, it should be turned through a sieve, bottled and corked tight. Keep it in a cool place.

MUSTARD.—*Sinapis.*

Two species of this well known plant are cultivated in the kitchen garden, viz.: the White (*S. alba*), and the Black (*S nigra*), both of which are annuals and natives of Europe. Commentators upon the Bible seem divided in opinion, in regard to the identity of this herb with the mustard spoken of by our Blessed Lord, the seed of which is represented as "the least of all seeds," but is yet capable of producing a tree so large that "the birds of the air come and lodge in the branches thereof." Some writers contend that reference was made to an entirely different plant, while others believe that this extraordinary size may be attributed to the difference in climate and soil. Our garden herb has been cultivated for many centuries. The seed, which is an article of commerce, was first imported from Egypt.

Culture.—In selecting the spot for a bed, choose a loam which is deep and mellow, as well as moist and fertile. In the summer season, it is desirable to have a situation that is shaded during the middle of the day; but at other times, the bed ought to have the full benefit of the sun, and be protected on the north from cold winds.

For salads.—The seed may be sown at all seasons of the year;—in the open air, when the weather will permit, or else in gentle hot-beds, or in boxes kept in warm windows. The seed is put very thickly in shallow drills, about four inches apart, and covered with fine mold to the depth of one third of an inch. The sowing must be repeated every week or two, according to the supply of leaves required. A proper degree of moisture appears to be very essential to quick germination, and, therefore, a generous sprinkling of water is to be given, when the sowing is not followed by showers. In the course of a few days, the plants will be of a suitable size for cutting,—which is a much better mode of gathering them, than to pull them up by your fingers. They ought to be used soon after being picked, and be carefully washed from dirt and grit before taken to the table.

For the production of seed,—as well for its use in the manufacture of ground mustard, as for subsequent sowings, the bed must be made in the middle of spring. The soil should be deep and mellow. Sow thinly in drills eighteen inches apart. When the plants have attained the fourth leaf, they are to be well hoed, and thinned to the distance of ten or twelve inches in the drill. During the season, the ground must be frequently stirred, and kept free from weeds. Should the weather be dry at the time the flowers open, water may be applied to the roots with advantage. The pods are to be collected when they change color, but not threshed until they become perfectly dry.

USE.—The leaves and seeds of both species are used for salads, pickles, and the manufacture of ground mustard; although for the latter purpose the black species is generally considered preferable. The seeds of both have valuable medicinal properties, in cases of rheumatism, palsy and asthma, and are of common use in emetics and poultices. Ground mustard as a condiment is spoken of highly by physicians, as it warms the stomach, creates an appetite, and strengthens the digestive organs.

NASTURTIUM.—*See* INDIAN CRESS.

NEW ZEALAND SPINACH.—*Tetragonia expansa.*

A large, spreading plant, the native country of which is sufficiently indicated by its name. It was carried to England by Sir Joseph Banks, and it has been introduced into this country within a few years, as a substitute for the common spinach. It proves to be a valuable addition to our gardens. The flavor of the leaves is excellent, and there is this additional advantage attending its cultivation, viz.: that it will flourish through a severe drought, when other vegetables are nearly destroyed by the heat. This is a very important consideration.

CULTURE.—The success of plants grown for their succulent leaves, depends more upon the character of the soil, than upon the degree of skill and care which may be manifested in the other details of their cultivation. For the New Zealand spinach we would prefer a bed of mellow loam, that is deep and has been made rich by the liberal application of manure. The situation should be open. Sow in the months of April or May, according to the forwardness of the season, in drills two feet apart. The seeds should be dropped thinly along the drill,—say six inches asunder, and covered with fine mold to the depth of one inch. Should the seeds all vegetate, the plants would be too much crowded, and they must be thinned out to distances of at least twenty inches. Those which are taken up may be set out in another bed. By keeping the ground well tilled, not only for the benefit to be derived from atmospheric influences, but also to prevent the encroachments of weeds, the plants will grow very luxuriantly. The number required for a family of moderate size is not large.

Use.—Besides the use to be made of the leaves like common spinach, the green seeds are excellent for pickling purposes. From the fact that the plant suffers but little inconvenience from hot weather, it seems well adapted to the notice of the reader.

OKRA.—*Hibiscus esculentus.*

The okra plant is an annual from the West Indies, where it is held in high esteem for use in soups and stews. It is frequently known under the name of Gumbo, and attains a height of four or five feet. It has not been much cultivated in this country until within a very few years, but it is now gradually acquiring popularity, in consequence of an impression that it is particularly wholesome. We do not rank it among the fancy vegetables, but think it eminently worthy of a place in every family garden. Those who make use of it one season, will not afterwards be willingly without it.

Culture.—Sow the seeds rather thickly, in drills three feet apart. The proper time for doing this, is in the first part of May, when the weather becomes settled, and about the usual period for planting Indian corn. The most congenial soil is rich and light, warm and dry. Cover the seed nearly an inch deep. Should the plants be destroyed by late frost, do not hesitate to make a second sowing. But, when they are considered out of all danger, they are to be thinned to distances of ten or twelve inches in the drill. Keep the ground mellow, and occasionally draw a little up around the stalks, to steady them against the wind. Under proper management, they will grow four or five feet high, and bear abundantly. The pods are best for use, when in a green state, and so tender as to snap easily; in fact, they are worthless when they become old and tough. Cooks who are not as well acquainted with this fact as they should be, may perhaps think that the excellence of the vegetable is much over estimated.

Use.—The young pods are excellent, if boiled and served with butter, and seasoned with a little pepper, salt and nutmeg; but they are most valued for the rich flavor they impart to soups, stews and sauces. It is said that the ripe seeds, after being properly roasted, form a very good substitute for coffee. The pods are easily preserved for use through the whole year, by being cut into narrow rings or slices, and then dried. Spread the slices on a board, or else put them in strings like dried apple. Keep them in paper bags. If picked when they are tender and juicy, they will be as good in winter as though fresh.

Gumbo.—Take equal quantities of the okra, chopped fine, and ripe tomatoes, which have been skinned, a sliced onion, a small piece of butter, together with salt and pepper to the taste; and stew the whole until tender, in a stew-pan, with a tablespoonful of water.

ONION.—*Allium cepa.*

Notwithstanding the many nice objections raised by over-fastidious people, to the use of the onion in the culinary department, it may justly be considered one of the most important vegetables, as well on account of its antiquity and general dissemination, as of its value for domestic purposes. The name onion is a corruption of *unio*, by which word the bulb is known in the Latin language. It came originally from Asia, and is described by modern travellers as growing plentifully in Egypt, where, on account of its mildness and easiness of digestion, it can be eaten with more satisfaction than in any other country. We read in Scripture that the discontented Israelites, in passing through the desert, murmured against the provisions of God, and lamented the loss of "the leeks, and the onions, and the garlic," to which they had been accustomed. The Egyptians are even reproached with the worship of the *Allium* tribe thus Juvenal says:—

"How Egypt, mad with superstition grown,
Makes gods of monsters, but too well is known.
'Tis mortal sin an onion to devour;
Each clove of garlic has a sacred power.
Religious nation, sure! and blest abodes,
Where ev'ry garden is o'errun with gods!"

The onion has been cultivated in this country since its first settlement, and in some sections very extensively for exportation. The inhabitants of Wethersfield, in Connecticut, a few miles distant from Hartford, are celebrated for their skill and success in this department of rural labor. Large tracts of land are devoted to this single crop, giving a comfortable support to quite a number of families. Much of the labor is performed by women and children, which, of course, diminishes the cost of cultivation and increases the profit. The best varieties for a family garden, are thought to be—the *New England White*,—the *Yellow Strasburgh*,—the *Red Dutch*,—and the *Silver-skinned*. The latter is excellent for pickling.

CULTURE.—The onion needs a light, rich soil, founded upon a dry substratum, and having a free, open exposure. In this plant we find an exception to the general necessity for a rotation of crops, as experience has demonstrated, that the onion can be grown on the same spot of ground for three quarters of a century, or more, without any apparent diminution in the produce. This fact, however, by no means affects the principle, or the philosophy, of rotation; because every one will admit that were it possible to restore to the land what is abstracted by a crop, economically as well as conveniently, the same grain or vegetable might be raised in one particular locality until the end of time. As the onion does not take much from the soil, which may not be returned to it by annual applications of manure, there is no necessity for alternating it with other vegetables. If the soil be poor, it ought to be deeply spaded in the autumn, enriched by a liberal application of well rotted dung, and thrown into ridges for exposure to the weather. In the spring, it may, perhaps, be well to give it a small dressing of the dung taken from an old hot-bed, or some rich compost. Indeed, many persons think there is but little danger of making it too rich. It should be borne in mind, however, that fresh dung is apt to breed maggots, and engender decay in the bulbs.

When the weather becomes settled in the middle of spring, it will be time to get the ground in readiness for the reception of the seed. The surface should be raked smooth, with care to pulverize all the clods which may have escaped the spade. The best bulbs are grown upon a hard bottom, and it is, therefore, advisable to roll the bed, or to beat it gently with the back of the spade. Draw drills one foot apart, so shallow as to be nothing more than mere guides for sowing the seed regularly.

Sow moderately thick, because it is difficult to thin the plants where they are much crowded, without doing them injury. A single ounce of seed will be quite enough for one rod of land. Cover the drills with a very little mellow dirt, and either tread them down with the feet, or smooth the whole surface by walking upon a board. After this has been done, many gardeners are accustomed to strew upon the bed a thin layer of sand, ashes, or soot, especially if the soil be stiff rather than light. The operation of sowing ought always to be performed in dry, pleasant weather.

The bed will require considerable attention at the beginning of the season. When the plants are three inches high, they are to be reduced in the drill to distances of two inches apart. Onions intended for pickling should stand thickly, in order to bring them early to maturity, as well as to prevent their attaining too large a growth. By performing this operation in damp, cloudy weather, the superfluous plants can be set out in another bed. As soon as they again crowd each other, they must receive a second thinning, so as to stand about four or five inches apart. Those which are pulled, can be carried to the kitchen, where they will be gladly welcomed for their small size and agreeable flavor. We must assure the reader, that onions and weeds do not agree well when cultivated together in the same bed. It is not necessary to stir the ground deeply, nor to bring it up around the plants; either of which would prevent the proper growth of the bulbs. Indeed, so objectionable is the hoe after the onions have once got fairly started, it is much the best plan to throw it aside, and make use of the fingers in keeping the drills clean.

Should there be danger of the crop running too much to blade, it may be advisable, in the latter part of July, to check the growth of the tops, and to throw the vigor of the roots into the development of the bulbs. This is very important with a late crop or in any case where there appears to be an undue luxuriance. It is effected by bending over the stems at the height of one or two inches above the bulbs. It may be done most easily by means of a hoe handle, drawn over the drills, from one end of the bed to the other.

The maturity of the crop will be indicated by the change of color in the stems. When the onions are drawn, they must not be housed immediately; but, on the contrary, be exposed to the sun for several days, being turned frequently, until they become dry and hard. They may then be separated from the roots and tops, previous to being spread upon the floor of a well-ventilated loft; or they can be strung in ropes, to be hung up until wanted for use, or carried to market for sale. It will be necessary to examine them often during the winter, to avoid loss by moisture, which causes decay, or by warmth, which promotes vegetation.

Where the cultivator desires larger onions than can be matured in a single season, under the course of culture above described, he must take up the bulbs at midsummer, to be planted in the following spring. The seed is to be sown thickly, and the young plants are to be kept free from weeds. By the middle of July, the bulbs will be about the size of small cranberries, and are then to be raised, dried, and stored in a dry, airy loft. In the next April, they shall be planted in ground which has been properly dug and manured, in drills one foot distant from each other. The beds should be well rolled, and the bulbs are to be set merely on the surface, without being covered with earth. The subsequent cultivation, —in the shape of weeding, storing, &c.,—is identical with that of the crop harvested in the same year in which sown.

For seed,—some of the best onions are to be planted in early spring, upon a bed of light, rich soil, and in rows some eighteen inches apart each way. They should be inserted so deep that the crowns are barely covered. The flower-stalks will need support, lest they should be broken down by violent winds. As soon as the seed ripens, the heads are to be gathered, and laid on a cloth to dry. The seed is best preserved in a cool, dry apartment.

USE.—Onions are known to afford considerable nourishment. When boiled, they seldom disagree with the healthy stomach, and, as a general thing, may be thought wholesome. The French introduced onion soup as a restorative after any unusual fatigue. Sir John Sinclair said, "It is a well known fact, that a Highlander with a few raw onions in his pocket, and a crust of bread or bit of cake, can work or travel to an almost incredible extent for two or three days together, without any other food." When eaten raw, they taint the breath considerably, but this difficulty may be partially overcome, by eating a few raw leaves of parsley directly after the onions. When roasted, they are sometimes employed as a poultice for tumors. The expressed juice is given as an expectorant in coughs, and is rubbed on the skin to remove blotches or the stings of insects. It would be a difficult matter to enumerate all the virtues which have been ascribed to this popular bulb. It is chiefly valuable in the family garden, however, for culinary purposes. Boiling renders it much more wholesome, and deprives it, in a great degree, of its strong taste and smell. Used in the raw state, it is not easily digested, and frequently remains in the stomach for a day or two. When roasted or fried, it is quite as objectionable, and must be eaten sparingly, if at all. It is a great favorite for seasoning dishes, particularly with the French cook.

To boil.—Peel the onions, and put them into boiling milk, or milk and water mixed. When they become tender, they are to be taken from the fire, salted, and served with melted butter. Changing the water when they are about half-boiled, relieves them of much of their strong flavor.

To pickle.—Peel the onions, and boil them for ten minutes in milk and water. To one gallon of vinegar, put one half ounce of cinnamon and mace, one quarter ounce of cloves, one half ounce of alum, together with a small teacupful of salt. The spiced vinegar is to be heated, and turned, when scalding hot, upon the onions, after they have been drained from the milk and water. Cover them tight until they become cold.

Onion Sauce.—Take peeled onions, boil them till quite tender, and then press out the water which they have absorbed. Chop them fine, add butter melted in milk, and place the dish again upon the fire.

Onion, (Potato).—*See* POTATO ONION.

Onion, (Tree).—*See* TREE ONION.

PARSLEY.—*Apium petroselinum.*

Parsley is a well known biennial, of hardy constitution, and a native of Sardinia. It is found growing wild in many different climates. Aside from the excellent properties for which it is esteemed in the culinary department, it makes a very ornamental appearance in the garden. There appear to be three varieties, viz.:—the *Common*,—the *Curl-leaved*,—and the *Hamburgh*. The first named is most generally cultivated, although the second is distinguished by the superior beauty of its leaves. Where the plant is used for its seasoning qualities alone, as in soups and stews, it matters little which may be the particular variety; but, for garnishing, the *Curled-leaved* is preferable. The *Hamburgh* is valued for its root, which is tender and palatable; it is cultivated and prepared for the table in the same way as the parsnip.

Culture.—Plants are obtained from seed, an ounce of which will sow about one and a half rods of ground. They may be raised in a bed by themselves, but they make a very pretty edging for the walks. In the first case, it will be necessary to sow in drills one foot apart, rather before the middle of spring. The seed should be dropped moderately thick, and covered to the depth of half an inch. It vegetates slowly sometimes not under a month, and it would be a good plan to steep it for twelve hours, either in warm water, or in sulphur-water. This steeping, together with an occasional application of water in dry times, will greatly expedite the process of germination.

It is often found, that where the plants are dilatory in showing themselves above ground, the weeds have opportunity to take undisturbed possession. No effort should be spared to prevent the settlement of these intruders, for which labor the gardener will derive much benefit from the thumb and forefinger, that are able to work in the drill where the hoe might occasion damage. The plants may be gathered as wanted for use, as soon as they are two inches high; at about which time, they ought to be thinned out to distances of six inches in the row. Where they seem disposed to grow too rankly, it is advisable to cut them down, in order to secure the formation of new shoots. If the cultivator wishes to raise none other than the *Curled-leaved* variety, he must be careful to eradicate every root of the *Common*, or plain-leaved, as quick as it appears in the bed.

Parsley may be grown for winter use, with very little trouble. The plants are to be cut down to the ground, in the first part of autumn, in order that new heads may grow before the approach of severe frost. They will grow well under a covering of straw, litter or evergreen branches; or in a rough board box; but a cold frame is better than any other kind of protection. In this way, continued supplies of fresh leaves can be obtained during extreme cold weather.

For seed,—permit some of the largest and best looking plants to throw up flower-stalks. They ought not to be closely crowded. The-seed should be well dried, before any attempt is made to thresh it.

USE.—The aromatic leaves are thought highly of, for seasoning various dishes, in addition to their value as a garnish. A few, eaten raw, will remove the unpleasant taste and smell of onions. When they cannot be obtained fresh throughout the year, a supply can be gathered in summer, dried before the fire, broken fine by being rubbed between the hands, and put in tight bottles. They have a high reputation in Holland for the cure of the dropsy. Among other curious properties ascribed to the plant, it is said to poison birds who eat of it, and sometimes to occasion epilepsy.

PARSNIP.—*Pastinaca sativa.*

According to Johnson, the botanic name, *Pastinaca*, is derived from the Latin word for a dibble, *pastinum*, in allusion to the long, tapering shape of the root. This is a very hardy biennial, of which the original is probably the common wild parsnip of southern Europe. In its natural state, it is of small size, woody and poisonous. It has been greatly improved by cultivation, and is at the present time much esteemed for culinary purposes, being found nutritious as well as wholesome. It is particularly valuable on account of its power of standing severe frost without injury, and continuing good for use until the latter part of spring. The varieties are not numerous, and the *Hollow-crowned* is undoubtedly the best adapted to the wants of the family gardener.

Culture.—In regard to soil, the parsnip has a preference for one that is dry and mellow, rich and of considerable depth. A good sandy loam seems to be most suitable; while only poor crops can be expected from a gravel or tenacious clay. Depth and fertility are particularly necessary, because thereon depend the length and size of the roots. In the latter part of autumn, or the very commencement of spring, the ground selected for the bed should be spaded or trenched two spits deep; and, if it be not sufficiently rich, some well decomposed manure ought to be dug in with the lower spit. Sea-weed, decayed forest leaves and bird's-dung, have been highly recommended as fertilizers, as being less liable to affect the quality of the roots, than common stable dung. In spading, care is to be taken to break up all the clods or large lumps of dirt, and to remove the largest stones.

Sow in drills, twelve inches apart, in April or May, according to the forwardness of the season. One ounce of seed is sufficient for rather more than a rod of ground. Drop the seed thinly, and cover it nearly an inch deep. In dry weather, vegetation will be hastened by rolling the surface of the bed, or by treading down the drills with the feet. When the plants have taken a good start, they are to be weeded and thinned out in the drills; but, it is not until they become firmly established, that they shall receive their final thinning. To ensure the formation of large roots, they ought to have plenty of room, and stand not nearer together than six inches. It is a bad plan to crowd vegetables like the carrot and parsnip. Make frequent use of the hoe, as well to keep the ground free from weeds, as to prevent its becoming hard or baked.

Parsnips do not attain maturity until cold weather is near at hand. They will be found fit for use as soon as the leaves decay, in the month of October, but their sweetness and agreeable flavor are much improved by frost. This fact is so well understood, that many cultivators are accustomed to let the roots remain in the bed through the winter; or, at least, to take up only a number sufficient for the wants of the family while the ground is closed, and to harvest the balance of the crop in the spring. They ought to be dug very carefully, without being cut or bruised by the spade any more than is unavoidable; and, for preservation, must be packed in layers of sand, in a shed or cool cellar.

For seed.—Some of the best plants should be left in the bed where grown; or else set out in a border, some time during the early part of spring. They ought to be in rows, about two feet apart each way. In continued dry weather, it will be found of advantage to apply water every three or four days. Lay the flower-heads upon a cloth, and suffer them to get fully dry, before you attempt to thresh out the seed.

USE.—The parsnip has many valuable qualities, which commend it to both the farmer and the gardener. It is thought highly of for feeding to domestic animals. Hogs and bullocks are fattened upon it in a very short space of time, and the flesh is considered of superior flavor; while in cows it produces an extraordinary yield of milk, having a rich color, and affording butter of an excellent quality. Its character in the kitchen is well established. Although disliked by some persons on account of its peculiar sweetish taste, it is certainly wholesome, and proves very acceptable at that season of the year when in perfection, and when other vegetables are so few in number. It excites appetite, and physicians think it wholesome for convalescents. It is sometimes manufactured into ardent spirits, wine and marmalade; while in Ireland, it is used with hops for brewing a kind of beer much liked by the peasantry. The seeds are occasionally employed in intermittent fevers.

To boil.—Wash and split the roots, lay them in a stewpan with the flat sides down, and just cover them with boiling water, into which a little salt has been thrown. When they are quite tender, pare and butter them, and carry immediately to the table. Cold boiled parsnips are good, when cut into thin slices, dipped into butter, and fried brown.

PEA.—*Pisum sativum.*

The original locality of this hardy annual seems to be unknown. It has been cultivated in India, China and Japan, for many centuries, and was introduced into this country at the time of its first settlement. It probably went to Great Britain from Italy. In the reign of Queen Elizabeth, the most delicate varieties were brought from Holland, and Fuller observes that they were "fit dainties for ladies, they came so far, and cost so dear." At the present day, the pea is very extensively diffused, and is well known as one of the most important culinary plants. The varieties are numerous, differing in stature, productiveness, the color of the flowers, and the time of ripening. We mention several of the choicest kinds, being such as we can recommend to the notice of the reader. Each one has some distinguishing feature which makes it worthy of cultivation, yet no more than four or five out of the list will be wanted in a small family garden. There is much deception practised in selling peas for seed, and the inexperienced purchaser will be very likely to discover a great similarity in the character of his crops. One variety is sometimes known under two or three names. This should be a caution to the reader to buy of those persons only, who have a reputation to sustain for honesty and fair dealing.

We enumerate—the *Prince Albert,*—the *Cedo Nulli,*—*Landreth's Extra Early,*—the *Early Frame,*—the *Early Warwick,*—*Bishop's Dwarf,*—the *Charlton,*—the *Blue Imperial,*—*Woodford's Marrow,*—the *Dwarf Sugar,*—and *Knight's Dwarf* and *Wrinkled Marrows.* If the reader desire a longer list, we must refer him to some seedsman who raises new varieties for sale. Those above mentioned are all excellent for the kitchen. The *Prince Albert* is the earliest sort with which we are acquainted, and should be sown for the first crop. The others are arranged in nearly their order of coming to maturity. The *Dwarf Sugar* peas are eaten with the pods, like string-beans.

Culture.—The dwarf kinds are best pleased with a soil that is light, dry, and moderately rich; while those of a lofty growth need a loam of greater depth and fertility. Where it is rank, the cultivator will find himself repaid by a very luxuriant set of vines, but the crop will be small. The application of fresh dung at the time of sowing, or shortly previous thereto, is positively injurious. Only well decomposed manure or compost should be given at that season of the year; and, after all, it is decidedly the best way, to select such ground as is in good condition after a crop, having been enriched some months previous.

Forcing under glass is often resorted to, but the majority of family gardeners are content with open air crops. To have green peas as early as possible in the season is, of course, very desirable; and there is frequently found, among persons living in the same neighborhood, a good-natured rivalry in obtaining the quickest returns. Many are in the habit of raising early plants on a gentle hot-bed, or even in a simple cold frame, to be transferred to the open ground as soon as it can be done with safety. The peas are sown in long, narrow boxes, formed of two boards put together in the shape of the letter V. The germs will be speedily roused into action under the glass, and, as the season advances, they must be gradually hardened, that they may not suffer injury from being transplanted. By taking off one end of the box, the earth, together with the young plants, can be easily pushed into the drill prepared for their reception. If done carefully, the roots will not experience the least inconvenience from the change. This simple process will hasten the crop many days.

The first sowing in the open air, should be in March, as soon as the frost leaves the ground, and there is a prospect of continued pleasant weather. Successive plantations can be made every fortnight or three weeks thereafter, until the middle of August, but the heat of summer is so unfavorable to the young vines that the sowings are often interrupted at the end of May, and resumed somewhere about the beginning of August. By doing this, the table can be kept supplied for several months together.

The earliest sowings in the open air should be in the warmest part of the garden, in beds having the full benefit of the sun's rays, but, at the same time, sheltered from cold winds which might retard vegetation. The border on the east or south side of a fence, is an excellent situation. Sow moder ately thick—say from an inch and a half to two inches asunder, —in drills, which are four feet apart for the dwarf varieties, and five or six feet apart for the other kinds. With some of the dwarfs the distance might be even less; the *Bishop's Dwarf*, for instance, can be grown in drills not more than two feet asunder. But a free circulation of air is so essential to the vigor of the plants, that we are always willing to allow them more room than they actually require, and to occupy the intervening spaces with cauliflower, cabbage, lettuce, and such other vegetables as will be benefited by their shade.

It is usual to make two rows in each drill, nine inches from each other, and about two inches deep; because then less ground is required for the plantation, while the cost of setting brush will be diminished one half. One quart of seed will plant from forty to eighty yards of row, and when the soil is dry, the seed ought to be soaked in warm water at least twenty-four hours before the time of sowing. When the weather becomes very warm, if water be poured into the rows before they are covered, the time required for the germination of the seed will be considerably shortened. The extent of the various sowings may, perhaps, be determined with tolerable accuracy from the experiments of Bradley, who ascertained that, on an average, three rods of land, containing eighteen double rows, yielded thirty-six quarts of shelled peas.

In early spring, should any injury from severe cold weather be apprehended, the sowings might be protected by thin layers of straw, litter, or evergreen brush. When the plants are two inches high, the soil should be thoroughly loosened by the hoe, and a little drawn up against the stems for their support. This must be repeated once or twice previous to the time of "brushing," with care to destroy every upstart weed. As soon as the plants show their tendrils, or when about nine inches in height, "brushing" should be performed. Gardeners generally make use of cedar tops, trimmings of apple trees, or some other refuse stuff with small twigs, for the support of the tendrils, sharpened at the lower end, and between four and seven feet high—according to the variety cultivated. They are to be firmly inserted between the rows, and sufficiently close together to sustain all the vines. It is a much neater plan, to stretch twine on each side of the drill, tying it to stakes that stand some six or eight feet asunder, by which means, the vines will be kept upright, without the assistance of the unsightly brush. The *Bishop's Dwarf* does not require staking.

When the plants of the early and late sowings are in blossom, and the flowers on the lower part of the stalks begin to fade, it is a good practice to stop the growth of the leading shoots, by pinching off the terminal buds. By doing this, the strength of the roots is spent wholly upon the development of the pods, thus hastening the maturity of the crop. In time of drought, and in certain situations, even during ordinary dry weather, water may be applied with marked advantage, by pouring it between the rows. We have saved entire plantations, with a few minutes' labor at evening, after the vines, in consequence of the heat and want of moisture, had turned yellow for several inches above the ground. When artificially watered, they continue in a vigorous state, resisting disease and bearing abundantly, while less favored vegetables are almost burned up. It is said, that if the pods be gathered regularly as they become fit for use, with care not to injure the stems, the produce will be larger and continued for a greater length of time.

The pea-bug is a small brown insect, which derives its name from its habits of preying on this vegetable. The egg is deposited by the parent fly in the soft pod, and the minute maggot works his way into the very heart of the pea, there to perfect its growth. Hence Dr. Harris observes, that few persons in eating a plateful of green peas, "are aware how many insects they unconsciously swallow." The beetle emerges from its hiding place, near the time for planting in the following spring. The germ is seldom injured, but the vegetable is rendered unfit for winter use. We would advise soaking the seed in boiling water for about a minute, and then rolling it in ashes or plaster, whereby the bug will be destroyed, and the germ roused at once into action. Care must be taken, however, to prevent the destruction of the seed as well as of the bug. With the crop intended for drying, it is advisable to plant late, after the time for the parent fly to deposit its eggs has passed. A disease called the "mildew," is caused by the want of moisture.

For seed,—save none but the best plants. New and improved kinds have been thus obtained, and what has been done once can be done again. Even if you cause no improvement in the variety, you will prevent its degenerating. The pods should be gathered when dry, and, after being kept several days in a cool place, for all surplus moisture to escape, are to be shelled, and stowed away in paper bags or boxes.

USE.—The anxiety manifested by gardeners in the neighborhood of cities to raise the first crops for market, is indicative of the general regard in which the vegetable is held. In the green state, peas are light and wholesome, and on account of their earliness, form a grateful addition to the dinner-table. They can be easily preserved for winter use by drying them on cloths in the shade, and keeping them from mildew; by soaking them a few hours in water, they will be as good as though freshly picked. When ripe, they are used in puddings and soups; and are considered nutritious, although unfit for very delicate stomachs. They have, moreover, an agricultural importance, being known to be one of the best kinds of provender for cattle and poultry.

To boil.—Green peas should be freshly gathered, and not shelled until a few minutes before the time of cooking. Wash them clean, and then put them into boiling water, with salaratus in the proportion of one quarter of a teaspoonful to one half peck of peas. When they are tender, take them up by means of a skimmer, put a piece of butter in the dish, and sprinkle on a little salt.

Pea Soup.—Stew one pint of green peas in a pint of water, with an ounce of butter, a few leaves of lettuce, onions, pepper and salt, till they become soft, when you are to add more water, and stew until they are quite tender. If the peas have been dried, they should be soaked for twelve hours in a warm place, boiled for an hour, drained, put in fresh water, together with a piece of salt pork, and further boiled till they are soft.

PENNYROYAL.—*See* MINT.

PEPPER.—*Capsicum.*

Capsicum is the name given to several species of plants found in South America, as well as in the East and West Indies. Though numerous, they all agree in their pungent properties, and are easily distinguished by their red or yellow pods, which contain many small, flat seeds.

CULTURE.—The best soil is one that is rich, mellow, dry and in a warm situation. One ounce of seed will yield between two and three thousand plants. The earliest sowing can be made in March, upon a gentle hot-bed; or delayed until the first part of May, in a sheltered border. Cover the seed near half an inch deep. When the plants are two inches high, they shall be removed to their final location, to be set in rows two feet apart each way. Until they become established, protect them from the noonday sun; and occasionally, during all dry weather, give them gentle sprinklings of water Keep the soil open and clean.

For seed,—plants bearing the most forward and best-shaped fruit must be selected. When the pods are ripe, they are to be hung up to dry in a warm room, where they can be kept through the winter.

USE.—In hot climates, the fruit of these plants is much used for culinary purposes, being eaten in large quantities with both animal and vegetable food, and mixed, in different proportions, with almost every kind of sauce. In family gardens of this country, it is generally cultivated for pickling, and should be gathered before it ripens. For the manufacture of Cayenne pepper, it is dried in the sun, and then ground. In addition to the value of Cayenne for seasoning dishes, it has some medicinal virtues, and is often rubbed upon meats to preserve them from insects.

PEPPERMINT.—*See* MINT.

POTATO.—*Solanum tuberosum.*

Sir Joseph Banks thought, that this well known vegetable was originally brought to Spain from the mountainous districts of South America, where it may yet be found growing in a wild state. Its history is involved in some obscurity, in consequence of its being frequently confounded with the sweet potato, from which root it seems to have derived its name. It was carried to England in 1586, from Sir Walter Raleigh's colony of Virginia, and was first cultivated upon his estate at Youghall, in Ireland. Clusius, a European writer, mentions it about the year 1588. Its character was then by no means settled, and for a long time the tubers were treated as fruit, being eaten with sugar, or baked in pies with wine and spices. They were purchased as a great delicacy for the table of Queen Anne, at the cost of two shillings per pound. So much opposition was manifested to its culture, that its introduction into many parts of the Eastern continent is of comparatively recent date. Thus, some writers did not hesitate to call it fit for swine alone, while even the celebrated Evelyn, at the very close of the seventeenth century, advised that it be planted in the worst land. Others based their objections on religious grounds, saying that what is "not mentioned in the Bible" cannot be fit for the food of man. It did not reach Switzerland until 1720, and the French were so much prejudiced against it, that its cultivation did not become general among them until during a time of scarcity in the Revolution. Nor did the peasantry of Italy receive it into favor, until their cupidity had been excited by the rewards which government offered to those who cultivated it most successfully; it is true, that they were afterwards so well convinced of its value during a severe famine, that they proudly refused to take the premiums to which they had become entitled. But this diversity of opinion has long since passed away, and the potato is considered one of our most important field and garden crops.

In consequence of the facility with which it is propagated by seed, as well as of the distinctive character which it acquires from a change of soil, climate and management, its varieties are very numerous,—being dissimilar in form, appearance, size, quality for the kitchen, and productiveness. Every section has its favorite sorts, which either improve or deteriorate by removal to another district. Thus, the far-famed Irish potato loses its valuable properties, when transplanted to this country; and a kind that is highly esteemed in one part of our broad Union, is only second or third-rate in another quarter. Prejudice has undoubtedly something to do in this matter, but it chiefly results from certain natural causes, which might easily be explained. It will be seen, therefore, that we can only enumerate the principal varieties, and leave the consideration of their respective merits with the reader: these are—*Fox's Seedling*,—the *Early Kidney*,—the *Mercer*,—the *Pink Eyes*,—the *Foxite*,—the *Liverpool Blues*,—and the *Blue Jackets*. We believe the above to be the very best in general cultivation; still, for the reasons just named, there may be other kinds equally good, and perhaps much better than some included in the list.

New varieties are obtained from seed. With the gardener who has time to spare, such experiments are very interesting, to say nothing of their actual importance in producing estimable kinds for cultivation. The apples should be gathered when ripe, and the seeds washed therefrom, dried in a warm window, and put away in paper bags. By the first of May following, the seeds are to be sown in drills, one third of an inch deep, and ten inches apart, upon a bed of fine, mellow earth. The plants, when three inches high, are to be thinned out to distances of eight inches in the drill, and those taken up in cloudy weather, can be set out in another bed. Cultivate carefully through the summer,—destroying weeds, and occasionally bringing a little soil around the stems. In autumn, at the time the vines wither, gather the small tubers, and keep them in separate paper bags; to be planted the next season, at such distances apart as will prevent any intermixture or confusion of sorts. When the crop ripens, such tubers as appear desirable for extraordinary size, flavor, early season of maturity, or productiveness, may be reserved for the following spring; while all others are thrown to the pigs.

Culture.—Potatoes are raised in nearly every kind of soil, although experience has shown the superiority of a light loam over all others. For the want of a little forethought in the selection of the ground, farmers often find the crop small, or, if large, of very poor quality. We think it generally understood, that a fresh loam which is light, moderately rich, and somewhat moist, is better than one of a wet, hard, or tenacious character. Unless it be quite loose and friable, it is always the best plan to dig it deeply in autumn, letting it lie in ridges to court the action of frost in winter, and levelling it in the spring. In regard to manures, unfermented barn-yard dung is by many considered objectionable, on account of a real, or fancied, unpleasant taste which it communicates to the tubers; and, for this reason, if it be necessarily used, it should be spread over the whole surface and dug under, rather than put in close contact with the seed. Lime or gypsum, ashes, bone-dust, charcoal, etc., make excellent additions to the soil, rendering it fertile without causing rankness.

To avoid disappointment and delay, the seed should be got in readiness some days before the time of planting. At this stage of our inquiry, we find another of those important questions which can never be put to rest, viz.: "Shall the potatoes be planted whole, or after being cut up into sets?" Each method has its advocates, and the respective advantages of each have been again and again ascertained by actual experiment, but with results as variable as the movements of the weathercock. From personal observation, we think that if the tuber be of a medium size, it may be planted whole, or if large, cut into four five or six pieces. At least two buds, or eyes, should be retained in every set. The point of the potato is found to come to maturity about a fortnight earlier than the root end,—a fact which may, with propriety, be noted for the first crops. When the sets are cut, they ought to be laid on a floor to dry, for about a week previous to the date of planting. Sprinkling them with water, and covering with a thin layer of mold, so as to sprout the buds, is attended with not a little trouble and considerable danger of injury to the young shoots.

Lay the ground out into drills, about two feet apart, and eight inches deep. In the bottom of each, spread three inches of manure, over which is to be thrown a little loose earth for the reception of the sets. Put them eight or ten inches apart, and with the eyes uppermost. When one drill is planted, fill it up with three or four inches of mold, and proceed to the next one. For the general crop, the time of planting will be somewhere near the middle of April, although a good yield is frequently obtained from seed planted a month earlier in the season. Forcing is often resorted to, in order to secure a quick return. Our general directions in the article headed "FORC-

ING VEGETATION," are quite sufficient. The hot-bed need not be very large, but it should have sixteen or eighteen inches of good soil upon the top, so as to afford plenty of room for the formation of roots.

When the young vines appear above the ground, the duties of after-culture commence. The soil should be thoroughly loosened by the hoe, as well to admit light and air, as to check the further progress of weeds. A little mold is from time to time to be drawn around the stems for their support, and for the benefit of the roots—both to prevent their pushing themselves through the surface, and to guard them against excessive moisture. Care must be taken not to make so large a ridge, as to occasion harm rather than good; the proper height is dependent upon such circumstances as climate, season, soil, and the variety cultivated. For a potato patch no part of the treatment is more essential, than the systematic and thorough use of the hoe; but it must not be continued after the blossoms have set, because it will then encourage a new growth of fibres, which, without being able to arrive at maturity, rob the first growth of the nourishment that is necessary to their perfection. After that period, the gardener will be obliged to make use of his fingers, in extracting such weeds as persist in showing themselves among the drills. Botanists and practical cultivators have decided, that the crop is much benefited by picking off the blossom buds before they are ready to open. Whether the trouble will be counterbalanced by the increased produce, can be decided by individual experiment.

The time when the potatoes are fully ripened, will be indicated by the decay of the vines. They are, however, taken up long before this, and exposed for sale under the tempting name of "new potatoes." We do not hesitate to condemn the practice, believing that these walnut-sized tubers are almost as destitute of nourishment, if not quite as unwholesome, as unripe cherries or apples. But, it is true that they are fit for use sometime previous to the withering of the stems, and can be dug as wanted. We object only to taking them up before they are scarcely half grown. The main part of the crop intended for storing, ought not to be harvested until vegetation has ceased.

In a large plantation, the drills are often opened by the plough, which is a cheap and expeditious way ; in a garden at that season, the team will be liable to do injury, and recourse must be had to the hoe, fork, or long-handled shovel. The latter is a very effective implement for the labor, particularly in the hands of an honest Hibernian. The roots will be injured by the heat of the sun, and, if not dug in cloudy weather, should be thrown into small heaps covered with a few of the dead vines, for the escape of the surplus moisture. Handle them carefully, so as not to bruise or injure them any more than cannot be avoided. They are generally stored in the cellar, in large bins, or common flour barrels,—a little straw being thrown upon the top, to prevent exposure to the air. At other times, they are piled in a pyramidal or conical heap, in some unoccupied part of the garden. The heap ought to be in a dry spot, thatched with straw, with ten inches of dirt upon the outside, made smooth so as to shed the rain, and encircled by a trench to conduct away the water. Such as are kept in the cellar must be frequently examined, for the purpose of picking out decayed ones, and preventing the growth of sprouts—which would injure their quality, both for use on the table and planting as seed.

The disease called the "curl," although long known, seems so far to have baffled investigation. Some experiments made in Great Britain indicated, that gathering the tubers for seed before they become fully ripe, adds greatly to the amount and certainty of the crop. We have yet said nothing in regard to the "rot," which has prevailed so extensively for a few years past, and showed itself, last season, in places where it had not before been known. It is a matter of so much importance to the gardener, that to pass over it without comment, might well be deemed inexcusable in the author of a work like this. And so, a few words in relation to it may be expected from us, even though we have nothing new to advance. The failure of the potato crop in Ireland and other parts of Europe, for several years in succession, and the consequent suffering among the poorer classes, are facts still fresh in our minds, and which, indeed, cannot easily be forgotten. The disease has been scarcely less fatal in our own country, although attended with less melancholy results. The attention of the most eminent scientific men has been drawn to the subject, and still, little or nothing of value has thus far been elicited. We are, probably, as ignorant as ever of the cause of the disease, and we, certainly, have not yet found a remedy. This little book would hardly contain all the alleged preventives, that have been brought forward in our agricultural journals, and a small number of which we ourselves have tested, with results varying from season, temperature, soil, exposure and manure. If we have any opinion of our own, it is briefly this—to plant upon new and long-uncultivated ground, with such fertilizers as lime, ashes, charcoal, and salt, instead of stable-dung, and especially that which is unfermented. The subject has been again revived, and is open for the exercise of learning and sagacity; but we much fear, that the great moving cause of the contagion will prove as mysterious, as the principle of "the pestilence that walketh in darkness."

USE.—The discovery of the potato plant has been of more benefit to mankind than the discovery of gunpowder. The one destroys, while the other feeds,—having, it is said, added millions to the population of Europe, and rendered unknown, until within a few years, those famines that were so frequent and so distressing. If we search the whole round of the vegetable kingdom, we find no member more generally valuable, as well as more extensively cultivated. The roots, when of a good quality and well cooked, are wholesome and nutritious, forming a staple article of food, of which the appetite never tires. With the poor they are one of the greatest blessings of the soil, being "flour without a mill, and bread without an oven." Mixed in certain proportions with wheat flour, they make a most excellent family bread; when ground into flour, they are used by confectioners; and they are manufactured into starch, tapioca, yeast, alcohol, and sugar. The stalk can be converted into potash, and a sort of flax; and the apples yield vinegar; while soap can be extracted from the tubercles.

Irish mode of boiling.—Wash the potatoes clean, but do not pare them; then put them into hot water, and boil them until a fork can be readily inserted. Dash in a pint of cold water, and in two minutes afterward, pour off the whole. Now set the pot, with the lid half drawn, either over the fire, or near it, for the steam to evaporate; when the potatoes may be peeled, and carried to the table in an uncovered dish. If they be of a good kind, this mode of cooking will render them sweet, dry and mealy, very different from the water-soaked lumps too often seen.

To roast.—Select potatoes of a nearly equal size, that they may all occupy about the same length of time in cooking. After they are washed clean, put them in a tin pan, and bake in a stove or oven. Send them to the table unskinned.

Potato Bread.—Boil the potatoes very soft, when they are to be peeled and mashed as fine as possible. They are then to be mixed with two thirds their weight of flour, and made into dough with lukewarm water. Add a little salt and butter, and work in the yeast, together with flour sufficient to stiffen the dough. It rises quicker than common bread, and is more economical, and continues fresh for a longer time. It should be baked as soon as risen, for it will, otherwise, turn sour in the course of a few hours.

POTATO ONION.—*Allium tuberosum.*

Not unfrequently called the under-ground onion, in conse

quence of its producing clusters of offsets from the roots. Plant in March or April,—the bulbs being ten inches from each other, in rows one foot apart, and having their crowns one inch below the surface. The soil should be moderately rich, and, for convenience of cultivation, laid into beds four feet wide. Make good use of the hoe throughout the summer, and occasionally draw a little earth around the stems. This practice of "earthing," as it is called, is generally followed, although condemned by many eminent authorities. The crop will be matured sometime during the month of August, and is to be harvested like the common onion.

POTATO (SWEET).—*See* SWEET POTATO.

PUMPKIN.—*Cucurbita pepo.*

We believe that the pumpkin is a native of India. It is one of the nine species of the gourd, or squash, family. The botanical term *Cucurbita* is derived from the resemblance which some of the species bear to certain vessels used by the chemist. This one is readily distinguished by the round shape of its fruit, and is sometimes known under the name of Pompion. For families the best varieties are, undoubtedly,—the *Cashaw*,—and the *Valparaiso*. Some other kinds attain such an extraordinary size, that they are better suited for taking premiums at agricultural shows, than for use in the kitchen.

CULTURE.—This vine ought not to be cultivated in the garden, where it will occupy much room that might be devoted to more profitable crops, and where it will, moreover, do great injury by hybridizing with the choicest melons and cucumbers;—unless the gardener have no other ground at his disposal. It is generally planted by the farmer, in the hills with Indian corn, and allowed to take care of itself. But, it is known to be most successful when grown in an open space, like the MELON;—the ground being properly manured, the seed sown in hills some eight feet apart each way, and the vines protected from the attacks of insects.

USE.—The pumpkin has a well-earned reputation. In Europe, it is used in soups, or when boiled like potatoes, or as a kind of baked preserve. In this country, where it is annually raised in immense quantities, it is considered very excellent food for cattle, and, in the hands of the skilful housewife, it makes a pie that is inferior to no other. It can be preserved through a great part of the winter, upon a shelf in a cool cellar, where the temperature is uniform and not below the freezing point. When discovered to be decaying, it may be cut up in strips, and dried near a fire; the dry strips to be stewed, when wanted for making pies. Or, it may be stewed, sweetened with sugar, and seasoned with ginger, and put in a jar to be kept in a cool place; when to be made into pies, the required quantity to be taken out, and put with milk and eggs.

Pumpkin Pie.—A pumpkin is to be halved, freed from the seeds, washed clean, and cut into small pieces. These are to be stewed gently until soft, then drained, and strained through a sieve. To one quart of the pulp, add three pints of cream or milk, six beaten eggs, together with sugar, mace, nutmeg and ginger to the taste. When the ingredients are well mixed, pour them upon pie plates having a bottom crust, and bake for forty minutes in a hot oven.

QUINCE.—*Cydonia vulgaris.*

"Quinces," says Columella, "yield not only pleasure, but health." The tree derived its botanical name *Cydonia*, from the city of Cydon, in Crete, where it appears to have first attracted notice. It is, however, found growing in a wild state in western Asia, as well as in the southern and eastern parts of Europe. The tree is of hardy habit, about twelve feet high, and of a spreading, irregular growth. The flowers are very ornamental, while nothing can be prettier than the ripe golden fruit in autumn. It is largely cultivated for market, and, under skilful management, yields a good profit. It occupies considerable room, and the roots are apt to do injury to such vegetables as may be in the immediate neighborhood; for which reasons, it is better adapted to the orchard than to the kitchen garden. We sometimes see it in the lawn around a house, where its richly laden branches of flowers or fruit have always a fine effect. The chief varieties are—the *Apple-shaped*,—the *Pear-shaped*,—and the *Portugal;* of which three, the first is most popular, although in flavor it is inferior to the last.

Culture.—Propagation is effected by seeds, cuttings and layers. But, as the character of the seedlings is uncertain, the last two methods are usually preferred. The cuttings are to be taken from young wood in early spring, each being twelve inches long, and planted in a moist, shady situation, with about one half its length below the surface. By giving a little water occasionally in dry weather, and keeping the soil light, the formation of roots will be encouraged, so that the plants will probably be fit for removal in the ensuing autumn. To propagate by layers, the shoots must be bent down into the ground, early in spring, and can be separated from the parent stock early in the first or second autumn thereafter, as may be most convenient.

The trees should be set about ten feet distant from each other, and in that portion of the garden where they will occasion the least injury. An idea seems to have become general, that currants, gooseberries and quinces, will be satisfied with a poor soil, and flourish without any special care or attention on the part of the cultivator. By the present method, the quince bushes are almost wholly neglected, and permitted to attain a rough, scrubby growth, that produces only a small, diseased crop. But, our observation has long since satisfied us, that no occupant of the garden or orchard can be more improved by systematic and thorough cultivation, than the one now under notice. In the first place, the soil selected for a plantation should be of the very best description—rich, deep and mellow,—be kept in good tilth through the summer, and enriched with a top-dressing of dung or compost in the autumn. Instead of having a thick clump of suckers, but three or four main stems should be allowed; while the only pruning necessary, is to remove the old wood, and such branches as interfere with one another. Under this treatment, the trees will be vigorous in their growth, and the crop will prove all that could be desired.

USE.—The fruit in its raw state is said to be good for the asthma, spitting of blood, dropsy and some other complaints; but its principal value is for making preserves, sauces, marmalades, jelly, wine, etc. It is also used with other kinds of fruit, for the sake of the agreeable flavor which it communicates to them. One pound of sugar mixed with one quart of quince juice makes a very excellent wine, that is thought to have performed many wonderful cures in cases of the asthma.

To preserve.—Pare the quinces, and cut them in halves or quarters,—at the same time taking out the cores. To every five pounds of the prepared fruit, add three pounds of sugar and one half pint of water. Put the whole upon the fire, where they are to simmer gently for three hours, the cover being kept upon the vessel to prevent the escape of steam. When the quinces are fully cooked, put them into a stone pot, which is to be kept in a cool, dry place. If the syrup ferments, draw it off, and return it while hot.

Another Receipt.—When the quinces are very ripe, pare and cut them in slices, or rings, an inch thick. Remove the cores carefully. To each pound of fruit, allow one pound of fine white sugar, which is to be dissolved in one half pint of cold water. After the fruit has soaked in this syrup for ten or twelve hours, put the whole into a preserving kettle, and let them boil gently, until a broom splinter will go easily through the pieces, when they may be taken from the fire. In the course of a week, draw off the syrup, and boil it down so that there will be just enough to cover the quinces.

Quince Jelly.—Halve and core the fruit, which is to be boiled very soft, and then drained through a flannel bag without squeezing. Add to every pint of the liquor, one pound of white sugar. Clarify by putting in the whites of eggs. When the liquor becomes clear, boil it over a moderate fire until a thick jelly is formed. Put the jelly in glasses, and cover them tight. The pulp remaining in the bag can be made into

Quince Marmalade.—Wash and quarter the quinces, without paring them, and stew them over a moderate fire. When they become soft, rub them through a sieve, and add brown sugar at the rate of "pound for pound." Then let the whole stew slowly, being stirred so as to prevent burning to the kettle. In about an hour, take out a little upon a spoon, and if it can be cut smooth on becoming cold, it is sufficiently cooked. Keep in jars or glasses.

RADISH.—*Raphanus sativus.*

This valuable plant came originally from China and Persia, but has been cultivated in Europe for time immemorial. It is an annual, having a stem about two feet high, which bears purplish white flowers. Formerly the leaves were boiled and stewed, and at the present day they are used with salad herbs; but the plant is chiefly esteemed for its root, which, containing little besides water, woody fibre, and acrid matter, cannot be very nutritive, although perhaps good as a stimulant. The best varieties for general culture, are—the *Early Short-top Scarlet*—the *Early Salmon*,—the *Long White Naples*,—the *White Spanish*,—the *Black Spanish*,—together with the *Red*, *White*, and *Yellow Turnip-rooted*.

Culture.—The early crops will require artificial heat. We have previously given general directions for the management of frames, and must refer the reader thereto. The best kinds of radish for culture under glass, are the *Early Short-top Scarlet*, and the *Early Salmon*. The bed of dung need not be large, because no great degree of warmth is necessary. The mold should be rich and light, about ten inches deep. As soon as it becomes warm, sow the seed rather thickly upon the surface, and cover with an additional half inch of mold. The plants ought to stand about two inches apart, and be freely supplied with air, although protected by mats during cold nights. Water must be occasionally given in moderate quantities. In the want of a regular hot-bed frame, a common box, set upon the dung, to be covered with loose boards whenever the weather is cool, answers a very good purpose. Should the gardener be so unfortunate as to be without manure which he can spare for a bed, he may hasten the maturity of the plants in no small degree, by the simple shelter of a close frame or box. Air must be freely admitted in all pleasant days. Early radishes are excellent on the breakfast table, and can be very easily obtained.

Sowing in the open air may be commenced sometime about the middle of March, provided the weather appear sufficiently mild. But, where we can depend upon frame crops, we prefer waiting a few days later. The first sowing should be made in a warm border, well screened upon the north side, and having the full benefit of the sun. The most favorable soil is one that is mellow, dry, and of average fertility. Sow either alone in drills eight inches apart, or in the same bed with carrot, spinach, lettuce, or any other vegetable which will come in after the radishes are removed. About one half ounce of seed will be required for a rod of ground; it should be covered evenly, and to the depth of half an inch. Throwing a quantity of litter or refuse straw on the bed, proves an excellent protection against frost, besides accelerating germination. Continue this at night, after the plants have started until all danger of their suffering from the cold be past.

A sowing ought to be made every two weeks until the middle of May, and occasionally afterward until September. For the summer crops, sow seed of the *Yellow Turnip-rooted* and *Long White Naples* varieties. The great difficulty in raising radishes during warm weather is, that the roots quickly become tough and bitter, when they are worthless for the table. In order to avoid this, they must be plentifully supplied with water, which renders them fleshy, with a mild, agreeable flavor. The winter supply of the *Black* and *White Spanish* varieties, shall be planted in the latter part of summer, or in the beginning of autumn, and harvested in November, to be packed away in sand.

When the seed leaves are well developed, the plants are to be thinned to one inch apart in the drill, and subsequently, to distances of two inches for the spindle-rooted, and of four or five inches for the turnip-rooted. Care must be taken to prevent their being too much crowded. A regular application of water is at all times of advantage, and particularly during a season of drought. The roots will not be eatable, unless they have a good supply of moisture. It has been recommended, to mix with the soil equal quantities of fresh horse-dung, and buckwheat bran, in order to hasten the growth of the roots, so as to get them out of the way of those worms which so greatly injure their appearance and quality. Snuff or air-slacked lime sifted upon the leaves, is a preventive of the depredations of small flies and beetles.

For seed,—leave some of the early spring plants in the bed where grown, or set them out in another bed, at distances of about three feet from each other. Endeavor to keep the varieties distinct, and having this object in view, you should not permit two different kinds to flower in the same neighborhood. Give them a little water after transplanting, and from time to time afterward, especially when the flowers are opened. The ripeness of the seed will be indicated by the pods turning brown; it may be threshed out immediately, or hung up with the stalks, until wanted for sowing.

USE.—The roots of radishes are eaten raw, and, when of good flavor, are highly relished at the tea or breakfast table. But, that they may be thus agreeable to the taste, as well as acceptable to the stomach, they must be young and tender. Physicians always condemn the use of such as are tough and stringy; and, indeed, on other considerations, we do not see how they can find favor with any person. The small leaves are sometimes put in salads, and the pods, while green and plump, are added to pickles, as a substitute for capers. The juice that may be extracted from the roots, is said to be good for diseases of the chest, such as hoarseness and difficulty of respiration.

RASPBERRY.—*Rubus Idæus.*

In its wild, unimproved state, the raspberry is a native of various temperate climates, to be found growing in thickets, woodland and rough mountainous districts. The species which is commonly cultivated in our gardens, appears to have originated from the *Rubus Idæus*, or Mount Ida bramble. Downing says, that the name of raspberry is derived from the Italian word *raspo*, probably in allusion to the rasping roughness of the wood. The root is creeping, and of a woody character. The stems are erect, attaining the height of three or four feet, and armed with short prickles. Several varieties are known, which differ from one another, in their habits of growth and hardiness, as well as in the quality and quantity of their fruit. Among those considered best for general cultivation, are—the *Red* and *White Antwerps*,—the *Colonel Wilder*,—the *Franconia*,—the *Fastolff*,—and the *Ohio Everbearing*.

The cultivation of the raspberry on an extensive scale for

market, is found to be very profitable, for the crop is generally large, and it always commands good prices. A Mr. Hallock, of Ulster County in the State of New-York, has a plantation covering three fourths of an acre of land, which, in the season of 1848, yielded thirty-three hundred baskets of fruit. He sold them in the City of New-York, at an average price of ten cents per basket, being at the rate of near four hundred and fifty dollars per acre.

Such a return cannot be expected from anything beside the very best management. An idea that the raspberry will flourish without cultivation, is very prevalent among those who consider themselves gardeners. On the contrary, it requires a good soil, the occasional application of manure, and regular pruning, quite as much as a cherry-tree, or a grape-vine. We frequently hear people complaining that the improved varieties, which they have procured at considerable expense, are but little better than the old-fashioned kinds to be found on the road side. The reason is obvious ;—the bushes are set in perhaps the most unfavorable part of the premises, and then allowed to take care of themselves. To expect that they will yield fruit in abundance, and of the best quality, is about as reasonable as it would be to suppose, that a boy left to follow his own headstrong will, and allowed to run wild with all kinds of associates, can become a respected member of society.

Culture.—The raspberry will grow well upon nearly every soil that is deep and rich, but it prefers a sandy loam, somewhat moist. Some of the most tender varieties, however, succeed best on a dry spot, where they are less liable to injury from frost. But, in no case is a strong, hard or heavy soil to be selected, where the cultivator has the choice of other ground. The situation should be free and open, that the bushes may have the full benefit of light and air.

New varieties are obtained from seed, and may be tested in the second or third year. For the propagation of established kinds, the most usual mode is by suckers or offsets from the roots. Some of the American varieties may be increased by layers,—that is, by bending a branch into a little hole, where it will take root. Set the canes in bunches of two or three, and in rows about three and a half feet apart each way, at almost any time when the ground is open between November and April. They will soon accommodate themselves to their new position, and throw up a growth of young suckers. In new plantations, in order to give the bushes an opportunity to strengthen themselves, rather than to perfect fruit the first year, it is a good way to cut the suckers down nearly to the ground, and the value of the crop in the following season will be considerably increased.

The management of a raspberry bush is certainly very simple, and renders the neglect and ill treatment so common quite inexcusable. During the summer, the ground ought to be kept mellow; no weeds nor grass being allowed to obtain a foothold. In autumn, the pruning is to be performed; or it may be delayed until the following spring, if that time be more convenient. The old canes, together with the feeble young wood, are to be cut down, leaving about half a dozen of the healthiest young shoots to bear the next crop. These shoots should be shortened some eight or ten inches, and then tied to a stake, in such a manner that the tops will spread out like a wineglass.

In cold latitudes, winter protection is necessary, and the reserved canes, instead of being tied up, are bent down upon the ground,—a small mound of earth being placed near the root to prevent their breaking,—and covered with earth, straw, or evergreens; in early spring, the covering is removed, and the stakes are set. Where a late crop is desired, the canes can be cut down in spring, to cause a new growth which will bear several weeks later than the other bushes. The soil should be thoroughly dug, and enriched with a liberal application of dung. Salt applied at this time also proves beneficial, and many cultivators are accustomed to spread litter, sea-weed, or salt hay upon the surface, to the depth of four or five inches, particularly in case the land be of a dry nature. Under high culture, the roots will continue in a good state of productiveness for six, ten, or fifteen years, each season yielding the owner a generous return for his trouble.

USE.—Succeeding the strawberry, the fruit of the raspberry is highly prized, not only on account of its value for the dessert, but also for making preserves, jellies tarts, etc. Wine, syrup and shrub are made from the juice. The fruit is wholesome, and of agreeable flavor; commending itself by its handsome appearance, as well as by its delightful fragrance. Raspberry syrup is excellent for dissolving the tartar that accumulates on teeth, and the wine, mixed with water, makes "a good reviving draught in ardent fevers."

Raspberry Jam.—For each pound of fruit, allow one pound of powdered white sugar, and place a layer of each alternately in a preserving-dish. After they have remained thus for half an hour, put them over a moderate fire, and let them boil slowly, stirring them frequently so as to prevent their being burned. Boil for half an hour, or until the mixture has become a thick jelly. This is ascertained by taking up a little in a cup, which is to be set in a dish of cold water.

Raspberry Shrub.—To three quarts of fresh, ripe fruit, put one quart of vinegar, and let them remain for twenty-four hours: at the end of which time, strain the liquor, and add to each pint one pound of white sugar. Boil the whole together for half an hour, and skim it clear. When it becomes cool, add to each pint of shrub, a wineglassful of French brandy. Three tablespoonfuls of this shrub, mixed with a tumbler of water, make a very pleasant drink, that is wholesome and refreshing in fevers.

RHUBARB.—*Rheum rhaponticum.*

Known in some sections of the country by the name of Pie-plant. It is a species of the genus *Rheum*, which furnishes the rhubarb of commerce. The leaves are broad and long, supported by large petioles. The roots, when not disturbed for a period of seven years or thereabouts, acquire a value for medicinal purposes; but the plant is cultivated in kitchen gardens for its stalks, which are to be used in tarts and pies. We should be glad to see it more extensively introduced, for apart from its value for culinary preparations, it is thought to exercise a peculiarly healthful influence upon the system. Its production for market is attended with profit, especially when brought forward in the early part of spring, before the season of fruit commences. The rhubarb family belong to the interior of Asia, and this species has been cultivated in England since the year 1573. The best varieties are, —*Buck's Scarlet*,—the *Tobolsk*,—the *Giant*,—and *Myatt's Victoria*. Either is worthy of the reader's attention.

Culture.—The most favorable soil is one which possesses the merits of depth, mellowness and fertility. A good succession of leaves cannot be expected from a spot that is either heavy, shallow or poor. And in making a plantation, it will be found of advantage to spade the ground deeply, and, where it is not naturally rich, to dig under a liberal quantity of manure. The situation is best when having a northern exposure, or partially shaded from the sun.

Plants are obtained from seed, or portions of old roots. Where the cultivator is in no hurry for the first crop, or where a large plantation is to be made, he will prefer sowing the seed to purchasing roots. The seed bed should be of light, rich soil, somewhat sheltered from the heat of noonday, and laid out in drills one foot apart, and near one inch deep. Drop the seed thinly. The proper time for doing this, is about the middle of spring, due attention being given to the character of the season. In the event of dry weather, the occasional application of water proves of benefit. When the plants are two inches high, thin them to distances of six inches in the drill; those which are pulled up, can, if the roots are not injured, be set out in another bed.

In autumn, when the leaves have withered, it will be time to remove the plants to their permanent location. After the ground has been manured and carefully spaded, mark out holes for the reception of the plants, thirty inches apart each way. For all varieties of moderate growth, this distance will be quite sufficient; but, with some of the giant sorts lately introduced, it may be advisable to allow more room. Bury the roots with their crowns two inches below the surface. As soon as cold weather arrives, cover the bed with about three inches of well rotted dung, to guard against injury from frost, and the next spring to be forked into the soil.

No crop is to be expected this season, and so to avoid the charge of keeping unoccupied land, quick-growing plants, such as lettuce and radishes, can be sowed between the rows. Good use of the hoe ought to be made at all times; and, in severe drought, artificial watering may be necessary. Every autumn, a top-dressing of old dung, or rich compost, should be given, to be mixed with the earth in the spring. Where the gardener does not choose to wait two or three years for his first crop of leaves, plantations are frequently made with portions of old roots. This is always a good plan, if the roots can be readily obtained, either at a fair price, or as a gift from some friend. Each offset should have at least one bud or eye, and be planted in well prepared ground, at the same distances apart as plants taken from the seed bed.

It is very common to blanch rhuburb, by placing over each stool an inverted barrel or box, which in a short period will be found almost entirely filled with the stems and leaves. Another way, is to cover each stool with a bushel of black peat earth, late in autumn. When thus blanched, they are delicate and of a most excellent flavor, being infinitely superior to those grown in the open air. To obtain a very early crop is easily done by forcing;—the barrel or box is placed over the stool in autumn, and in midwinter entirely covered with dung and forest leaves. By reason of the warmth, the growth of the tops is rapid, and, owing to the absence of light, they will be white and sweet.

USE.—The common garden rhubarb, or pie-plant, is cultivated for its stalks, which when young and tender, make an excellent pie, tart, or sauce to be eaten with bread and butter. They are sometimes converted into wine and jelly. They should not be gathered after they appear to have attained full size, because they have then lost a good part of their fine flavor. It is better to slip them gently off the root, than to make use of the knife. But few garden plants are more worthy of notice, for their useful and wholesome properties. As we have before intimated, the roots, after a certain length of time, may be used for their medicinal virtues, although decidedly inferior to the other species.

Rhubarb Pie.—Take the young stalks, remove the skin, and cut them into thin slices. Line a deep plate with pie crust, and put in the rhubarb, together with layers of sugar. Cover the whole with a thick crust, pressed down at the edges, and pricked by a fork. Bake for about an hour in a slow oven. Some persons are accustomed to stew the fruit before baking, by which means a greater quantity can be put in the plate.

Rhubarb Jam.—Boil gently, for three hours, an equal weight of fine sugar and rhubarb stalks. The juice and grated rind of a lemon to each pound of the stalks, will correct their peculiar flavor, which is unpleasant to some persons.

ROSEMARY.—*Rosmarinus officinalis.*

Rosemary is a hardy shrub, and a native of southern Europe. Its botanical name is composed of two Latin words—*ros*, dew, and *marinus*, of the ocean,—in allusion to the beautiful appearance of the plant, when glittering with dew on the sea shore. The stem varies in height from three to six feet; the leaves are distinguished by being of dark green upon the upper side, and whitish gray beneath; and the flowers are pale blue. Every part of the plant has a strong odor, and the tender leaves are possessed of a sharp, aromatic taste. One fourth part of the oil is camphor. From an old notion that rosemary has the property of strengthening the memory, it has been made the emblem of remembrance and fidelity; and this was undoubtedly the origin of a custom in some parts of England and Wales of wearing it at weddings and funerals. It is not much cultivated.

Culture.—The soil best suited to the wants of rosemary is both poor and light; in rich ground, the plant grows luxuriantly, but loses its fragrant properties, and becomes more susceptible of injury from cold weather. The finest plants are raised from seed, which is sown in early spring, in drills one inch deep, and six inches apart. They are also obtained from cuttings of the young shoots, six inches long, and inserted in mellow ground, at the same season of the year, two thirds of their length—which part has been previously divested of leaves,—being below the surface. Give water freely, until the roots have fairly started, and no longer need an artificial supply of moisture. Keep the ground in good tilth. You may remove the plants to their final location, either in autumn, or in the following spring. The work ought to be performed during damp, cloudy weather. Set the plants in rows two feet apart each way.

Use.—On account of their pungent taste, the leaves are used in Italy for seasoning certain dishes. They yield an essential oil, which is the principal ingredient of Hungary water; and they also enter into the composition of Eau de Cologne. Rosemary has lost much of its reputation as a medicinal herb; or, at least, it is rarely employed as such. It is a stimulant, and has been recommended for nervous headache and hysteria.

RUE.—*Ruta graveolens.*

A hardy perennial, known to antiquity, and a native of the south of Europe. It possesses a very strong and disagreeable smell, with a bitter taste. The leaves have the power of blistering the hand that touches them, and the plant has, therefore, been adopted by the poets to express disdain. Shakspeare calls it the "sour herb of grace."

Culture.—Rue flourishes best on a poor loam, rather approaching the nature of a clay, and it may, therefore, be located upon the most barren part of the garden. Plants are obtained from cuttings of young wood, set out in early spring, in some shaded situation. Water should be given freely until they are established. The seed may be sown at the same time of year, in rows six inches apart; the plants, as soon as they crowd one another, being thinned out to distances of five inches therein. In autumn, transplant the cuttings and seedlings to their permanent position. Keep the ground loose, and free from weeds; dressing it with the rake, both in spring and in autumn; and removing all dead leaves or branches to the compost heap.

Use.—The leaves were used by the ancient Romans for culinary purposes, and, it is said that, at the present day, they enter into the composition of certain dishes in middle Europe.

Their medicinal virtues seem to have been much exaggerated; nevertheless, they are ranked among the anti-spasmodics, and considered of great benefit to persons of cold, phlegmatic habits. Mr. Wilson, in his "Economy of the Kitchen Garden," says that, the most certain remedy for expelling worms ever brought to his notice, is an infusion of rue leaves in gin, to be taken in the morning on an empty stomach.

SAGE.—*Salvia officinalis.*

Sage is a well known garden perennial, a native of southern Europe. It has a pleasant, although powerful, smell; while its taste is sharp and aromatic, somewhat resembling camphor. It was formerly much celebrated for its medical qualities, and, indeed, its botanic name, *Salvia*, is derived from the Latin *salveo*—to be in good health. It was once an adage, "*Cur moriatur homo cui salvia crescit in horto?*"—how can a man die, in whose garden there grows sage? Time has, however, stripped it of this reputation, and we now cultivate it principally for culinary purposes. Of the several different varieties, those most esteemed by the cook, are—the *Green*,—and the *Red* or *Purple*. The *Broad-leaved Balsamic* is most valuable in a medicinal point of view.

Culture.—Select for the bed a dry, mellow soil, with an average character as regards fertility. Experience has shown that, although the plant flourishes luxuriantly in a rich or moist situation, it is thereby rendered more susceptible to injury from cold weather. The best method of propagation is by seed, but it is frequently accomplished by cuttings or rooted slips. Sow the seed, in the middle of spring, in drills about six inches apart, and one half inch deep. When the plants are of a suitable height, thin them to distances of six inches in the drill; and those which are drawn, can be placed in another bed, if the weather be favorable for transplanting. In autumn, or the following spring, they may be removed to their permanent location, in case they are not permitted to remain in the seed bed.

Cuttings of the young shoots are generally set out in July or August. They should be of a strong and healthy growth, about six inches in length, and divested of their lower leaves. Put them in a shaded border, eight inches apart each way, and give them occasional sprinklings of water until the roots have taken firm hold. They can be transplanted, either at the end of the season, or in the following spring. Rooted slips are most successful, when planted in the middle of spring, and in the place where they are to remain. Care should be taken to preserve as many of the fibrous roots as possible, and to supply artificial moisture if necessary.

Keep the ground in good order,—mellow, as well as free from weeds and dead branches. It ought to be dug over in early spring, in such a manner as not to injure the crowns of the roots, and every second or third year to receive a small top-dressing of good manure, at the same time. In cutting the tops, avoid taking off too many late in the season, lest the plants have not sufficient vigor to withstand the severity of winter. Whenever the main stalk shows a disposition to run to seed, it can be cut down, to encourage the growth of lateral branches.

For seed,—select fine plants, and water them frequently when in flower. Pull up the stalks as soon as the seed becomes ripe, and after they are well dried, it will be easily threshed. Keep it in a cool, dry room.

Use.—We have already noted the change in public opinion, as to the value of sage for medical purposes. It is, however, yet allowed to possess some aromatic and astringent powers; and a decoction, or "sage tea" as it is called, is found useful in debility of the stomach, and in nervous cases. This decoction is thought highly of by the Chinese; in fact, they are said to prefer it to their own tea. The leaves are used to a considerable extent in many kitchens, to season stuffings and sauces, as well as to correct the too great lusciousness of strong meats. They are gathered in August and September, when in their greatest perfection, dried before the fire, powdered fine, and kept in tight bottles for winter use.

SALSIFY.—*Tragopogon porrifolius.*

By many gardeners this truly excellent plant is known as the Vegetable Oyster,—the root, when well cooked, having somewhat the flavor of the oyster. It is a biennial, of a hardy constitution, and to be found growing wild in the southern part of Europe. The stems are two or three feet high, bearing beautiful blue flowers, and rising from a long, white, fleshy root, which resembles a small parsnip. It is a valuable addition to every family garden worthy of the name, and particularly to those in the interior of the country, where the oyster cannot readily be obtained.

Culture.—Select a soil which is mellow, deep and fertile, and lay it out into drills, one foot apart, and towards an inch deep. Sow from the middle to the latter part of spring, as the season may be early or late. It will be necessary to drop the seed rather thickly, in order to be certain of a sufficient number of plants. A single ounce will be enough for at least one rod of ground. When the plants have made their appearance, and have attained the height of an inch, they are to be thinned so as to stand six inches apart. The soil should be kept entirely free from weeds, and often stirred by the hoe, for the benefit of atmospheric influences. In dry times, artificial watering is of great advantage; and some cultivators recommend the addition of half an ounce of guano to every gallon of water. The root is hardy, and will not suffer injury from severe cold weather. When a long frost is expected, a supply for the table should be dug, and packed away in sand.

For seed,—it is only necessary to suffer some of the most healthy plants to remain in the ground through the winter, and they will yield abundantly in the following season. Or, they can be set out in the spring, after having been kept in the cellar.

USE.—The tender shoots of the second year's growth, when some four or five inches high, make an excellent substitute for asparagus. The root is palatable and wholesome—being good, it is said, for consumptive patients in particular. It is very inviting when prepared in the following way:—

Artificial Oysters.—After the root has been scraped, and laid in water for several minutes, in order to abstract a part of its bitter flavor, it is to be boiled tender, and either cut in thin slices, or grated and pressed into little cakes, of the size of oysters. Dip the slices, or cakes, into a batter made of wheat flour, milk, and eggs; roll them in crumbled bread or crackers; and then drop them into hot lard. When of a light brown color, they are sufficiently cooked, and ready to be carried to the table.

SAVORY.—*Satureja.*

An aromatic herb, the leaves of which have a warm pungent taste. The two species cultivated in the kitchen garden, viz.:—the *Summer* (*S. hortensis,*) an annual, and the *Winter,* (*S. montana,*) a perennial,—are believed to be both natives of Italy.

CULTURE.—Both species will grow upon poor soils, and are propagated in early spring by seed sown moderately thick. The *Winter Savory* is also grown from slips, and it is managed like SWEET MARJORAM. For directions as to the culture of the other kind, the reader is referred to SAGE.

USE.—The leaves are gathered in the latter part of July, or the beginning of August, and dried for the use of the cook. Their agreeable warmth and flavor are much esteemed in salads. Formerly, they were employed for medicinal purposes, and, according to Professor Bradley, they possess the power of "expelling fleas from a bed."

To preserve Herbs for Winter use.—They should be gathered on a pleasant day, at that time when they are in their greatest perfection. When freed from dirt, they are to be put in a common Dutch oven, and dried quickly before the fire, without being scorched. They shall then be placed in a mortar, and pounded fine; passed through a sieve, and put away in closely-corked bottles. They will thus retain their fragrance and flavor much longer, than when kept in paper bags, and exposed to smoke and steam; besides being more convenient for the use of the cook.

SCORZONERA.—*Scorzonera Hispanica.*

Many cultivators prefer this vegetable to the salsify, which it greatly resembles in appearance, habits of growth, and taste of the roots. It is a native of Spain, and has long been cultivated. It being so similar to the salsify, we do not choose to recommend it to our readers, except to such as desire to have a great variety in their grounds, rather than a selection of the very choicest plants for domestic purposes.

CULTURE.—Scorzonera prefers a soil that is mellow, deep, and moderately fertile, in an open situation. Sow during the month of April, or in the first week of May, in drills ten or twelve inches apart, and half an inch deep. The seed is to be dropped thinly, and when the plants are two inches high, they are to be thinned to distances of six or eight inches in the drill. Keep the soil at all times clean and light, and give regular applications of water in dry weather. The roots are fit for use when the leaves begin to decay, and may be allowed to remain in the ground all winter, as they will not suffer from frost, or be preserved in a box of sand in the cellar.

Use.—The roots are nutritious and palatable; and are used in soups, boiled like Carrots, or cooked in the same manner as Salsify. In Spain, scorzonera is considered a certain cure for the bite of a serpent called the *scurzo.*

SEA-KALE.—*Crambe maritima.*

Kale, as this plant is often called, is a species of sea-cabbage growing wild upon the sandy coasts of Europe,—particularly of England and Ireland. From time out of mind, its value as a pot herb has been known to the peasantry of those countries where it is found in a natural state, who, upon the appearance of the young shoots, in early spring, cut them off several inches below the surface, and boil them as greens. When these stalks are tender, before the leaf has opened, they make an excellent dish for the table. Although the merits of the plant were long since understood by the common people, yet it did not acquire much of a reputation for garden culture, until the beginning of the present century. Within a few years, it has been gradually extending itself in public favor, and is now an esteemed inmate of most English gardens; but in this country, it is by no means as common as it ought to be. Such is its value as a table esculent during a season of many weeks, in addition to a hardy habit, and a ready growth, that we cordially recommend it to the reader's notice.

Culture.—As regards soil, sea-kale is best suited with a sandy loam, which is moderately rich, two or three feet deep, founded on a dry substratum, and having a free, open exposure. The spot selected for the bed should be brought into this condition, before the plantation is made. Sand or coal ashes will correct tenacity; and a wet subsoil can be avoided by draining. Decayed leaves are better than hot dung for enriching the ground, and, owing to the marine character of the plant, the application of salt, at the rate of one pound to four square yards, proves very beneficial. Upon starting right, depend the gardener's subsequent satisfaction and profit.

Propagation is effected by seed and slips of old roots, but the first mode seems to be the one most generally adopted, as the plants are thought to be healthier and longer-lived than those obtained from slips. Lay the piece of ground, after it has been prepared in the manner above directed, into beds five feet wide. Through the middle of each, draw a drill about one inch deep, and another on each side, two feet distant from the first. Sow the seeds in clusters of six or eight, eighteen inches apart in the drills. Water the ground freely during dry weather, and when the plants appear well established, pull up all except the strongest one in each stool. Little care is needed, other than keeping weeds under, and giving occasional waterings. The beds should have a winter protection of earth, dung, leaves or sea-weed, three or four inches in depth; which is to be removed on the approach of warm weather, or, if well rotted, to be then forked into the ground.

The only attention required on the part of the gardener, during the second summer, is to keep the ground in good order—light, clean, and moist in continued dry weather. Occasional applications of brine are found to be advantageous. By autumn, the plants will have attained a suitable size for bearing the first crop. To obtain shoots during the winter months, recourse must be had to

Forcing.—The roots can be put in the forcing-pit, or in a hot-bed frame,—the glass being covered, so as to exclude light, and the ground frequently sprinkled with water. Or, they may be allowed to remain in the bed, covered with some fermenting substances to induce artificial heat. This is undoubtedly the best plan. In the latter part of October, or in the beginning of the following month, the dead leaves and branches should be removed, and a little dung worked into the soil around the stools. Then, light earth or sand must be spread over the whole surface, to the depth of about three inches, and each stool covered by a small box, or a large-sized flower pot, the edges of which are pressed down into the sand, to prevent the entrance of steam from the dung which is to be placed around them.

The pots are now to be covered with a compost of forest leaves and fresh dung, which were mixed in equal quantities some two or three weeks previous, in order that a regular heat might be obtained. This compost is either to be spread evenly over the bed to the depth of twenty-four inches, or put around each pot to the thickness of eight or ten inches. The temperature ought not to fall below 50°, and in extreme cold days, a covering of litter may be required, or perhaps the addition of warm dung. When the heat is much above 60°, some of the covering should be removed. In four or five weeks, the pots can be examined, and the shoots will be found fit for use, when three inches high. In cutting, the dirt is scraped away from the sprout, which is then taken off close to the crown, with care not to injure the young buds. The bed will continue productive for about two months, when the covering should be gradually reduced, that the plants may not suffer from sudden exposure to the cold, after having been so long a time confined in a hot atmosphere. In spring, the surface is to be cleared, properly levelled, and enriched by a little of the rotten compost, so that the roots can have a healthy, natural growth during the summer. A top-dressing of salt, at the same time, proves as beneficial as upon the asparagus.

It has been noticed that, unlike the generality of vegetables, the shoots of sea-kale obtained by artificial heat, are always more crisp and delicate than those produced in the natural way, later in the season.

The open-air crop—is easily managed. Some persons recommend covering the whole surface with layers of straw or leaves, or by inverting flower pots and boxes over the stools. Others are accustomed to spread upon the bed, early in spring, after the removal of the winter covering, ten or twelve inches of sand, through which the tender stalks will speedily show themselves, well blanched and pleasant to the taste. When the roots stop bearing, the sand is to be taken away, and a little rich compost dug in around them, that they may strengthen themselves for the next crop. A much better mode than either of the foregoing, is to spread over the whole bed, in autumn, a layer of black peat earth to the depth of fourteen or fifteen inches. This keeps the frost from penetrating to any considerable depth, and by its dark color attracts the sun's rays, so that the roots are excited into an earlier growth in the coming spring. When the season of cutting is over, the peat is to be removed to the compost heap, or to another part of the grounds.

By a little management, the gardener can have sea-kale through a good part of the winter and spring months, thus furnishing his table with an excellent dish, at a small expense. The same bed will continue productive for near a dozen years; and to avoid weakening the roots, it may be advisable to have two plantations, which are forced alternately. In this way, the season of the vegetable will be prolonged, and, every other spring, those roots which suffered from being forced the year previous, have an opportunity to regain their strength and vigor. Unless seed be wanted, no plant should be allowed to throw up its flower-stalks.

For seed,—the plant must be permitted to grow without being blanched or deprived of its young shoots.

Use.—Physicians and others speak highly of the sea-kale as an esculent. Dr. Curtiss remarks that, used with rhubarb, "it may save many pounds for medical attendance, and people may soon say, 'I grow my own medicine.'" Another authority has declared it to be "one of the most valuable acquisitions made to culinary vegetables within the last fifty years." The young shoots and stalks of the unfolded leaves, when blanched and tender, are boiled and dressed like asparagus. They also form an excellent ingredient in soups.

To cook Sea-kale.—Soak the stalks in water for thirty minutes, and tie them up in small bundles. Boil them very tender, over a brisk fire, with a little salt in the pot; drain off the water, and lay them on a slice of toast which has been moistened in the liquor. Dress with melted butter, pepper and salt.

SHALLOT.—*Allium Ascalonicum.*

This member of the *Allium* tribe was originally found growing wild near Ascalon, in Palestine, whence has been derived its botanical name. It is supposed to have been introduced into England by the returned Crusaders, and is now known under the several appellations of Shallot, Escalot and Eschalot. The root is bulbous, resembling the garlic, in being divided into cloves enclosed in a single membrane. From the circumstance of its rarely sending up a flower-stalk, it received from ancient authors the name of Barren-onion.

CULTURE.—The shallot is best suited with a light loam, of rather a sandy character, fertile, and free from excessive moisture, besides being in a free, open situation. Rank manure is apt to produce maggots, which will oftentimes do the crop great injury; and we, therefore, advise the use of compost, soot or bird's-dung, when the ground is not already sufficiently rich.

Propagation is effected by offsets of the roots. Where the bed is dry, the offsets are best planted in the autumn; but, otherwise, the labor should be deferred until the first part of the following spring. Put them in rows, eight inches apart each way. When planted in autumn, they are to be set about three inches deep, but they must be uncovered in May, so that they may bulb well, and be less likely to suffer from the canker. When planted in spring, they shall be placed almost on the surface. The soil ought to be kept light, and free from weeds. As soon as the tops turn yellow, say in July or August, the roots must be taken up, and gradually dried in a place shaded from the noonday sun, by which means they may be preserved throughout the winter without difficulty.

For seed,—the offsets must be kept in a dry, airy place until spring, when they are to be put in the open ground.

USE.—Although the shallot has a more pungent taste than some other members of the same family, yet it is rather more agreeable, and is often preferred to the common onion for use in pickling, seasoning soups, gravies, hashes and various other dishes. It is with some a favorite accompaniment to beef-steak.

Shallot Sauce.—Put a few shallots in some clear gravy, together with half the quantity of good vinegar; season with salt and pepper, and then boil for half an hour.

SKIRRET.—*Sium sisarum.*

Skirret is a perennial, and a native of China, which has been cultivated in England for upwards of three centuries. It was much esteemed by the ancient Romans. The stem rises about a foot high, and is crowned by an umbel of white flowers. The root is composed of several long, fleshy tubers, each one as large as the little finger, and joined together at the top. These, in times back, were thought highly of for the kitchen. A distinguished English horticulturist by the name of Worlidge, in the year 1682, speaks of them as "the sweetest, whitest, and most pleasant of roots."

CULTURE.—New plants are obtained from seed and offsets of old roots, but the first method is decidedly the best. The soil should be light, of a moderate degree of richness, and somewhat moist; whenever it is to be manured, the dung ought to be dug in with the lower spit. In dry ground, the crop will probably be small, unless the season should prove wet.

Sow in the latter part of March, or any time during April, according to circumstances, in drills ten or twelve inches apart, and near one inch deep. As soon as the seedlings are two inches high, they must be thinned out to distances of six or eight inches in the drill. No opportunity should be given the weeds to establish themselves, to the injury of the young plants. When the leaves decay in autumn, the roots are fit for use, and will be good until they begin to sprout in the following spring. They are to be stored in the cellar, in a box of dry earth or sand.

For seed,—it is only necessary to permit some of the plants to throw up their flower-stalks, in the second season.

USE.—The tubers abound in saccharine particles, having somewhat the flavor of a parsnip. By some persons, they are considered much more palatable than that root. They are prepared for the table in various ways;—stewed; boiled, and served with butter; boiled, rolled in flour, and fried; or boiled to be eaten cold with vinegar and oil. They possess diuretic qualities, and are in a slight degree stimulant.

SORREL.—*Rumex acetosa.*

A perennial weed, which is found growing naturally in poor, barren soils. It has a long root, with a stem one or two feet high. The leaves are oblong and arrow-shaped; they are remarkable for their acidity. The French sorrel, so highly valued in cookery, seems to be of a different character,—being round-leaved, and having a much pleasanter flavor. Only a few plants will be required by a single family.

CULTURE.—The most favorable soil is light and rather moist, in an open situation. Propagation is effected by sowing seed, or dividing old roots. Both methods can be practiced in spring, and the latter also in autumn. Sow in drills ten inches apart, and one half inch deep. The seedlings are subsequently to be thinned out to ten inches in the row; and, in making a plantation of old roots they are to be set at similar distances. An occasional watering may be necessary in dry weather,—particularly when the plants have not become well established. Keep the ground free from weeds, give it a slight dressing of manure in the spring, and, at the approach of frost, put on a little manure, or a covering of leaves. In summer, when the stalks show a disposition to run up to seed, they should be cut down, to encourage a new growth of herbage; they ought also to be cut down late in autumn.

For seed,—allow some of the seed-stalks to perfect themselves, and they will yield abundantly.

USE.—The acid juice of sorrel is often recommended for refreshing drinks in febrile complaints, but, as it is well known that it contains oxalic acid, a deadly poison, some degree of caution should be exercised in its use. It is valuable for taking spots of ink or iron-mould from linen. The leaves are by many highly esteemed in soups, sauces, salads, or when boiled plain like spinach.

SPINACH.—*Spinacia oleracea.*

A very hardy annual, which has for a long time been a favorite in the kitchen garden. Its name is derived from the Latin word *spina*, a thorn, in allusion to the prickly character of the seed. Its native country cannot now be determined, but it is by different individuals attributed to both Spain and Persia. In the monasteries on the continent of Europe, it was in use as early as the year 1351, five centuries ago. The stem is smooth, and about two feet high; the leaves are of various sizes and shapes, according to the varieties; while the male and female flowers are produced on separate plants,—the former growing in long, terminal spikes, and the latter in clusters about the stalk. The principal varieties are by no means numerous, viz.:—the *Round-leaved*, or *Round-seeded*, for the spring sowings;—and the *Prickly-seeded* for the winter and spring crops. The New Zealand Spinach has been spoken of on page 213.

Culture.—With all spinaceous plants, or those which are cultivated for their succulent leaves, the principal point of good management consists in providing a fertile soil, and keeping it in excellent tilth throughout the growing season. Spinach is called "a gross feeder," and can scarce ever be placed in ground that is too rich,—for the quality of its leaves depends mainly upon the rapidity of their growth. The roots must be well supplied with food, or a good crop cannot be expected. In summer, moisture in the soil is desirable, as the roots suffer much from drought, while the situation should be open; but, with the autumn sowings that are to be protected through the winter, for obvious reasons, a dry, warm, and rather sheltered border is to be preferred.

For the winter and spring crops, the seed is to be sown, first about the middle of August, and again near the middle of September. The beds ought to be protected through all inclement weather by thin coverings of straw, leaves, cedar-brush, mats, or something which will not press too heavily upon the plants. By judiciously removing the cover in pleasant days, and carefully guarding against extreme cold, the gardener will be able to have a good supply of leaves from the first sowing through the whole winter.

The *Round-leaved* variety can be sown as early in the spring, as the ground is in good order. The sowing may be repeated every fortnight or three weeks until the last of May. When continued longer than the time mentioned, the plants will be affected by the hot weather of June, and the following months, which causes them to run quickly to seed, without having a good growth of leaves. For the sowings even in the latter part of spring, it will be well to allot ground between the drills of peas and pole beans, for the benefit of the shade afforded by the tall vines.

After the ground has been properly dug and enriched, it is to be laid out into beds four feet wide. Spinach is often sown broadcast, but, while we see no advantage in this practice, we find much to condemn. When put in drills, the general appearance of the garden is improved, and the labor of subsequent cultivation is considerably diminished. We recommend having the drills ten inches apart, and one third of an inch deep. One ounce of seed is sufficient for one hundred, or one hundred and twenty-five, feet of drill. It should be dropped thin, and covered evenly. When the ground is dry, it ought to be rolled, or pressed by a person's walking upon a long board, or gently beaten by the spade.

The young plants will present themselves above the surface in the course of ten days. As soon as they appear to be well established they should be hoed and thinned out to distances of three or four inches in the row. When they are so much grown as to be in danger of crowding one another, every other one can be drawn for boiling, by which means the others will have a fair chance to mature. A very little experience will satisfy the cultivator, that spinach does not flourish when confined in close quarters. Unless plenty of room be given, the stalks will be tall and spindling, and the leaves small. It is ever necessary that the soil be kept light and permeable to atmospheric influences. In hoeing, care ought to be taken not to choke the heart of the plant by covering it with earth.

In dry weather, great benefit will be derived from the regular application of water at evening. Where there is a deficiency of moisture, the whole top of the plant is ever found dry and hard, instead of large and succulent. The principles of management appear to be simply:—having a rich soil, in an open situation; giving the plants sufficient room; preventing the growth of weeds; keeping the ground light; and supplying moisture during dry weather.

For seed,—let the flower-stalks grow up without molestation. It will not be wise to pull up the male-flowering plants, lest the others prove unfruitful. When the number of the first is too large, a portion can be immediately removed; and the whole can be taken, as soon as the female blossoms are set. Put the seed-stalks, when gathered, upon a cloth, and let them become perfectly dry, before you attempt threshing them.

USE.—The leaves, when green and tender, are put in soups, and boiled as greens. Physicians do not agree in regard to the effects of spinach upon the system. The French esteem it "not only food but physic," terming it figuratively "the broom of the stomach," as sweeping that organ of many ill affections and disorders; and, we believe, that it is generally considered innocent, although devoid of nutriment, and may be eaten when other vegetables are not allowed by the medical attendant. It certainly is a familiar dish at table, and with most families is thought indispensable in its season.

To boil Greens.—Under the general name of "greens" is comprised the succulent leaves of several vegetables, such as spinach, beet, mustard, etc. They should be washed very clean, and, if not freshly gathered, ought to be soaked in salt and water for thirty minutes before being put in the pot. Boil in a little water, with salt and salaratus added, to preserve their color. Take off the scum as it rises. When sufficiently cooked, they are to be drained, and seasoned with butter and pepper. A hard-boiled egg, cut in slices, and laid on the top of the dish, much improves its appearance.

SQUASH.—*Cucurbita melopepo.*

This well known and highly esteemed vegetable is a member of the *Cucurbita*, or Gourd, family, some species of which are very beautiful and are cultivated for ornament, while others are considered curiosities, on account of their immense size, and others are used for culinary purposes. The squash has been thought the link which connects the melon and the pumpkin. It is so much of a favorite in this country, that it is generally raised in the kitchen garden; but, on account of the large space it occupies, as well as of its liability to intermixture with other vines, we advise that it be kept without the garden limits, whenever the cultivator has other ground at his disposal. The best varieties are—the *Early Orange,*—the *Early Bush,*—the *Large Green Striped,*—and the *Autumn Marrow.* The *Valparaiso,* which sometimes attains the weight of near one hundred pounds, is a very excellent kind, and should be brought into general use.

Culture.—As the squash is quite sensitive to cold, and will not start well in spring, until the weather becomes fine, it is not advisable to plant the seed before the first week of May. It will flourish on any good soil, and requires much less care than the cucumber or melon. The ground should be marked out for hills, at distances of six to ten feet apart each way, according to the variety cultivated. In making the hills, a hole is to be dug for each to the depth of a few inches, filled with compost or rotten dung, and covered with three or four inches of loam, upon which half a dozen seeds are to be planted. At this rate, one ounce of seed will plant from sixty to eighty or a hundred hills. Keep the surface light and clean at all times, and draw a little soil around the stems for their support.

Three vines are quite enough for a single hill, and their leading shoots may be stopped, so as to induce the speedy formation of fruitful laterals. For advice in regard to the attacks of insects, we refer the reader to our article on the "DESTRUCTION OF VERMIN." The squashes are fit for use, when as large as a cocoa-nut, and continue in season until the rind becomes hard.

USE.—No American needs to be told the value of the squash as an addition to the dinner table. Much of its excellence, however, depends upon the manner in which it may be cooked, for some persons will send it from the kitchen so hard, or so full of water, that it is scarcely fit to be eaten. Many housewives are accustomed to prepare it in the shape of pies, after the same receipt as given for the PUMPKIN.

To boil.—If very young and tender, it may be boiled whole; but, otherwise, should first be freed from its seeds, pared, and cut into strips. When quite soft, it is to be mashed, drained, and then seasoned with cream or butter, pepper and salt.

STRAWBERRY.—*Fragaria.*

This fruit has been aptly termed "the most delicious and the most wholesome of all berries." It is a native of the cold and temperate regions of both hemispheres, and is very extensively diffused, particularly in Europe and America. The root throws out many slender, creeping shoots, which fasten themselves to the ground at intervals, and form so many new stalks. The leaves are each composed of three leaflets, supported on a long footstalk. After the season of flowering, the seed-receptacle increases, acquires a pulpy and succulent consistence, and finally a red color when it has attained maturity. The name is said to have arisen from the ancient practice of putting straw around the plants, for the purpose of keeping the berry free from dust and sand. The botanical appellation is derived from *fragrans*, in allusion to the delightful fragrance of the well ripened fruit.

It is not many years since it has been brought into general cultivation, and the course of treatment pursued in early times was about as imperfect, as the number of varieties was limited. The poet Tusser, who wrote in 1557, says that the best plants were to be found "growing abroad, among thorns in the wood," and turns them over to the female members of a family, as though unworthy the attention of the men. Modern skill and care, however, have brought the strawberry into high repute. It now occupies a conspicuous position in most private gardens, while in some sections of the country it is extensively cultivated for market. One grower, in 1846, picked one hundred and twenty-eight bushels daily at the height of the season. Under proper management, it can be made very profitable: instances are recorded of crops being at the rate of from $1000 to $1600 per acre; but the fair average product is probably not far from $350, which is certainly a good return upon the investment. In fact, it is so productive and easy of cultivation, that it is really a matter of wonder why so many families are willing to be without it.

In its wild or natural state, the plant produces "perfect" flowers, or such as contain both stamens and pistils—the male and female organs. When brought under high culture, many varieties lose this character, and the flowers become what is called "imperfect,"—that is, either the stamens, or the pistils, as the case may be, are *imperfectly* developed. Where the stamens are wanting, or so small and imperfect as to be incapable of fertilizing the pistils, the plant is termed "pistillate, or female." Where the pistils are defective, the plant is then known as a "staminate, or male," variety. As a natural result of this change, the berry either does not set, or else it is of small size and little value. Gardeners, therefore, are accustomed to associate the two classes of plants, in order to secure a crop. In Fig. 25 the staminate flower is indicated by the letter *a*, and the pistillate flower by the letter *b*, and the perfect flower, in which both stamens and pistils are developed, by the letter *c*. In Fig. 26 are represented portions of the first two, as they appear in a microscope; the stamens being marked *a*, and the pistils, *b*. The greatest bearers being pistillates, they are usually selected for the beds, a smaller number of the less productive staminates being placed in the neighborhood to secure fertilization.

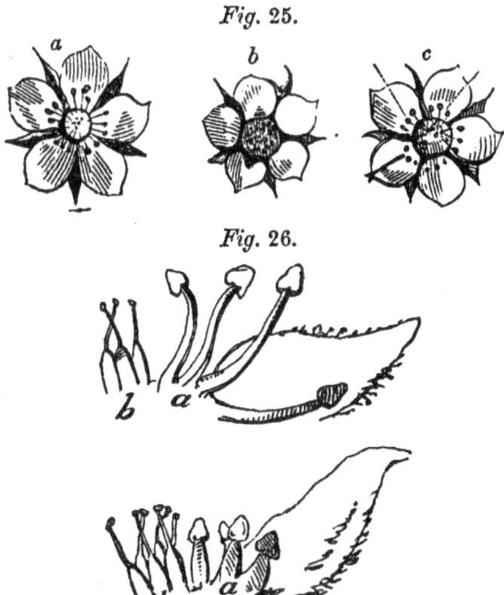

Fig. 25.

Fig. 26.

The varieties have become very numerous, and within a short period many have been introduced to the public, that are of peculiar excellence. Nevertheless, it is well understood that most of the "seedlings" brought forward from time to time, with high-sounding names and finely-drawn descriptions of their good qualities, are of little or no value. Aided by the published experience of others, we venture to present the following select list of the choicest kinds,—the class to which each belongs being designated, by the letter S for staminates and by the letter P for pistillates. We enumerate—the *Large Early Scarlet* (S),—the *Boston Pine* (S),—*Hovey's Seedling* (P),—*Burr's New Pine* (P),—and the *Dundee* (P). As with all fruits, these varieties differ in quality according to climate, season, soil, exposure, etc.

CULTURE.—Four things appear to be essential to success in the cultivation of the strawberry, viz.: a good selection of varieties,—a favorable situation,—careful culture,—and a renewal of the bed once in every three or four years. The labor, apart from the formation of the bed, is but trifling, and is, indeed, often over-estimated; while the necessary annual outlay, is of small account in a garden of common dimensions. A moderate crop yields a rich reward for the expense incurred. When we see our own vines literally covered with fruit, tempting to the eye, and pleasant to the taste, we cannot but inquire how it happens, that a farmer, or a *gardener*, or any person in the country having a rod of spare ground, can be without a plantation of strawberries.

The situation of the bed ought always to be open, away from close fences, trees and buildings, so that the plants may not suffer from the want of light and air. To have a succession of crops, one bed may lie towards the south, and a second have an inclination to the north. Where the soil is not naturally of a suitable character, it should be brought into that condition before the plants are set out. A good loam, light rather than heavy, deep, rich, and somewhat moist, is undoubtedly to be preferred. It needs to be friable so as to be easily worked, and yet not so light as to suffer from drought. It would seem that a slight degree of moisture is indispensable to the full perfection of the fruit. Moreover, the soil should be both deep and rich, that the roots may have plenty of room in which to extend themselves, together with a good supply of food suited to their wants. To prepare the ground for a plantation in the best manner, we would recommend trenching and manuring it several months previously, taking care that the manure shall be well incorporated. Instead of using common stable dung alone, we should rather apply it in connection with leaves, decayed wood, ashes, plaster, salt, or bone-dust. It sometimes happens that too large a supply of dung, causes a rank growth of vines, without a corresponding return of berries.

After the ground has been properly dug,—all the lumps being pulverized, and the surface raked smooth,—rows are to be struck out at distances of two, or two and a half, feet from each other. In our own garden, we should be willing to allow even more room, being under the impression that there is such a thing as crowding the plants, and thereby injuring their productive powers. The months of April and May, or August and September, are the proper seasons of the year for making new plantations. The first season is undoubtedly the best, because the newly-transplanted vines then require less attention than they would in the heat of summer, and the first fair crop will be a twelvemonth earlier.

The best plants are the young, healthy-looking runners from old stocks. They are to be set out at distances of twelve or eighteen inches in the rows. A hole is made by means of a small dibble, and before the root is inserted, it should be dipped in mud, a semi-fluid mass of dung and water, or even simple water, in order that the freshly-stirred earth may adhere to the fibres. We have already noticed the necessity of putting staminate plants in the immediate vicinity of the pistillates. Still, to prevent the first named from usurping the place of the latter, as by reason of their greater luxuriance they would be apt to do, the two classes must be kept distinct, and only near enough together to secure fertilization.

Thus, every fifth or sixth row may be of staminates exclusively, and by keeping their runners confined within proper bounds, there will be no chance of their crowding out the more valuable pistillates. Perhaps, our idea will be better understood by the following diagram, in which the classes of the plants are designated by the letters S and P.

S P P P P S P P P P S
S P P P P S P P P P S
S P P P P S P P P P S

Every root ought to be set firmly, and when the operation is not followed by a shower, the ground ought to be well watered. If the season be autumn, the new beds require not a little attention, and the liberal application of water will be frequently necessary, until the roots become established. Whenever practicable, transplanting ought to be performed in dull, damp weather.

It will not be long before runners show themselves, and instead of being allowed to roam over the bed at will, they must be trained along the rows so as to form parallel lines of plants, with good, wide paths between them. This system of culture is preferable to every other for many reasons, and principally on account of its being more convenient of access for weeding and gathering the fruit. Light and air are freely admitted to the leaves, while the roots have a large foraging ground beneath the unoccupied paths. The hoe must be often used, as well to keep the surface light and porous, as to eradicate the young weeds before they have taken possession. A full grown weed in a strawberry bed, speaks but little in praise of the owner's industry, or skill in gardening. In severe hot weather, the plants ought to be examined every day, to ascertain whether they be suffering from the want of moisture. This is particularly necessary where the situation is dry and in a warm exposure. But, in most cases, frequent stirring of the soil will attract sufficient moisture from the atmosphere Mulching, or covering the surface with straw or leaves, is to be recommended, as checking evaporation, and preventing the parching effects of drought.

In the beginning of winter, a covering of leaves, straw or any light litter should be given, to prevent injury from frost. When the land is not quite rich enough, this is a good time to dig a little compost into the paths, to keep the roots warm through the winter, and cause them to start thriftily in the spring.

As soon as the weather becomes settled in March or April, the covering is to be removed, and the ground ought to be frequently stirred, until the flowers open. At this time, clean straw, sea-weed, or coarse hay, can be spread around the plants, for the purpose of protecting the berries from sand; this also is useful in keeping the soil moist, and, when decayed, it forms an excellent manure. After the blossoms fall, the growing berries ought to be occasionally watered, in case the season prove dry. Throughout the summer and autumn, the runners are to be confined to the rows from which they start, unless new plants are wanted, when they may be permitted to root themselves in the paths. No room should be allowed a weed or a blade of grass. The same course of management is to be pursued annually thereafter.

A strawberry bed cannot be expected to remain in perfection longer than four years, and to ensure a regular supply of fruit, it is advisable to make a new plantation in every second year. There is, however, a plan of renewing the bed at the end of each season, which is simple, and answers a good purpose. The rows are about three feet apart, that the paths may be as wide as the spaces occupied by the plants. After the crop has been gathered, the runners are allowed to strike themselves into the paths, which have been previously enriched by manure when not sufficiently fertile. With a little care, they will cover the ground very regularly. In the latter part of summer, the old plants are to be spaded under, and the spaces which they occupied are now to be used as paths. At the close of the next season, the process is to be repeated, and so henceforth until the land has become tired of the berry, when the plantation may be removed to another part of the garden. It will be observed that the strips of land are every other season at rest, while their principal production, the old vines, are dug under for the benefit of the roots.

USE.—No reader needs to be told in what universal favor this luscious and wholesome fruit is held. It consists almost entirely of matter soluble in the stomach, and never grows acid by fermentation. Hence, it is found very nourishing, and may not only be eaten with safety by invalids, but is furthermore known to exercise a healthful influence in many cases of disease. The great Linnæus was cured of the gout by partaking freely of strawberries. In fact, they disagree with but few constitutions. The flavor is equalled by the delightful perfume which they exhale. Even the muse has sung of

"A dish of ripe strawberries, smothered in cream."

Eaten alone, or with sugar and cream, they are highly prized for the dessert; and they are invaluable for pies, tarts, ices, jams, and preserves. The juice, which has rather a subacid taste, is made into a cool, refreshing drink, known as *bavaroise à la grecque*, as well as into a very pleasant wine.

Strawberry Preserve.—The berries, after being hulled, are put in a large dish, in layers with an equal weight of fine white sugar,—a layer of fruit being at the bottom of the dish. At the end of an hour, pour in a gill of cold water. Set the whole upon a moderate fire, which is to be increased from the time the juice runs freely until the syrup boils quite brisk. Let it boil for half an hour, then turn the sweetmeats into a dish, and before they are cold, put them into bottles, which are to be sealed tight and kept in dry sand.

Strawberry Jelly.—Bruise the ripe fruit, and let the juice run through a flannel bag without pressure. To each pint add one pound of powdered white sugar; and for every three pounds of sugar, add the beaten white of an egg. In boiling the syrup, the vessel should always be taken from the fire when it is to be skimmed. The jelly is boiled enough, when a little of it will drop in a solid lump to the bottom of a tumbler of cold water. Keep in glasses, covered with clean paper.

SWEET POTATO.—*Convolvulus batatas.*

A convolvulus, deriving its name from the agreeable sweetness of the root. It is believed to be a native of the East Indies, although ascribed to many different countries by various authors. Formerly, it was imported into England from Spain and the Canaries, and sold as a great delicacy. It was supposed to have the power of restoring decayed vigor. It is said to be the potato of Shakspeare, and cotemporary writers, as at the time he wrote, the common vegetable of that name was scarcely known in Europe. Thus Falstaff, in the "Merry Wives of Windsor," cries "Let the sky rain potatoes, let it thunder to the tune of 'Green Sleeves,' hail kissing-comfits, and snow eringoes." The sweet potato is now cultivated in all the warmer portions of the globe, where, owing to the favorable influences of climate, it may be had on the table for many months. In this country, it is a great favorite with the people of the southern and middle states, and large tracts are annually devoted to its production. The roots are large, fleshy, and spindle-shaped; containing much sugar mixed with farina. The vines are herbaceous, taking root at intervals; while the leaves are smooth, and generally three-lobed. The varieties are numerous, but those cultivated at the south are much superior to our own northern kinds.

Culture.—The best soil for the sweet potato plant is light,

dry, of rather a sandy character, and in a warm situation. It should be prepared for planting, by being deeply dug or ploughed, and enriched by a liberal application of manure. All the large clods ought to be pulverized. The ground can then be laid into beds three feet wide, with a very shallow drill through the middle of each, or marked out in hills, three feet apart each way.

Where the season is of sufficient length, the seed potatoes may be planted immediately in the beds prepared for their reception; but, in northern climates, artificial heat is necessary to procure early plants. In the latter case, the roots are to be split and placed about three or four inches deep in the soil of a hot-bed, sometime during the latter part of spring. This bed is composed of good, warm dung, to the depth of twelve or fifteen inches, covered with eight inches of sandy loam. Where the gardener is without sash-lights, he can shelter the bed with half a foot of litter, well pressed down, and protected from rain by a roof of old boards. The soil should be examined every day, to ascertain whether the heat of the dung be too great; in which case, air must be admitted freely in all pleasant weather. The runners will show themselves in the course of a fortnight or three weeks, and the bed ought, during the process of sprouting, to receive an occasional sprinkling of water. When three inches high above the surface, they are of the right size for removal to the open ground. In taking them up, place the left hand on the potato, to keep it from moving, and draw them, one by one, with the right hand. If they be planted in drills, they should be set about nine or ten inches asunder; but, if in hills, two plants must be allotted to each. The operation is most successful, when performed at evening, or in damp, cloudy weather; and, in a dry time, frequent applications of water, until the roots have taken hold firmly, will be found of great advantage. The potatoes in the bed will continue throwing up sprouts, for as much as three or four weeks.

Where the climate is so mild as to render forcing needless, the split potatoes are, in early spring, placed in the open ground, at similar distances. It is found better to split large potatoes, than to plant small ones uncut. The covering of soil is to be near two inches deep, and rather hollowed upon the top, so as to catch the rain.

The bed ought to be carefully cultivated, particularly in the early part of the season. The roots must have plenty of light and warmth during their young growth; and, after they become well established, the soil is to be drawn up around them by means of the hoe, but not so as to form a ridge to turn off the rain. It is recommended that, when the vines attach themselves to the ground, they be forcibly torn up, by slipping a rake-handle, or other long stick, under them, and raising it gradually. This will throw the vigor of the runners into the roots.

The crop is fit for harvesting, when the tops decay. Keeping the roots through the winter is usually found a difficult matter. The best plan is to dry them in the sun, until their moisture is evaporated, then to sweat them in heaps, previous to being packed in dry sand. We know of some northern cultivators, who even take the trouble to wrap each root in a piece of paper, before putting it in the barrel. Probably, the most suitable place for the barrel or bin is a dry cellar, which is perfectly free from frost. In order to ensure success, it seems to be necessary to keep the potatoes from frost, dampness, light and air. Sometimes, the crop is placed in heaps, five or six feet high, built upon a dry situation in the field. A foundation is made of cornstalks or brush, and the heap is covered with the same, and with a foot of earth upon the outside. The top should be sheltered from rain, by a roof of boards; and there ought to be a ditch around the heap, to prevent any water getting to the interior. A hole in the top, partially closed with straw, gives the heated air a chance to escape.

For seed,—the roots must be taken very carefully from the

ground, as the least bruise engenders decay. They are to be packed in leaves or sand, which have been exposed to the influence of the sun or a fire until perfectly dry, and then stored in a room where no injury is to be apprehended from the cold.

USE.—The peculiar, agreeable flavor of the root has long rendered it a favorite at the table. It is called easy of digestion, wholesome and nutritious. Containing more saccharine matter than the potato, it is better liked by most people. It is not so good when boiled as when baked, a fact that will be readily admitted by those who try it both ways. It also makes an excellent bread, for which consult the receipt on page 239. The young, tender vines are by some persons esteemed as a pot-herb.

Sweet Potato Pie.—Boil the potatoes very soft; then peel and mash them. To every quarter of a pound, put one quart of milk, three tablespoonfuls of butter, four beaten eggs, together with sugar and nutmeg to the taste. It will be much improved by the addition of a glass of wine.

SWISS CHARD.—*See* BEET.

TANSY.—*Tanacetum vulgare.*

Tansy is a perennial, which is to be found growing wild in many parts of Europe, and is now naturalized in this country. The stem rises about two feet above the ground, bearing golden yellow flowers. The whole plant has a sharp, bitter taste, together with a powerful, aromatic odor, which are agreeable to some persons. The *Curled-leaved* variety is about the only one cultivated for culinary purposes.

CULTURE.—It is propagated in spring by seed, rooted slips or divisions of the roots. The plants should stand from twelve to eighteen inches asunder. The best soil is one of a dry, light and moderately fertile character, in an open situation. It is sometimes necessary to water a new plantation, when dry weather succeeds. The ground is to be frequently stirred, and all upstart weeds are to be eradicated. Cutting down the large stalks will encourage a growth of young leaves. In autumn, the decayed branches should be removed, and a little good loam spread over the bed.

USE.—Tansy is now but little regarded by the herb-doctor, although formerly thought highly of for its virtues as a stimulant and carminative. The young leaves are sometimes, though not frequently, shredded to color and flavor puddings, omelettes, etc.

TARRAGON.—*Artemisia dracunculus.*

A perennial, originally from the northern part of Asia. It was brought to England in 1548, and has there obtained the name of Dragon s-wort. It has a fragrant smell and an aromatic taste, for which it is greatly esteemed by the French. Only one variety is grown for culinary purposes.

CULTURE.—Plants are obtained from seed sown in the spring, or from cuttings, slips or offsets of the root, set out in either spring or autumn. They should be about one foot distant from each other. They flourish best in soil which is poor and dry, in a warm situation, because they often suffer from frost when they grow too luxuriantly. A little water, applied every now and then, is of great benefit to the roots before they become well established. The ground should be kept clean, and the stalks must not be permitted to run up unless seed is wanted. Some winter protection ought to be afforded the plants, by a covering of straw or any coarse litter.

Use.—In Persia it has long been customary to use the leaves of tarragon to create an appetite. Together with the young tops, they are put in salads to correct the coldness of other herbs, in pickles, and in vinegar for fish-sauce. They are also eaten with beefsteaks, served up with horse-radish. They are in the best state to be dried for winter use, in July and August. The superior vinegar of Maille, in France, owes its flavor to this plant.

THYME.—*Thymus vulgaris.*

An evergreen shrub, originally from southern Europe. It has a strong, penetrating odor, together with a sharp, pungent taste. Its name is derived from the Greek word for courage, in allusion to its supposed qualities for reviving the strength and cheering the spirits. On account of its fragrance, it was formerly used in sacrificing. The varieties are,—the *Narrow-leaved,*—the *Broad-leaved,*—and the *Variegated;*—the last of which is grown almost wholly on account of its ornamental appearance.

Culture.—The best soil is one that is poor, light and warm, in a free, open exposure. Plants are obtained either from seed, sown in shallow drills six inches apart, or from rooted slips, set out in rows six inches apart each way. Early spring is the most suitable period for making a new bed, and it should be done, if possible, on a damp, cloudy day. In dry weather, the surface of the seed bed ought to be gently pressed by the spade or board, and the rooted slips must receive an occasional sprinkling until they become well established.

When the seedlings are one or two inches above the ground, they are to be thinned to distances of six inches in the drill, and those pulled can be set out in another place, where they will take a good start, if kept moist. The ground should at all times be clean and light. In autumn, the decayed branches are to be removed, and the stools covered with a little mold.

For seed,—the stalks must be permitted to flower. Cut the stalks before the rain has an opportunity to wash out the seed, and dry them in the shade.

USE.—Owing to their aromatic qualities, the young leaves and tops are valued for seasoning soups, sauces and other culinary preparations. An infusion is excellent as a tonic for the stomach, and as a cure for the headache. They are preserved for winter use, by being cut when the flowers have just opened, in June or July, and dried before the fire, to be powdered and kept in tight bottles. The whole plant yields an essential oil, which is highly charged with camphor.

TOMATO.—*Solanum lycopersicum.*

One of the most interesting facts in the history of this vegetable, is its sudden rise in public favor in this country. It was formerly known as the Love Apple, and cultivated in the flower garden for its ornamental appearance, the fruit being by some persons considered poisonous. Within a very few years, however, it has attained a high reputation among esculents, and, in the neighborhood of cities, large fields are annually devoted to its production for market. It belongs to the same genus as the potato and the egg-plant. It was introduced into Europe from South America in the year 1596, and derived the name of tomato from the Portuguese. The plant is an annual of rank growth, the leaves somewhat resembling those of the potato, but the flowers are yellow, while the fruit is about the size of a small apple, with an acid flavor that is quite disagreeable to those unaccustomed to it. The principal varieties have received their names from the peculiar shape and color of their fruit, viz:—the *Large Red*,—the *Large Yellow*,—the *Pear-shaped*,—and the *Cherry-shaped*,—the last two of which are mostly used for pickling purposes

CULTURE.—As with every other choice vegetable, the first supply of tomatoes in the season commands an unusually high price, and affords a good profit. It is, therefore, an object with market gardeners to bring the first crop to maturity as soon as possible. To other cultivators this should be not less desirable, because early vegetables are highly prized in all kitchens, and must certainly reduce the expense of living.

In order to obtain early plants, many small cultivators are in the habit of sowing the seed, somewhere about the last of March, in boxes which are to be placed in the windows of a warm room. When the weather becomes mild and pleasant, the seedlings will have attained a suitable height for removal to the garden, where they ought to be protected during nights and cool days until they are accustomed to the change of situation.

But those persons who are supplied with the necessary conveniences, will find it most for their interest to make use of a gentle hot-bed. The heat should not be violent, and the covering of mold may be about six inches in depth. The seed—one ounce of which is considered sufficient for from three to four thousand plants,—is sown quite early in spring, thinly, and covered one third of an inch deep. As soon as the plants are two inches high, they must be properly thinned, or they will be injured by standing too close together. For this first thinning, the right distance is near three inches apart. Those which are drawn can be set in a similar bed, to be watered and shaded until well rooted.

The cultivator must be careful to admit air freely to his seedlings under glass during all pleasant weather. The observance of this rule seems to be indispensable to a successful result, for, when confined in a warm atmosphere without a free circulation of air, they soon become spindling and weak. It being desirable to remove them to the open ground, without doing the roots any more injury than is unavoidable, it is a good plan to put some of those which are most advanced into pots, to be kept in the frame until May, and then set out with balls of earth attached. This single thing may make a difference of several days in the maturity of the crop,— a circumstance by no means to be overlooked.

At the latter part of April, or the beginning of May, according to the character of the season, the most forward plants are to be placed in a border, sheltered from cold winds and having the full influence of the sun. The most suitable soil is one that is rich, light, easily worked, and neither wet nor dry. When the border is not sufficiently rich, it will be well to set the plants in holes, which have been filled with good compost. They should stand about three feet apart, and, if possible, against the south side of a fence or trellis. They are to be gradually hardened, and during all inclement weather, as well as during cold nights, must be screened by hand-glasses, small boxes or flower pots. Shade may be necessary at noonday, until they appear well established. Careful attention will be required to prevent loss of vigor by the change of situation.

The seed for the main crop is to be sown as soon as the weather becomes settled in April or May. It should be got into the ground as early in the season as may seem prudent, because there is some danger of the crop being overtaken by frost in the following autumn. Make the bed in a warm border, and transplant in the latter part of May.

The duties of the cultivator are simple and easy of application. He must hasten the growth of the plants by all means in his power. The surface soil is to be stirred frequently with the hoe, and a little drawn up to the stems for their support. Where the branches are not kept erect by being trained upon the fence or trellis, it is usual to put brushwood around them for the same purpose. Covering the ground with refuse straw or litter, is found beneficial as checking evaporation, preventing injury from drought, and keeping the fruit clean. It is a good plan to cut off the tops of the stems, not long after the blossoms fall, which accelerates the ripening of the crop

Some persons are in the habit of pulling up the plants when frost is expected, and either hanging them in a dry, airy apartment, or laying them in an empty hot-bed frame, with the glass kept close. By so doing, the season of the fruit can be still further extended.

For seed,—some of the most forward fruit is to be left on the bushes until it becomes perfectly ripe. Then the seed is to be washed from the berry, and after being dried, put away in paper bags.

USE.—Perhaps no fruit or vegetable described in this volume, is prepared in such a variety of ways as the tomato When green, it is made into pickles and sauces; and, when ripe, into soups, stews and sauces; besides being pickled, preserved, roasted, and made into catsup. But, it is said, that compared with the Italians, we have little idea of the many forms in which it can be brought to the table. We have room for only a few receipts.

To cook.—If the tomatoes are not quite ripe, dipping them into hot water will loosen their skins so that they may be easily peeled. Put them in a stew pan, together with a tablespoonful of water, in case they are not very juicy. Add a little butter and salt, and stew the whole for half an hour.

Another way,—is to put them in a deep dish, with layers of bread crumbs or powdered crackers, being well seasoned with salt, pepper, nutmeg, and sugar. The top layer should be of crumbs. Bake for half an hour.

Tomato Omelette.—Take a stew pan, and melt a piece of butter the size of a nutmeg. Mince up an onion very fine, and fry it quite brown. Add ten peeled tomatoes, seasoned with pepper and salt, and stir them until cooked to a soft pulp. Then stir in four beaten eggs, until the underside of the mass becomes brown. Lay a plate on top, turn the pan upside down, and the omelette is ready for the table.

Tomato Marmalade.—Gather full-grown tomatoes when

quite green. Stew them until soft, when they are to be rubbed through a sieve, again put over the fire, and seasoned highly with pepper, salt, and powdered cloves. Let the pulp stew until it becomes very thick. It will then keep well, and be excellent for seasoning gravies.

Tomato Catsup.—To one quart of ripe tomatoes, put two tablespoonfuls of salt, two tablespoonfuls of black pepper, two tablespoonfuls of good mustard, a half-tablespoonful of all-spice, and three red peppers ground fine. Simmer the whole together with a pint of vinegar, in a tin vessel, slowly for three hours. Strain through a sieve. Bottle and cork tight. The later in the season it is made, the better it will keep.

To preserve for winter use.—Put perfectly-ripe fruit in a stone pot, or a glazed earthen jar, and cover them with salt and water strong enough to bear an egg. Before being cooked. they ought to be soaked in fresh water for several hours.

Another receipt.—Scald the ripe fruit, which should be of small size, and, after the skins are removed, squeeze them slightly. Spread them on earthen dishes, which are to be placed in a brick oven after the bread has been taken out, and let them remain there until the next morning. Then put them in bags, and keep them in a dry place. The tomatoes are in the best condition for preserving, in the months of July and August. Before being cooked, soak them in fresh water for a few hours.

To preserve Tomatoes.—For the sake of variety, we append a poetical receipt for preserving tomatoes, furnished to the "American Agriculturist," by some fair reader:—

"Six pounds of tomatoes first carefully wipe,
Not fluted, nor green, but round, ruddy and ripe ;
After scalding, and peeling, and rinsing them nice—
With dext'rous fingers 'tis done in a trice—
Add three pounds of sugar, (Orleans will suit,)
In layers alternate of sugar and fruit.

In a deep earthen dish, let them stand for a night,
Allowing the sugar and juice to unite.
Boil the syrup, next day, in a very clean kettle,
(Not iron,—but copper, zinc, brass, or bell metal,)
Which having well skimmed, 'till you think 'twill suffice,
Throw in the tomatoes, first adding some spice—
Cloves, cinnamon, mace, or whate'er you like best,—
'Twill add to the flavor, and give them a zest.
Boil slowly together, until they begin
To shrink at the sides, and appear to fall in;
Then take them up lightly, and lay them to cool,
Still boiling the syrup, according to rule,
Until it is perfectly clear and translucent—
Your skill will direct you, or else there's no use in't.
Then into the jars, where the fruit is placed proper,
Pour boiling, the syrup, direct from the copper.
After standing till cold, dip some paper in brandy,
Or rum, or in whiskey, if that be more handy;
Lay it over the fruit with attention and care,
And run on mutton suet to keep out the air;
Then tie a strong paper well over the top,—
And, 'now that I think on't, the story may stop.'
If you'll follow these rules, your preserves never fear,
Will keep in good order till this time next year."

TREE ONION.—*Allium proliferum.*

This hardy perennial species of the onion family is sometimes called the Canada Onion, because it is much cultivated in cold countries where the other kinds do not flourish well. Small bulbs are produced at the top of the stalks,—hence its name. Propagation is effected by planting the offsets of old roots in spring or autumn, or the top bulbs in the middle of spring. They should be set about six inches apart, in rows that are one foot distant from each other. The only care required, is to keep the ground well tilled, and to support the stems by stakes. The bulbs are to be gathered when the tops decay, dried in a shady place, and preserved in a dry, cool apartment.

TURNIP.—*Brassica rapa.*

Little is known of the history of this valuable plant. Its origin appears uncertain, but the choicest English varieties, from which our own are descended, were brought from Hanover. For culinary purposes it has been prized from the earliest periods, long before it was considered important in an agricultural point of view. Columella recommends its extensive cultivation, because that portion of the crop not wanted for the table, will be greedily eaten by the farm-cattle. At the present day, however, its merits are generally acknowledged, and in some countries it occupies a conspicuous position in every system of husbandry. It must be yet fresh in our minds, how, in the recent dearth in Ireland, the people placed their whole trust upon the success of the turnip crop. The varieties are numerous; but the best are those known as—the *White Dutch*—the *Red-top*—the *Early Garden Stone*,—the *White Flat*,—the *Yellow Dutch*,—the *Yellow Aberdeen*—and the *Improved Swedish.*

Culture.—Experience has proved the best soil to be one of a light character, such as a sand or gravel mixed with loam. On land of this description the roots will be found sweet and well flavored. It should be rich,—capable of yielding abundantly, and yet not so rank as to injure the quality of the product. Guano, bone-dust, ashes, gypsum and salt, are considered excellent manures.

The first sowing ought to be made in March or April, soon after the frost is out of the ground, and in a warm, sheltered border. For this early crop, the best varieties are the *White Dutch* and the *Red-top*. The *Improved Swedish* should be sown about the last of July, and the other kinds sometime during August. The latter part of the month is the best for the winter and spring supplies.

Sowing is best performed in damp, cloudy weather, immediately before a shower. The soil should be freshly dug, and raked smooth upon the surface. The seed—one ounce being sufficient for two hundred square feet,—is to be dropped thinly in drills, one foot apart, and half an inch deep. To avoid wasting it, some persons are in the habit of mixing it with dry sand, which secures a more regular distribution. Many different methods of protecting the young plants against the ravages of insects, have been proposed. It is recommended to press or roll the surface immediately after sowing, when performed in dry weather.—to soak the seed in some liquid that will not only accelerate the growth of the germ, but also impart a disagreeable taste to the first leaves,—to put ashes, lime, plaster, bone-dust, charcoal or poudrette, in the drill with the seed,—or to burn a quantity of light brush upon the bed before sowing. Watering the ground at evening will bring up the plants in a few hours' time, and where danger is apprehended, it is advisable to sprinkle them, when moist, with ashes, plaster, soot, or anything calculated to disgust the nostrils of the destroyers. Should all these precautions fail, the gardener must not despair at seeing the tender leaves entirely cut off, but sow again and again until his efforts are crowned with success.

When the plants have the rough leaves about an inch in breadth, they should be thinned out to distances of three or four inches in the drill. As soon as they appear perfectly well established, every other one is to be drawn, leaving the bulbs six or eight inches apart, so that they may have plenty of space to acquire a good size. The ground ought to be frequently stirred, but not drawn up around the roots. About the middle of autumn, when frost is expected, the bulbs for winter and spring use are to be taken up and stored. The leaves should be cut off within an inch of the crown, and the roots are then to be put in a dry cellar, or piled in the open field, with a covering of straw and earth. When properly managed, they will retain their freshness throughout the winter, and prove excellent for the table in the succeeding spring.

For seed.—Some of the best-shaped and medium-sized roots should be set out, in March or April, in rows eighteen inches apart each way. The stalks are to be supported by being tied to stakes, and, as soon as the seed becomes hard, to be cut and laid in a shed to dry. It will there ripen without being wasted, and can at any time be beaten out by means of a small stick. That which is fresh germinates most readily.

USE.—The tender tops, gathered in spring, make a very good dish of greens. The roots are considered a nutritious and wholesome esculent, although difficult of digestion in some stomachs. Owing to the scarcity of grain in England many years since, the poor people made bread of equal proportions of wheat flour and boiled turnips. In common cookery, they are generally boiled plain. When tender, they are drained, mashed, and seasoned with butter, pepper and salt. They are also put in soups and stews. The syrup, extracted by baking, and mixed with honey, is excellent for coughs, hoarseness, and complaints of a kindred nature.

VEGETABLE OYSTER.—*See* SALSIFY.

WATER CRESS.—*Sisymbrium nasturtium.*

"Eat cress and learn more wit," says an ancient proverb. It would seem that the plant once had a high reputation for its cordial and stimulating qualities, being thought to invigorate persons of a cold, phlegmatic disposition, and to quicken the understanding. Although its medicinal virtues are now rated much less, it has become a favorite vegetable in Europe and some parts of this country. It is grown in immense quantities for the London markets, and is in considerable de-mand at the markets of New-York and Philadelphia.

CULTURE.—The water-cress is best pleased with a clear, moderately-swift stream, one and a half inches deep, and having a sandy or gravelly bottom. The nearer the stream may be its source, the more successful will be the plants. Where the bottom is naturally of mud, it should be covered with gravel. The plants are sometimes thrown on the surface, when the seed will fall to the bottom, and germinate. At other times, they are set in rows parallel with the course of the stream, and according to its depth, the rows will be from eighteen inches to three feet apart. Again, cress is cultivated on low ground, which can be irrigated at pleasure. The bed is deeply dug with the spade, and, in spring or autumn, as most convenient, laid out into shallow trenches. The plants are set in these trenches six inches, asunder, and must be plentifully supplied with water at all times during their growth.

USE.—Water cress is well known as an anti-scorbutic, and is generally considered a purifier of the blood The warm, pungent taste of the leaves renders them a favorite for early spring salads. We are surprised that the plant is not more extensively cultivated.

WATER-MELON.—*Cucurbita citrullus.*

Upper Egypt, Bokhara and the island of Cyprus, are the countries most distinguished for the culture of this fruit. It is there brought to great perfection, and is highly esteemed for its sweet, succulent flesh, and gratefully cool juice. It is justly pronounced one of the most delicious refreshments that nature, amidst her constant attention to the wants of man, affords in the season of violent heat. Dr. E. D. Clark, in his travels through Egypt, gives an interesting account of the melon cultivation on the Nile. When the water subsides, after the periodical inundations, the rich sediment that is left on the banks, is manured with pigeon-dung and planted with melons. The product is astonishingly large, and is said to perfume the air to a great distance. It is eaten by the Egyptians, and those of the lower classes in particular, so freely that it has been called their meat, drink and physic. In cases of ardent fever, it is their most common medicine. This well explains the regret expressed by the Israelites for the loss of this fruit, which had so often quenched their thirst and relieved their weariness, and would have been so grateful in a dry, scorching desert.

The water-melon is very popular in the United States, as one might well infer from the enormous quantities yearly carried to market. It has not the fragrance, nor the rich flavor, of the common melon; but its refreshing coolness, together with its beautiful appearance, cause it to be a general favorite during the hot season. The following are the varieties most worthy of notice:—the *Black Spanish*,—the *Imperial*,—the *Mountain Sweet*,—and the *Mountain Sprout.*

Culture.—This is almost identical with that of the melon. The best soil is of a sandy character, but very rich, and having the full benefit of the sun. In those countries where the vine proves most successful, it is always grown on a sand. And, where the soil is naturally wet and heavy, it is advisable to dig out deep holes, to be filled up with a light compost for the reception of the seed. In field culture, the finest crops are raised upon an old meadow sod, turned over by the plough in the middle of spring.

To have the fruit in perfect purity, it should not be in the neighborhood of other vines of the same family. Let the hills be at least seven feet apart, so as to afford ample room for the spread of the foliage, and three or four inches above the surface of the ground. Plant nine or ten seeds in each, somewhere about the first week of May, to be covered half an inch deep. One ounce of seed will thus supply near fifty hills. When the plants have two rough leaves, reduce their number to three in a hill; and when the blossom-buds are presented, pinch off the ends of the shoots, to induce the production of fertile laterals. Keep the earth mellow, and draw a little around the stems as high as the seed-leaves. Guard against the attacks of insects, by the use of the vine-shield, and by sprinkling soot, tobacco-dust, etc., upon the hills. For more particular directions, reference is to be made to the article upon the culture of the MELON.

USE.—Apart from the use of the water-melon for the dessert, it may be pickled, or baked in sweet wine, or preserved as sweetmeats. The inspissated juice makes a very pleasant syrup, and in some parts of Europe is brewed into beer.

To preserve the rinds.—Cut the rind in small strips, which are to be boiled fifteen minutes in a weak pearlash-water. Then drain them, and to every pound add one pound of loaf sugar. Boil the whole for twenty minutes, or until the rind becomes quite soft. The syrup will probably require scalding several times.

WORMWOOD.—*Artemisia absinthium.*

Wormwood belongs to the same genus of plants as the tarragon. It is an erect under-shrub, of a hardy constitution, and to be found wild in nearly every part of Europe, growing by the road-side and on heaps of old rubbish. The leaves and flowers are warm and bitter, with a strong, nauseous smell; the roots are warm and aromatic. "As bitter as wormwood," has become a common expression, no less significant than that every-day phrase, "As cool as a cucumber."

Culture.—This plant is best suited with a light, dry and poor soil, for when its growth becomes very luxuriant, it loses a good part of its aromatic qualities, and is less able to endure the rigors of winter. It is propagated by seed, as well as by slips and cuttings. Sow thinly in early spring, or in autumn soon after the seed ripens. When the plants have attained a height of two inches, thin them to distances of six inches apart. The slips and cuttings are to be taken off at midsummer, and set out in a shaded border, in rows six or eight inches apart each way, to be watered regularly until they have become established. Transplanting to the permanent location, is to be performed in the following spring. Keep the ground light and clean, and clear away the dead stalks in autumn.

Use.—Wormwood is cultivated chiefly for medicinal purposes. It has tonic properties, and is sometimes employed as a stomachic. A considerable quantity of oil rises from it in distillation, which is used to destroy worms. An infusion of the leaves, with the addition of a fixed alkali, makes a powerful diuretic in cases of dropsy. Before the use of hops was known, wormwood was much employed by the brewer in the composition of beer and ale; and it now enters into the French beverage called *eau d'absinthe*, which is thought to create an appetite, and exercise a healing influence upon the system

INDEX.